Word, Text, Translation

Other Books of Interest

About Translation
  PETER NEWMARK
Annotated Texts for Translation: French – English
  BEVERLY ADAB
Annotated Texts for Translation: English – French
  BEVERLY ADAB
'Behind Inverted Commas': Translation and Anglo-German Cultural Relations in
Nineteenth Century
  SUSANNE STARK
The Coming Industry of Teletranslation
  MINAKO O'HAGAN
Constructing Cultures: Essays on Literary Translation
  SUSAN BASSNETT and ANDRE LEFEVERE
Cultural Functions of Translation
  C. SCHÄFFNER and H. KELLY-HOLMES (eds)
Culture Bumps: An Empirical Approach to the Translation of Allusions
  RITVA LEPPIHALME
Discourse and Ideologies
  C. SCHÄFFNER and H. KELLY-HOLMES (eds)
Linguistic Auditing
  NIGEL REEVES and COLIN WRIGHT
More Paragraphs on Translation
  PETER NEWMARK
Paragraphs on Translation
  PETER NEWMARK
Practical Guide for Translators
  GEOFFREY SAMUELSSON-BROWN
The Pragmatics of Translation
  LEO HICKEY (ed.)
The Rewriting of Njáls saga:Translation, Ideology, and Icelandic Sagas
  JON KARL HELGASON
Translation and Quality
  CHRISTINA SCHÄFFNER (ed.)
Translation and Norms
  CHRISTINA SCHÄFFNER (ed.)
Translation, Power, Subversion
  ROMAN ALVAREZ and M. CARMEN-AFRICA VIDAL (eds)
Words, Words, Words. The Translator and the Language Learner
  GUNILLA ANDERMAN and MARGARET ROGERS
Written in the Language of the Scottish Nation
  JOHN CORBETT

*

Please contact us for the latest book information:
Multilingual Matters, Frankfurt Lodge, Clevedon Hall,
Victoria Road, Clevedon, BS21 7HH, England
http://www.multilingual-matters.com

What was it that attracted me [about translation]? A lot of things: . . . because it's how people communicate with each other . . . and because it's a crossword puzzle, it's something very attractive; I love to translate for the same reasons: because you have to try to fit things in; it's not only work, it's a game as well as work and it helps you to understand people.

(Peter Newmark in interview with Monica Pedrola, June 1997)

Photograph: Gunilla Anderman

Word, Text, Translation

Liber Amicorum for Peter Newmark

Edited by
**Gunilla Anderman
and Margaret Rogers**

MULTILINGUAL MATTERS LTD
Clevedon • Buffalo • Toronto • Sydney

Library of Congress Cataloging in Publication Data and British Library Cataloguing in Publication Data

Catalogue records for this book are available from the relevant libraries.

ISBN 1-85359-461-X (hbk)
ISBN 1-85359-460-1 (pbk)

Multilingual Matters Ltd

UK: Frankfurt Lodge, Clevedon Hall, Victoria Road, Clevedon BS21 7HH.
USA: UTP, 2250 Military Road, Tonawanda, NY 14150, USA.
Canada: UTP, 5201 Dufferin Street, North York, Ontario M3H 5T8, Canada.
Australia: P.O. Box 586, Artamon, NSW, Australia.

Typeset by Archetype-IT (http://www.archetype-it.com).
Printed and bound in Great Britain by WBC Book Manufacturers Ltd.

Contents

Part III. Text

Part IV: And Beyond

List of Figures

List of Tables

Contributors: A Short Profile

Gunilla Anderman is the Director of the Centre for Translation Studies, and teaches Translation Theory on the Diploma/MA in Translation in the Department of Language and International Studies at the University of Surrey, UK.

Reiner Arntz is Professor of Romance Linguistics and Dean of the Faculty of Languages and Technology at the University of Hildesheim, Germany.

Patrick Chaffey is a translator, particularly concerned with the translation of statutes and regulations, who teaches Theory and Practice of Translation at the University of Oslo, Norway.

Simon S.C. Chau received his Ph.D. in Translation Pedagogy from the University of Edinburgh. An author and a translator, he helped to launch Translation Studies at the Hong Kong Baptist University, Hong Kong.

David Connolly, an author and a published translator of Greek poetry has taught translation for many years in Athens and Corfu, Greece.

John M. Dodds is Dean of the School of Languages for Interpreters and Translators and Director of the Language Centre of the University of Trieste, Italy.

Jan Firbas is Professor Emeritus and teaches Functional Syntax on the Postgraduate Diploma/Ph.D. in English Linguistics in the Department of English and American Studies, Masaryk University, Brno, Czech Republic.

Janet Fraser, Senior Lecturer in Translation, teaches on both the BA Modern Languages and the Diploma/MA in Technical and Specialised Translation at the University of Westminster, UK.

Viggo Hjørnager Pedersen, a translator and lexicographer, teaches English and Translation at the University of Copenhagen, Denmark.

Piotr Kuhiwczak is the Director of the Centre for British and Comparative Cultural Studies and teaches MA courses in the fields of Translation Studies and Comparative Literature at the University of Warwick, UK.

Hans Lindqvist is Senior Lecturer in English Linguistics and Associate Chair of the Department of Humanities, Växjö University, Sweden.

Sylfest Lomheim, a consultant on New Norwegian and writer on Translation Theory and Subtitling, is Associate Professor at Agder College, Norway.

Gerard McAlester is a professional translator and lecturer in Translation at the Department of Translation Studies, Tampere University, Finland.

Albrecht Neubert is Professor Emeritus, author and lecturer on Translation Theory and Applied Translation at the University of Leipzig, Germany.

Eugene A. Nida , an author and lecturer on language and culture, received his Ph.D. from the University of Michigan, USA.

Eithne O'Connell has a special interest in Irish and other lesser-used languages as well as in the translation of children's literature. A lecturer in Translation Studies, she specialises in Screen Translation (Dubbing/Subtitling) at Dublin City University, Ireland.

Monica Pedrola is a student in the School of Languages for Interpreters and Translators at the University of Trieste, Italy.

Margaret Rogers is the Deputy Director of the Centre for Translation Studies and teaches Text Analysis and Terminology on the Diploma/MA in Translation in the Department of Language and International Studies at the University of Surrey, UK.

Candace Séguinot is the Director of the Programme in Technical and Professional Writing at York University, Canada and also teaches graduate and undergraduate courses in translation in York's School of Translation.

Mary Snell-Hornby is Professor of Translation Studies at the Institut für Übersetzer- und Dolmetscherausbildung, University of Vienna, Austria.

Gideon Toury is the author of many articles and books on Translation Theory and the holder of the M. Bernstein Chair of Translation Theory at Tel Aviv University, Israel.

Acknowledgements

The appearance of this volume owes much to the hard work and patience of many people, a few of whom we would like to mention in particular. We are very grateful to Multilingual Matters for helping us to keep our project under wraps for longer than would have been thought either possible or desirable, and for being supportive from inception through to production. In-house, our special thanks go to Gillian James of the Centre for Translation Studies who has worked with enormous patience and fortitude at all stages on the preparation of the manuscript and has kept us on the straight and narrow. We are also happy to acknowledge our debt to Rob Dickinson whose expertise guided us through the intricacies of copy editing and are grateful to the Croatian National Tourist Office for permission to reproduce the map of Croatia in Piotr Kuhiwczak's chapter. With regard to the contents of the volume, we are particularly pleased to be able to include material from Peter Newmark himself, based on an interview which was conducted by Monica Pedrola in June 1997 and for which she was kind enough to provide us with a transcript. Last, but of course not least, we would like to thank all the contributors for their efforts, patience and enthusiasm. We hope the result is a fitting collective tribute to the work of our friend and colleague, Peter Newmark.

Gunilla Anderman
Margaret Rogers

Guildford
March 1999

Chapter 1

Introduction

Gunilla Anderman and Margaret Rogers

This *Liber Amicorum* dedicated to Peter Newmark includes contributions from a sample of his many friends all over the world. Our choice has been guided *inter alia* by the wish to demonstrate the geographic breadth of Peter Newmark's circle of friends; the difficulty of this choice attests to his international standing in the world of Translation Studies as well as to the present bouyant state of the subject as an academic discipline, a development in no small measure due to Peter Newmark's teaching and writing on the subject.

Characteristic of Peter Newmark's approach to translation, throughout, has been his reluctance to endorse, unquestioningly, ideas on the subject which happen to be in vogue. At the same time, however, he often acknowledges, although at times implicitly, the value of contrasting views. And translation has, throughout the ages, been a controversial subject attracting conflicting opinions. Debates about the degree of latitude permitted to the translator in reproducing the source text (ST) in the target language (TL) date back to Antiquity and have continued to attract scholarly attention up to modern times. The early ideal of fidelity to the word associated with the translation of sacred texts came, however, to be contrasted with a 'freer' rendering of the ST in order to meet the demands posed by the social context of the target text (TT).

Anyone familiar with Peter Newmark's work knows his commitment to the WORD, his concern that lexical items in the source language (SL) are accurately and faithfully rendered in translation. '[W]e have to get the words right. The words must stretch and give only if the thought is threatened' (Newmark, 1988: 73). Still, in spite of the great importance which he places on the translation of the individual word, at the same time he acknowledges the need for 'freer' forms of translation. This is implicit in his proposed division into 'semantic' and 'communicative' translation. While 'semantic translation' remains within the original culture, communicative translation 'addresses itself solely to the second reader . . .' (1981: 39). Rather than keeping to the words of the original, the translation seeks to convey the meaning or the sense of a text.

A prerequisite for rendering the sense of the text is, however, an understanding of its CONTEXT. And in spite of Peter Newmark's insistence that due attention be given to the accurate translation of the word, this has not prevented him from acknowledging the importance of context: 'in translation, the translator indeed has to be aware of all the varieties of contexts — so many it is

1

idle to list them again — but this does not mean that context is the overriding factor in translation . . . ' (1988: 80).

In the 1950s–1960s, the breakthrough of modern linguistics and the so-called Chomskyan revolution provided scholars interested in translation with a ready-made framework for a description of their observations of translation phenomena. In the interview with Monica Pedrola in this volume, Peter Newmark emphasises his belief in the creative force of language, acknowledging his debt to Noam Chomsky. But at the same time as he is influenced by the psycholinguistic approach to language as propounded by Chomsky, he does not fail to recognise the value of contributions based more closely on work anchored in the field of sociolinguistics, acknowledging the importance of the work of Halliday, and Halliday and Hasan. 'Language has various resources to ensure the cohesion of thought beyond the sentence, and the translator comes to rely on them as guide-lines' (1981: 176). Nor does he fail to recognise the advantages of the linguistic framework of the Prague School of linguists including the powerful tool of analysis inherent in Functional Sentence Perspective and the concepts of 'theme' and 'rheme': 'Functional Sentence Perspective (FSP), the Prague School's enormous contribution to linguistics which is now spearheaded by Jan Firbas . . . links the study of discourse, sentence and emphasis. It is intimately related to translation problems' (1988: 60–1).

As translation may be viewed as the conversion of a TEXT, written in one language for a certain situation or purpose into another language, it was only to be expected that interest among translation scholars was soon to focus on text linguistics, the branch of linguistics that studies written or spoken texts. Peter Newmark, too, readily acknowledges the importance of text but, characteristically, goes beyond the thinking of the time, back to where he feels the original source is to be found: 'Many theorists have divided texts according to subject-matter (literature, institutions, technology, etc.) but it is perhaps more profitable to begin with Bühler's statement (1934) of the functions of language which had a wide influence on the Prague School and has been used by some translation theorists (Reiss, 1971; Hartmann and Vernay, 1970)' (1981: 12).

In providing a systematic framework for the description of language, the relevance of linguistics to translation is indisputable. It is not, however, the only discipline to interact with translation. By the 1980s, the importance of other disciplines had become obvious and a new interdisciplinary as well as culturally-oriented approach to Translation Studies was beginning to emerge. An increasing number of literary scholars also started to turn their attention to translations as instruments of mediation between national literatures and cultures and, in the 1990s, Translation Studies officially took the 'cultural turn', moving BEYOND the word and even the text.

As readers of Peter Newmark's books are well aware, his work has always been informed by strong literary and cultural interests, his inspiration and examples drawn from his knowledge of European culture and familiarity with its major literary figures throughout history. Writing on the question of the cultural value of translation, he remarks: 'My short answer would be that not only are all thriving intellectual and artistic cultures heavily indebted to translation — take our debt to Greek, Roman and Arabic literature, as well as to the Icelandic Sagas, but many of the finest writers, the poets in particular, have translated and written about translation' (1981: 185).

In September 1989, Peter Newmark began to contribute, once every two months, to *The Linguist*, the journal of The Institute of Linguists. He is likely to continue, he points out, 'as long as I go on teaching' (1993: ix), reminding us of his love of teaching and of the importance it has had for the development of his approach to translation. His contributions to *The Linguist* are now available in two volumes, *Paragraphs on Translation* (1993) and *More Paragraphs on Translation* (1998). In the preface to the first volume he points to what he feels are three subtexts. The first one is political:

> I am committed to some human, animal and environmental rights, many of them generally, some not yet generally accepted. All of these rights are reflected in an attitude to language and a treatment of translation method [1993: x].

The second one is artistic:

> I love certain musical works, poems, plays, fiction and paintings, and I want, rather too concisely, to convey the love to any readers I have. I admit that the connection between the works and translation is sometimes rather tenuous and artificial. For instance, I have not the slightest interest in the title of Goya's most impressive masterpiece; nevertheless, the Prado should produce an authoritative translation of The Third of May [1993: x]

The third subtext is linguistic:

> I am absorbed and fascinated by language, and I attempt to make a small contribution towards its understanding and appreciation (1993: x).

The extraordinary boom in Translation Studies in the 1990s has meant an increase in the number of research publications and an extension of its subject boundaries, ranging from standardisation, sub-and sur-titling and corpus-based studies to new genres such as the translation of children's literature. Approaching the millennium, a number of questions also need to be asked. Where do we go from here? What are the directions for Translation Studies in years to come? In *More Paragraphs on Translation*, his most recent book, Peter Newmark stresses the importance of asking such questions. 'My opinion is that, in many cases, translation scholars are more interested in the history and "archaeology" of translation than in its present or its future . . . ' (1998: 187). It is hoped that the present volume may in some sense reflect the abundance of Translation Studies at present, while also indicating some ways ahead.

The contributions to this *Liber Amicorum* dedicated to Peter Newmark divide roughly into the categories outlined above: WORD, CONTEXT, TEXT and BEYOND. The contributions are preceded, however, by an interview with Peter Newmark undertaken by Monica Pedrola in the summer of 1997, forming part of her Bachelor's dissertation at the University of Trieste, which attempts to shed some light on aspects of Peter Newmark's life that can be seen to have influenced his writing.

Anyone interested in finding the TL equivalent to an individual WORD is likely to consult a bilingual dictionary. Janet Fraser's contribution, 'The Translator and the Word: The Pros and Cons of Dictionaries in Translation', starts from Peter Newmark's comments on the importance of the bilingual dictionary for the translator. Fraser argues that the use of such dictionaries is, according to what she identifies as good practice demonstrated by professional translators, often complemented by 'intelligent guessing'. She bases her observations on think-aloud protocols or TAPs, transcripts which record translators' verbalised introspections as they work. In this case, 21 practising professional translators were asked to translate a French text from *Le Monde de l'Education* for publication in the *Times Higher Education Supplement*. Her analysis of the translators' searches for culturally-bound educational terms is preceded by some interesting comments on the scepticism which the translators in her sample expressed about the value of bilingual dictionaries (cf. also a recent investigation of the expectations of users of multilingual technical dictionaries — including translators — conducted by the Centre de Terminologie in Brussels (Hermans, 1995) which suggested that greater experience and training are associated with less reliance on dictionaries as a sole source of translation solutions). Fraser points out that the more alert translators demonstrated a healthy scepticism in their attempts to interpret the equivalents offered by the chosen dictionaries. And on occasions when a word or phrase did not feature in the bilingual dictionary or where the definition was inadequate, these translators used information from the ST to get them to a point where they could search elsewhere and take a decision on the best translation. According to Fraser, what distinguishes the better translators in her sample is their willingness to use a variety of sources, including monolingual SL dictionaries, TL documentation and TL human informants, in order to arrive at an acceptable translation. In her conclusion, Fraser argues that in addition to becoming familiar with the strengths and weaknesses of a range of reference materials, trainee translators need to learn how to release the rich resources within their own memories. In balancing their recourse to these resources, translators need to calculate the trade-off according to their translation task and deadlines to reach the optimal solution to a lexical problem.

In 'On the Perils of Particle Translation' Gunilla Anderman is similarly concerned with the solution of a lexical problem, i.e. the difficulties involved in the translation of particles such as *denn* in German, *dog* in Danish, *nok* in Norwegian and *väl* in Swedish. Anderman points out that failure to render particles, described as 'invariable word[s] with pragmatic function' (Davidsen-Nielsen, 1993: 16), accurately in translation may drastically change the style of the original, as in the case of Hans Christian Andersen whose fairytales often emerge in a more formal style in English than in their Danish original (Jones, 1992: 18). She first discusses the treatment of particles in the linguistic literature and shows that, with the exception of English, the Germanic languages may be viewed as 'particle-rich' in contrast to French and other Romance languages. A brief discussion of the origin and development of particles then follows, a process explained in terms of semantic 'bleaching' whereby grammatical and pragmatic functions develop from a lexical source. The function of particles in a number of different Germanic languages is also examined as well as the

problems in capturing accurately the intended meaning of particles in translation. Anderman then focuses her attention on the findings of specific studies of
particles in translation, in particular corpus-based studies. In an early corpus
study (Jakobsen, 1986), in which English novels in translation into Danish are
compared with novels originally written in Danish, particles show a much lower
frequency of occurrence in the translated texts, a finding suggesting that
translators do not always make full use of particles to express modality functions
in translation from 'particle-poor' languages. The findings for Danish are also
shown to hold true for Swedish (Aijmer, 1996; Gellerstam, 1996). As particles
tend to occur with high frequency in the spoken language, the importance of
rendering them accurately in the translation of drama texts is particularly pressing
as this is a genre of translation almost exclusively concerned with dialogue. Thus,
the last part of the chapter is devoted to a discussion of the translation of particles
in some works by Ibsen, Strindberg and Ingmar Bergman. The translator of
drama faces, according to Anderman, a 'trilemma'. The strong pull towards finding
a one-word equivalent in the TL may result in stilted adverbial constructions,
but omission of the modality effect, on the other hand, may result in a dialogue
lacking in nuance; and full semantic interpretation may not be an ideal solution
either as paraphrasing may threaten succinctness of the line in the ST. Anderman
concludes with the suggestion that more studies of the different ways cultural
relativity is reflected in the modality systems of the languages of the world might
help to shed some light on the problem inherent in particle translation.

The springboard for Viggo Hjørnager Pedersen's contribution is Peter
Newmark's observation that 'we . . . translate words, because there is nothing
else to translate' (1988: 73). In 'Accuracy in Translation', Hjørnager Pedersen
discusses the concept of accuracy in the context of literary translation, more
obviously associated nowadays with technical translation. In order to
exemplify his notion of 'accuracy', he turns to various nineteenth- and
twentieth-century translations of the Anglo-Saxon text *Beowulf* into Danish,
English, French and Norwegian. He sees the translations of literary works not
only as translations, i.e. as a set of choices which can be described, analysed and
explained, but also as literary texts in themselves which must be evaluated
accordingly. Picking up Jennifer Draskau's distinction between a 'literary
translation' and a 'translation of literature', he argues — from a functionalist
perspective — that accuracy is relative to the purpose of the translation. So, for
instance, if the purpose is to shed light on the original, then a close translation,
even at word level, is both acceptable and appropriate (as a translation of
literature). If, however, the purpose is to produce a text for a new literary
audience (as a literary translation), then the degree of closeness (still a guiding
principle) must be tempered by other factors to do with the TL and its culture
and its match with the SL and its culture. In the case of *Beowulf*, these factors
include, according to Hjørnager Pedersen, poetic forms and rhythms, metaphors, compounds, and names. He argues, for instance, that language typology
is a particularly important factor influencing the ability of the translator to
reproduce the poetic forms of the original, closely-related languages showing
greater aptitude in this respect. But his definition of accuracy does not
presuppose the typological proximity of language pairs: for Hjørnager Pedersen,

accuracy is multifaceted, i.e. the translation should not only render 'a fair proportion of the content', but also function as a work of art in its own right and do justice to the 'splendour' of its original. He concludes by pointing out that this can only be achieved through a certain degree of freedom for the translator. But perhaps, we could add, returning to Hjørnager Pedersen's first remarks, the words of the original are the starting point.

John Dodds's contribution, 'Friends, False Friends and Foes or Back to Basics in L1 to L2 Translation', deals with the frequency of students' errors, in particular students' treatments of words, when translating out of their mother tongue. Although controversial, this is in many situations a professionally necessary skill in countries where a lesser-used European language is spoken and the shortage of English mother-tongue speakers with a knowledge of the language makes translation out of L1 necessary (cf. Campbell, 1998 for Australia; Mackenzie, 1998 for the situation in Finland). John Dodds prefaces his remarks with a short exposition of the situation with respect to the teaching of translation in Italy, including an outline of different approaches to the issue of translation theory in the translation classroom. Having established the need for translation into English as L2, the main part of Dodds's argument is concerned with the frequency and nature of students' errors when translating in this direction. He maintains, on the basis of an error analysis of students' examination translations, that even advanced students experience significant difficulties with what he calls the 'basics', i.e. the 'grammar, the lexis, and the idiom' of the TL. Of particular interest in this respect is the treatment of individual words, which seem to account for the largest number of errors in both intermediate and advanced students' work. Dodds presents arguments for and against a literal approach to translation, using student data to illustrate the balance which is required between the creativity of the non-literal approach and mastery of the L2.

Reiner Arntz's contribution, 'Training Translators in a "Third Language" — A New Approach', is concerned with words in closely-related languages and their usefulness in a training programme for translator trainees. Starting with a description of the development of Translation Studies in a pedagogical context, Arntz sets out to outline how the acquisition of yet another language can be coherently situated in a translation curriculum by drawing on previous linguistic knowledge and language-learning experience, linking language learning and translation to Linguistics, and practising translation skills. The Hildesheim model described by Arntz rests crucially on the notion of 'cognate language learning' — a timely topic of increasing interest to the European Commission in relation to the objective of a multilingual Europe (cf. Slodzian & Souillot, 1997) — whereby typologically-related languages (often also genealogically related) form the basis of accelerated tuition on the assumption that the learner already knows a great deal about the new language. The particular language pair discussed and illustrated by Arntz is German (known language) and Dutch (new language). In this context, he emphasises the importance for learners of recognising different types of relation between lexical entities: three relations are identified, namely, the traditional 'false friends', but also what he calls 'good friends' and 'distant acquaintances'. Having established a thorough receptive competence (module 1), students' competence is activated — both oral and written — in a second module. In the third module, the new language knowledge is applied to translation practice. Parallel to the development of their receptive competence, students may follow a course in Linguistics which lays the foundation for comparative analyses of structures, terminologies and parallel and translated texts. This section is illustrated by examples from Italian. Arntz reports that evaluation of the method is ongoing but that the marriage of theory and practice is a promising one.

The first contribution focussing on CONTEXT, succinctly presented and richly illustrated, comes from Eugene A. Nida, and is entitled 'The Role of Contexts in Translating'. Nida presents the task of the translator as a multifaceted one, in which translation decisions of many kinds are influenced by a range of interdependent factors. Nida's understanding of 'context' is a broad one and includes not only syntagmatic and paradigmatic contexts within the text, as well as the type of text, but also factors such as language variation, prior translations, subject matter, style of the author, the publisher, the editor, the reader, and the medium of the translation. Peter Newmark's own translation typology of contexts overlaps considerably; he has distinguished the linguistic (for example collocations); the referential (the topic); the cultural; and the individual (the ideolect of the writer) (Newmark, 1991). Contextual factors notwithstanding, Nida concludes by emphasising the importance of the translator's personal contribution, acknowledging the role played by interlingual competence as well as subject knowledge. However, above all, he commends the personal integrity of the translator as the most important component in the translation process.

In 'Translation Theory, Translating Theory and the Sentence' Candace Séguinot tackles the ever-difficult concept of the sentence from a translation perspective, relating it to units of translation and translating. She starts by pointing out and illustrating that the 'reading of meaning' is both subjective and ideologically constrained. In investigating the relationship between meaning and the sentence in the context of translation, she considers a number of quotations from Peter Newmark showing different facets of the issue: the sentence as an operational unit of translating, as the individual translator's choice of unit (not, however, a choice supported by Séguinot), as a construct in translation theory when seeking a definition of the unit of translation, and as a cognitively-defined 'basic unit of thought'. Noting that a definition of 'sentence' is still missing, Séguinot goes on to develop the question of whether the sentence is a translation unit from an operational point of view, opting for an empirical rather than what she calls a probabilistic approach. Using think-aloud protocols, she demonstrates that meaning within sentences is constructed — and reconstructed in translation — through the interplay of many factors, including knowledge outside the immediate text. It seems to be the case, according to Séguinot, that the translating behaviour of more experienced translators can be characterised by an ability to look above the word level for solutions, leading her to conclude that the sentence has some kind of cognitive reality for people regularly engaged in professional translation. She therefore distinguishes between the sentence as a theoretical construct, which she finds hard to sustain, and the sentence as an operational unit in routine use, a view which she claims can be supported from a process view of translation.

The topic of Mary Snell-Hornby's contribution, 'The *ultimate confort*: Word, Text and the Translation of Tourist Brochures', draws attention to the mistakenly low professional priority given to translation in the tourist industry. Snell-Hornby situates the tourist brochure within Reiss's well-known text typology as being predominantly operative with the focus on the reader. Acknowledging the wide range of competences required in the translation of advertising, ranging, as indicated elsewhere by Candace Séguinot, from linguistic through legal to marketing, Snell-Hornby remarks on the paucity of research and training in this area, despite the complexities posed by the translation of such texts. She goes on to report on her own recent study of English and German written advertisements, highlighting linguistic and cultural differences but also identifying certain similarities, such as the pattern of 'clear, terse, rhythmical prose' and 'simple syntax', as well as the use of wordplay, metaphor and fixed idioms. The result of this analysis of model prototypes then provides the framework for the analysis of sample advertising texts and their translations. Snell-Hornby demonstrates how, as a result of the interplay of many different factors, the chosen translations fail to function as texts. In conclusion, a parallel Portuguese/English text promoting a seaside hotel in Brazil is refashioned by Snell-Hornby in the English version, showing how the judicious choice of words and phrases with positive connotations, combined with appropriate metaphors, stock images and straightforward syntax, work together to produce a coherent operative text for the target European readership. Interestingly, the refashioning also includes recommendations for a shift in the information content and its pictorial representation, reflecting the importance of recognising the cultural expectations of the European readership.

While the translation of tourist materials as operative texts presents clear cultural problems, it is often assumed that the translation of informative texts in technical areas is less problematic, particularly where technical terms are concerned. In her contribution on 'Translating Terms in Text: Holding on to Some Slippery Customers', Margaret Rogers argues that the view of terms as intralingually-interchangeable labels — in which context plays little or no role — can be a misleading one. From her analysis of two parallel extracts from an automotive handbook in English and German, she shows how terms at the textual level enter into many complex relations as word forms which cannot be related in any straightforward way to the kind of abstract representation often found at the system level of dictionary representation where terms are lexemes, not word forms. Such representations typically represent relations in hierarchical patterns such as 'X is a part of Y' or ' X is a kind of Y'. In contrast, Rogers goes on to show that terms in text are not necessarily constrained to one type of relation or dimension, but may exhibit multidimensionality. This in turn raises problems for translation, since such relations are likely to be differently mapped in each language, as her analysis shows.

The relationship between the word and the TEXT — at the same time a relationship of tension and interplay — is the topic of Albrecht Neubert's closely-argued contribution entitled 'Words and Text – Which are Translated? A Study in Dialectics'. Examining the popular view that translation is about words, Neubert moves on to show how the 'matter' behind the words is the essence in translation. Treading the slippery slope of associating language — or words — and thought, he argues that context is only rarely backgrounded as in the case of aphorisms. By their nature generic, universal and minimally contextual, aphorisms exhibit a high degree of translatability precisely because the words they contain follow closely their prototypical dictionary definitions. In most other types of text, however, context is foregrounded, since, as Neubert argues, 'meanings are funnelled through specific textual contexts'. He illustrates the importance of context in deciding the translation of words with reference to notices and titles. The translation of the title of John Updike's short story 'Slippage' is discussed in the linguistic context of the metaphors, literal usages, and mutations of words in the text and in the narrative context of the character of the story's anti-hero. The word in the title is therefore seen as an amalgam of the various meanings contained in the text. Neubert concludes on an open note, which we can take to mean that the new, i.e. translated, text, true to the dialectic, can be viewed as a synthesis of words as individual items and words as 'pointers to a complex and total textual experience'.

By looking beneath the level of text to sentences, and then in turn to clauses, phrases, words and even morphemes, in his contribution 'Translating the Introductory Paragraph of Boris Pasternak's *Doctor Zhivago*: A Case Study in Functional Sentence Perspective' Jan Firbas links the lower levels of linguistic analysis with the high-level concept of communicative purpose, thus providing an actual methodology for evaluating translations from a functional perspective. The text chosen for analysis through the application of Functional Sentence Perspective (FSP) is the opening paragraph of Pasternak's *Doctor Zhivago* in translation into four languages. Firbas's detailed treatment of this short literary extract leads to an insightful comparison of translation alternatives in terms of the distribution of information in the ST and the TTs using a set of semantic functions (Dynamic Semantic Functions or DSFs) which are then linked to their status as thematic or non-thematic in the sentence perspective. In this way, Firbas's theoretical framework provides a means of judging 'faithfulness' in translation in relation to the communicative purpose of the original. Throughout the discussion, Firbas stresses the interpretative aspect of his analysis, reflecting the 'potentiality' of utterances, particularly in literary as opposed to 'professional' texts, and leaving the reader to contemplate the complexity of the interacting and interdependent decisions open to the translator. The translator is therefore understood in the first instance as the 'interpreter' of the original text. The chapter includes a useful summary of FSP for those who are unfamiliar with Firbas's work.

Jan Firbas is not alone in his choice of literary text as a focus for analysis. Two further contributions in this section are also concerned with aspects of literary translation, in both cases poetry, although vastly different in nature. In the first of these contributions, 'Translating Prismatic Poetry: Odysseus Elytis and *The Oxopetra Elegies*', David Connolly, himself a writer and published translator of Greek poetry into English, provides some valuable insights not only into the translation of what his chosen author Elytis has called 'prismatic' poetry, but also into the creative processes of the poet himself. Of particular interest in the context of translation is Connolly's choice of a poet who himself has expressed doubts about the translatability of prismatic poetry. Prismatic poems are said to achieve an integration of form (both phonic and graphic) and meaning such that a fragment of a poem can still retain its poetic function when isolated from its source. This is said to characterise the true Greek poetic tradition. Connolly rejects the expedient of paraphrase as a translation approach, since the very form of the words contributes to their meaning: 'the words *are*, they do not *mean* something else'. Connolly also rejects the 're-creation' approach to the translation of such poetry on the ground that the poet's ideas and their verbal expression cannot be separated. In fact, he argues towards a precedence of form over meaning, illustrating this from his own translations of Elytis's work. He points out that even in cases where the form is difficult to retain, some compensation for the loss may be possible. Connolly distinguishes, following Harvey (1995), a number of different types of compensation, effectively raising the question of equivalence in an unfamiliar context. Moving on to the equally important image created in Elytis's poetic writing, primarily through, for instance, the use of metaphor, Connolly stays true to Elytis's own maxim that the juxtaposition of unexpected words — and therefore images — is intended to shock. The third poetic function described by Connolly is that of conveying emotion or sentiment. The context for this well-illustrated discussion is that of cultural equivalence in terms of connotational meaning. For the translator, the problem is one of deciding whether, for instance, to opt for 'olive tree' in an English translation (with its different connotations for that readership) or to substitute the prototypical English 'apple tree'. Connolly answers this question by reaffirming the translator's primary responsibility to the author and the SL culture. The last poetic function discussed is what Connolly calls the 'incantatory' function, in which words evoke another reality through their recitation: a contemporary kind of magic. Connolly sums up his own approach to the translation of prismatic poetry by emphasising the importance of a close correspondence to what Elytis calls the 'poetic nucleus' — the words or phrasal units — rather than the creation of a new poem or the re-creation of the poet's vision.

Another quite different poetic genre, namely the limerick, is used by Gideon Toury as an example to discuss literature in the context of translation. He sees literature as an example of a general phenomenon, encompassing many models of text types which are situated in and influenced by the cultural system in which they function. In 'How Come the Translation of a Limerick Can Have Four Lines (or Can It)?', Toury chooses to focus on the partly nonsensical, partly comic form of the limerick, a relatively value-free text type which, he claims, helps to avoid the overlay of ideology in the discussion of translation issues. The concept of model, understood as a 'set of guidelines for the production of an infinite number of texts recognised as belonging to one and the same type', is the basis for discussing the form of the limerick as typically a five-line stanza with an *aabba* rhyme scheme, in which lines 1, 2 and 5 consist of three metric feet, lines 3 and 4 of two. This, at least, is the prototypical form for the English limerick, whose most well-known proponent is Edward Lear, the nineteenth century British artist and author. The form of the limerick — or more specifically the five-line stanza — is the focus of Toury's discussion since it is one of the most salient features of the English limerick model. In terms of the model feature hierarchy then, the number of lines is what he calls 'high-level'.

In extending his discussion of the text type in the source culture to translation, Toury speculates about the relationship between the acceptability of features of the source-culture model in the recipient culture and their relative place in the hierarchy of features. His own studies so far suggest that it is not, as one may suppose, the less important features (i.e. those lower in the hierarchy) which are the first to be rejected, but rather the most salient. Indeed, in the translation of the limerick, it is precisely the five-line form which may be lost in the translation. Nevertheless, the issue is deserving of more extensive descriptive study before such rules could be uncovered: an approach which may, according to Toury, lead to explanations of the relationship between changes in the feature hierarchy of a model introduced through the act of translation and the circumstances under which these arise. Toury's perspective, as elsewhere in his writing, is a target-oriented one, placing considerable emphasis on the influence of the recipient culture on the acceptability of particular translations. Arguing along these lines, 'literary translation' may be understood as the translation of any text which is accepted as literary in the target culture (regardless of its status in the original) as opposed to its original role in the source culture. Accordingly, the translation of a limerick may involve the suppression of some of the ST features, even those salient ones by which the 'literariness' of the model is judged in the source culture. The change from five to four lines in the translation of the English limerick is just such a case in point, argues Toury. Changes of this kind may be regarded as conforming to what he calls the literary conditions of translation, compared with the more specific conditions of general textual and linguistic well-formedness.

Concluding the contributions to this section is a chapter on a different but nevertheless timely topic which also, eventually, looks to a TT orientation for a solution. Writing from his perspective as an experienced teacher of translation, Gerard McAlester discusses the assessment of translations — and eventually translators. His chapter on 'The Source Text in Translation Assessment' starts by reviewing some of the literature on translation quality assessment, focusing on what McAlester calls *evaluation*, namely the placing of a value on a translation by means of a grade or pass mark. He moves from the pre-functionalist view of evaluation to later, more functionally-oriented views, pointing out the shift away from the dominance of the ST as an evaluation measure at all levels from word to text. Most approaches to the assessment of translations depend on the concept of error, rather than what is correct i.e. a positive evaluation. But McAlester points out that both approaches lead to problems when attempting to quantify what is acceptable as an indication of translation competence. Systems of evaluation which incorporate errors in representing the ST (as well as errors violating the norms of the TL) do not, McAlester argues, replicate the situation of a real end-user, who may not be aware of the ST. Yet it is this kind of comparative evaluation which is the approach usually adopted in the academic context, particularly for purposes of accreditation. McAlester suggests that the choice of examination texts, for example, may be motivated by the apparent objectivity and suitability for quantification which a faithful rendering of a ST may provide. Even though the possibility of continuous assessment makes it easier for the translation teacher to broaden the range of translation tasks in a university context (hardly possible for the accreditation bodies, which must rely on examinations), the question of the position adopted by the translation assessor remains open. McAlester offers three potential answers: the position of the translator, of the end-user and of an expert judge. Rejecting the first two positions, he argues for the third, in which the comparison of the ST and the TT is *one* basis for the assessment but without the assumption that the ST sets what he calls the *functional standard*. The task of the translation evaluator is, McAlester concludes, one of balancing the need to reward imaginative translations whilst retaining some reliable, objective and practicable criteria for evaluating the communicative success of the translation. For the future he suggests that work on criterion-referenced testing, already familiar in foreign language testing, may be a fruitful avenue of exploration.

Looking BEYOND the present, posing the questions Peter Newmark would have us ask about the future, there seems little doubt that one of the most valuable resources for future research in translation theory is provided by the study of corpora of texts in translation: particularly when compared with texts originally written in the TL, they may yield important insights into different aspects of translation. In his doctoral dissertation, Hans Lindquist (1989) broke new ground in Translation Studies through his corpus study of English adverbials in translation into Swedish. 'Electronic Corpora as Tools for Translation', Lindquist's contribution to this volume, shows how the translator can benefit from developments in the availability of various sources for electronic text corpora, including CD-ROMS, on-line resources and the World Wide Web. He argues that such resources yield up many texts of different types which the translator can then process automatically in order to identify what he calls a 'natural' translation. Illustrating how various types of search, using key lexical words and what might be called 'linking' or 'pointer' words can produce valuable terminological 'hits' for the translator, he suggests that paper dictionaries, both general and specialised, are not only less accessible from the user's point of view but also less informative. This contribution illustrates well the usefulness of text as a rich source of lexical data for translators, enabling them not only to identify appropriate collocations but also to interpret lexical elements in their pragmatic and linguistic contexts. Lindquist concludes that electronic corpora may, in fact, be of more practical use for translators than machine translation systems.

In the smaller nations of Europe where lesser-used European languages are spoken, the subject of subtitling is increasingly attracting greater attention. Sylfest Lomheim's chapter on subtitling springs from his own extensive research and writing about this highly-specialised type of speech-to-text translation — or what he prefers to call *transfer* — as well as from his interest as an academic in translation theory (cf. Lomheim, 1995). Lomheim's contribution, entitled 'The Writing on the Screen. Subtitling: A Case Study from Norwegian Broadcasting (NRK), Oslo', falls into three main parts: a discussion of the form of subtitles and their presentation, their content, and a model for representing subtitling strategies. Remarking that reduction is intuitively a typical characteristic of subtitling, Lomheim addresses the question of how this can be measured. In settling on a practicable metric, he turns to words, showing how reduction is a consistently present but variable feature in the subtitling of the three television productions he has chosen to analyse, namely *Maigret chez les Flamands, Allo! Allo!* and *Golden Years*. Moving on to the distribution of the words on screen in terms of their division into lines, Lomheim demonstrates that while cinematic and readability considerations speak for a shorter first line, considerations of syntactic cohesion also play a role. These criteria notwithstanding, Lomheim is able to show inconsistencies in practice from his chosen TV productions. Just as line division is shown to be the outcome of interacting considerations, so also are exposure time and rhythm. While of importance for the former (most obviously) are the length of the subtitle, its level of difficulty for the readership, and the pace of the action, the two main factors relevant to the latter appear to be the subtitler's personal style and the pace of the dialogue.

With regard to the content of the subtitles, Lomheim starts by discussing Gottlieb's typology of strategies based on Danish TV subtitling practice (Gottlieb, 1994). Arguing that a proliferation of strategies is problematic in many respects, he goes on to establish a typology with fewer strategies, maintaining a distinction between those strategies which are characteristic of subtitling and those which are used in translation in general. Analysing the subtitles of his three chosen TV productions, he concludes that differences in the distribution of the strategies identified reflect genre differences rather than style differences between subtitlers.

As Eithne O'Connell remarks in her contribution, more than ten years have now passed since the Swedish educationalist Göte Klingberg pointed to potential areas of research in the field of translation of children's literature. Still, this genre remains a largely unexplored field of research among translation theorists. In 'Translating for Children', O'Connell starts from the imbalance between the high level of activity in the translation of children's literature and its low profile in Translation Studies research and training. Acknowledging the difficulty of defining what is meant by 'children's literature', she adopts a functional definition: literature for children and young people are those books published with a young readership in mind. Children's literature, however, happens to be written by adults who do not belong to the primary target group, nor do translators, publishers, parents, educationalists or critics, who all feel they have a say in children's choice of literature. As adults are more likely to wield power than children, the response from the readership is not always listened to sufficiently closely, nor has children's literature succeeded in achieving the status awarded other genres of literature. As O'Connell points out, the confluence of children's literature and translation, itself often viewed as a low-prestige activity, leads not surprisingly to low rates of pay and poor recognition in the professional world, and a paucity of research in the academic world. In looking ahead, she argues for a descriptive TL and target culture-ori-ented approach to the translation of children's literature, following the polysystems approach. This seems particularly well motivated in the light of O'Connell's own research into the screen translation (dubbing) of an animated German TV series into Irish, a lesser-used European language. The preference shown for a lower register in the Irish version reflects, according to O'Connell, the fact that Irish is for most native speakers a means of oral communication, whereas German has a much broader base. In conclusion, she emphasises the many factors which shape translations and the wide scope for future investigations of a descriptive kind, building on the early work based on the translation of Scandinavian and German children's literature.

It is not only in children's literature, however, that the translator is in the position of wielding power; in numerous other situations translation also has a political role to play. This is the topical and challenging theme of Piotr Kuhiwczak's contribution on 'Translation and Language Games in the Balkans'. Kuhiwczak's central argument is that translation can be both a force for enlightenment, revealing duplicities and misrepresentations, and a part of a game to maintain a pretence. He starts by reminding the reader of the huge changes which the former Yugoslavia has undergone in the past decade, the linguistic implications of which could not be foreseen by linguists writing in the 1970s and 1980s. He views the languages of Yugoslavia as an exemplification of conflicting attitudes: on the one hand universalist, reflecting a desire for global communication, on the other hand preservationist, respecting the language rights of the smallest community. The Serbs, Croats and Bosnians are said to share the same language, formerly known as 'Serbo-Croat', albeit with two possible scripts, Latin and Cyrillic. Rather than reflecting the Herderian principle of 'one nation—one language', historically the newly-unified Yugoslavia followed the principle of one language—one nation. Following the subsequent partition of Yugoslavia and the recognition of Croatia and Bosnia by the European Union, 'two politically distinct' languages as Kuhiwczak puts it, emerged: Serbian (written in Cyrillic script) and Croatian (written in Latin script), for which philological justifications were sought. Finally, following the establishment of Bosnia as an independent state, the language 'Bosnian' also emerged, apparently supported by standard orthographic guidelines, a translation of *The Q'ran*, and bilingual dictionaries. On closer analysis, it is Kuhiwczak's view that 'Bosnian' turns out to be the old Serbo-Croat. The political role of translation is exemplified by the use of interpreters by all post-Yugoslav delegates in the negotiations concerning Bosnia, despite mutual comprehensibility. Further examples are given by Kuhiwczak from tourist and product advertisements to illustrate the continuing attempts at linguistic and cultural diversification underpinning political developments. However, Kuhiwczak ends on an optimistic note, expressing the wish that translation in the new Balkan states should no longer play a divisive but rather a democratic role.

The role of democracy in a translation problem of a different kind emerges as an issue in Patrick Chaffey's contribution on 'ADNOM — A Project that Faded Away', in which he discusses a consensual attempt to standardise English translations of Norwegian administrative and institutional terms from the perspective of a lesser-used language. He describes some of the thinking which led to the publication of two major bilingual Norwegian-English dictionaries in the 1980s in what was, at that time, a terminological vacuum. Against a background of university translation classes which avoided the problems of administrative and institutional terminology, Chaffey starts by outlining the need for a standardised set of terms in which the need for consistency is primary. The translation of such terms is important if non-Norwegian speakers are to be able to understand and communicate about important aspects of Norwegian society. It was this perceived need which gave rise to the ADNOM project (the *Norwegian Project for Multilingual Administrative Nomenclature*) in 1982, a collaborative enterprise between Chaffey at the University of Oslo and Odd Sandal of the Translation Division of the Ministry of Foreign Affairs. Early on in the project a useful distinction was made between 'administrative nomenclature' and 'administrative terminology', the latter referring to culture-bound terminology including, for instance, legal terms, the former to the names of Norwegian institutions. Chaffey argues that a systematic nomenclature is essential for efficient communication and that this can only be achieved through standardisation with the aim of eliminating polysemy (for example *school* referring to an institution in both secondary and higher education) and synonymy (for example a university being referred to by *college, institute, academy, university,* etc.). It is well known, however, that in democratic societies standardisation operates through consensus and Chaffey describes some of the problems of achieving such a consensus, particularly in an area such as institutional names. Chaffey's contribution also raises interesting broader questions about the roles of universities, civil servants and academics (who are also civil servants in Norway) in the process of terminological standardisation, centring on the issues of authority, competence and power.

The notion of power as an issue in translation is at the heart of Simon Chau's contribution on a topic of close interest to Peter Newmark, namely campaigns to improve human and animal rights, both crucially dependent on making available relevant information to a wider audience. And outside the West, as Simon Chau points out in 'From Anonymous Parasites to Transformation Agents — A "Third World" Vision of Translation for the New Millennium', translators are key players in the process of transferring information. Using Peter Newmark's interpretation of the role of the translator in the past and the present, as well as his vision of the future, Chau makes an interesting and committed case for viewing the role of the translator outside the Western countries differently, with implications for the translator's allegiance. Outside the West, it is the social role of the translator *qua* activist that is, in his view, of primary importance. He compares this to the relative invisibility of the translator currently evident in Western countries. The amateurism of the leisured translator of the nineteenth century has given way in the West to a greater degree of professionalisation, i.e. translators are already important contributors to the flow of information across cultural and linguistic boundaries. Nevertheless, Western translators are — in Chau's words — 'efficient but characterless' or 'transparent'. Chau argues that campaigns such as those to improve human and animal rights can only succeed outside the West if information is available: in other words, action is predicated upon information. And it is translators in his view who are the key figures in transferring information in countries outside the West. Hence, he makes the strong claim that 'what gets translated, and how, charts the future of such societies'. In this sense, the translator can be viewed as 'subversive' with the ultimate goal of action for change, resulting from a chain of events starting with attracting attention, then passing on information, and finally triggering decisions which lead to action. To this end, the translator's primary allegiance, according to Chau, is to the social cause rather than to the author, the ST, the source message or the client.

This *Liber Amicorum* covers a wide range of themes and issues. Hopefully they will, if only in a small way, reflect Peter Newmark's many interests and concerns, illustrating his prescient and unique contribution to the development of Translation Studies.

References

Aijmer, K. (1996) Swedish modal particles in a contrastive perspective. *Language Sciences* 18 (1–2), 393–427.

Campbell, S. (1998) *Translation into the Second Language*. London & New York: Longman.

Davidson-Nielsen , N. (1993) *Discourse Particles in Danish*. Prepublications of the English Department of Odense University, Vol. 69. Odense: Odense University.

Gellerstam, M. (1996) Translation as a source for cross-linguistic studies. In K. Aijmer, B. Altenberg and M. Johansson (eds) *Languages in Contrast* (pp. 53–62). Papers from a Symposium on Text-based Cross-linguistic Studies, Lund 4–5 March 1994. Lund: Lund University Press.

Gottlieb, H. (1994) *Testning. Synkron billedmedieoversættelse*. Copenhagen: Center for Oversættelse, Københavns Universitet.

Harvey, K. (1995) A descriptive framework for compensation. *The Translator: Studies in Intercultural Communication* 1 (1), 65–86.

Hermans, A. (1995) Specialised dictionaries. Expectations of users, practices of authors and publishers. *Language International* 7 (1), 29–33.

Jakobsen, A.L. (1986) Lexical selection and creation in English. In I. Lindblad and M. Ljung (eds) *Proceedings from the Third Nordic Conference for English Studies* (pp. 101–12). Stockholm: Almquist and Wiksell.

Jones, W.G. (1992) HC & PC. *Professional Translator and Interpreter* 3, 18–20.

Lindquist, H. (1989) *English Adverbials in Translation. A Corpus Study of Swedish Renderings*. Lund: Lund University Press.

Lomheim, S. (1995) *Omsetjingsteori: Ei elementær innføring*. 2nd edition Oslo: Universitet-forlaget.

Mackenzie, R. (1998) The place of language teaching in a quality-oriented translators' training programme. In K. Malmkjær (ed.) *Translation and Language Teaching: Language Teaching and Translation* (pp. 15–19). Manchester: St Jerome's Press.

Newmark, P.P. (1981) *Approaches to Translation*. Oxford: Pergamon Press.

Newmark, P.P. (1988) *A Textbook of Translation*. London: Prentice Hall.

Newmark, P.P. (1991) *About Translation*. Clevedon: Multilingual Matters

Newmark, P.P. (1993) *Paragraphs on Translation*. Clevedon: Multilingual Matters.

Newmark, P.P. (1998) *More Paragraphs on Translation*. Clevedon: Multilingual Matters.

Slodzian, M. and Souillot, J. (eds) (1997) *Multilingual Comprehension in Europe*. Proceedings of the Brussels seminar, 10–11 March 1997 under the auspices of the European Commission. Centre de Recherche en Ingénierie Multilingue (CRIM) de l'Institut National des Langues et Civilisations Orientales (INALCO), Paris.

Chapter 2
An Interview with Peter Newmark

Monica Pedrola[1]

Although Peter Newmark's writing is well known throughout the world and considered one of the most important contributions to the development of Translation Studies, little is known about his life and the influence it has had on his work. What follows is a summary of a series of interviews with Peter Newmark, undertaken during the summer of 1997, with the aim of tracing the origin and the evolution of his thinking, giving particular attention to the events in his life which are linked, significantly, to his approach to translation.

Born in Czechoslovakia, Peter Newmark left his home town of Brno to move to England at the age of five but remained, throughout his life deeply attached to his place of birth. From the age of six to eighteen, he received a classical education. His memories of those years dwell, in particular, on the years spent at Rugby, a period of time in his life which he would describe as anything but happy. He describes life at Rugby as restricting individual development and, unable to conform, he felt he could not share the educational values propagated, principles such as reason is superior to emotion and knowledge for its own sake is the highest form of knowledge (Newmark, 1982). In 1934, however, Peter Newmark left the sombre world of Rugby to embark on a university career at Trinity College, Cambridge, where he studied Modern Languages, graduating with honours in French, German and English Literature three years later. While at Rugby he experienced education as something imposed on him, study and learning were given new life to him at Cambridge through discussion and debate. As a result, a dynamic and fascinating world started to open up to him. Three men in particular were to have a great influence on his thinking: his French tutor, Anthony Blunt, the art historian; his English tutor, the literary scholar Frank Raymond Leavis; and Sean O'Casey, the Irish playwright. The approach of these three men to art and literature captivated Peter Newmark, contributing towards the shaping of his own approach to translation:

> They influenced me because they took what they did very seriously.[2]

In particular, Peter Newmark grew to share the importance Leavis and O'Casey attached to moral and aesthetic aspects of literature which they primarily considered to be comments on human existence.

> Basically, literature boils down to two things. The first is a serious and moral comment on human behaviour; the second which goes hand in hand with

the first one, is a delight, a form of joy, a sensual delight. And because of the first one I always take literature seriously. . . . The situation parallels that of translation in the sense that I take translation very seriously. I don't think translation is a matter of fashion.

The encounter with Sean O'Casey contributed to a strengthening of many of Peter Newmark's political beliefs, in particular his firm conviction that all people are equal and his rejection of any form of discrimination:

Sean O'Casey was a wonderful person, a very strong personality, sharp, shrewd, interesting, fair. . . . He was a natural Communist who believed in equality and in this respect he had a strong influence on me.

Years later, Peter Newmark was to assert the role of translation as a political weapon that can and must be used to defend human rights and to favour understanding and peace between nations as well as individuals.

While still at University, Peter Newmark started to write drama critiques, first contributing to an undergraduate publication called *The Gownsman*, later to the more prestigious *Cambridge Review*. His contributions included reviews of some of O'Casey's plays which were welcomed by the playwright, as reflected in their exchange of letters where the two had the opportunity to air more general views about theatre and drama.

At the outbreak of World War II, Peter Newmark joined the British Army and after two years of service in the UK he was stationed overseas. In 1943, he landed in Italy where he remained for some time even after the end of the war. His prolonged stay in Italy was beneficial in that it provided him with the opportunity to learn yet another language, adding Italian to French and German, the two languages with which he was already familiar.

On his return to the UK, Peter Newmark started to work as a modern language teacher, first at a secondary modern school in Hull, then at a grammar school in London, and, in 1948, at Guildford Technical College. In fact, Peter Newmark's professional career as a teacher spans a period of gradually changing attitudes towards the role of translation within the educational system in the UK. The 1950s and the 1960s were characterised by widespread reluctance to acknowledge any role played by translation in the teaching of modern languages. Instead the so-called direct method of teaching was favoured, giving priority to the spoken over the written language. From the very beginning of his teaching career, Peter Newmark' approach to teaching contrasted with prevailing trends of the times. His ten years of experience as a modern language teacher at the Guildford Technical College led him to develop teaching methods which included both oral and written skills, making use of translation as a profitable instrument of comparative and contrastive analysis between source and target language.

In 1958, Peter Newmark was appointed Head of the Modern Language Department at the Holborn College of Law, Languages and Commerce, later to become the Polytechnic of Central London and, more recently, the University of Westminster. His particular approach to language teaching found a close match with the vocational aims of the College, which, under his guidance, expanded rapidly , soon to become one of the leading institutions for the training of translators in the UK. Within a few years, the number of languages taught had increased and new courses had been introduced, often the forerunners of their time. Owing to the close relationship of the College with the business and industrial community, courses were mainly concerned with technical and commercial translation with less attention given to the translation of literary texts. Moreover, some courses were specially designed to meet the needs of organisations and companies which had established contacts with the College. Then, in 1967, in order to meet the increasing demand for technical translators, Peter Newmark, together with Anthony Crane, at the time the Chairman of the Confederation of British Industry's Working Party on Technical Translation, launched the first Postgraduate Diploma in Technical and Specialised Translation.

Throughout his time as Head of Department, Peter Newmark combined his administrative duties with teaching and writing. The articles which he wrote at the time were primarily concerned with the subject of language teaching, some of which were published in *The Incorporated Linguist*, the journal of The Institute of Linguists of which he had become a member in 1962. His articles show a distancing from any views in current fashion which he felt would lead to educationally unsound teaching methods. Faced with what he experienced as an overemphasis on the importance of the spoken language, he would advocate a balanced use of translation at all stages of language learning. Peter Newmark's conception of language also emerges clearly in his articles, such as his rejection of what he experienced as an overemphasis on the social dimension of language. Acknowledging the importance of the communicative function of language, his overriding interest remained in a view of language as an instrument of thought and self-expression. Later Peter Newmark would reaffirm these views in his writing, acknowledging the influence on his work of Vygotsky, the Russian psychologist as well as of Noam Chomsky whose ideas would help to develop his concept of 'semantic translation', which, together with that of 'communicative translation', were to constitute cornerstones in his translation methodology.

Towards the end of the 1960s, translation as a language activity started to attract new interest and the status of translation began to be reassessed. With the injection of linguistics into the discipline, translation, which had often been viewed as a misused technique in language teaching programmes, began to gain academic respectability. And once again, Peter Newmark's initiatives proved to be influential in the process. In 1974, he was appointed Professor of Translation at the Polytechnic of Central London and, not long after his appointment, he introduced, as part of a four-year degree programme, approved by the Council for National Academic Awards (CNAA), the first courses in Translation Theory, together with an applied component involving translation of non-literary as well as literary texts. At about the same time, Peter Newmark also started to write his first articles dealing, exclusively, with topics in translation:

> I did actually write my first article about translation in the Journal of Education quite early on, but I only started to write seriously about it in the 1960s. What was it that attracted me? A lot of things: . . . because it's how people communicate with each other . . . And because it [translation] is a

crossword puzzle, it's something very attractive, I love to translate for the same reasons: because you have to try to fit things in; it's not only work it's a game as well as work and it helps you to understand people.

Peter Newmark's approach to translation had started to take shape, based on a continual interplay between theory and practice, generalisation and exemplification. Although he acknowledges his debt to Nida, it was teaching that was soon to become one of his most important sources of inspiration:

> I think my classes are a corrective: they stop you being abstract, they stop you being dogmatic, because all the time translation is a matter of compromise of some kind. There is no perfect translation, there is no ideal translation. A translation is never finished anyway and you can always change your mind. Classes make you face up to reality, I think even more than just reading.

In 1978, Peter Newmark was appointed Dean of the Faculty of Modern Languages at the Polytechnic of Central London, a position he held until 1981. By that time, the number of languages offered had increased to around forty. In several ways, 1981 was a significant year for Peter Newmark; not only did it see the honour of the title of Professor Emeritus conferred upon him but also the publication of *Approaches to Translation*, his first book which, a few years later, was translated into Italian as well as Arabic. Although he had given up full-time teaching, Peter Newmark continued to teach on a part-time basis as a Visiting Professor in Translation at the University of Bradford. And in 1982, at the time of the establishment of the Centre for Translation Studies in the Department of Linguistic and International Studies at the University of Surrey, he was appointed Visiting Professor in Translation Theory at that University, the first position of its kind in the UK.

As time has progressed, Peter Newmark has continued to add depth and refinement to his thinking on translation, resulting in further development of his translation methodology. More recently, he has shifted to a somewhat different approach to the subject which, however, does not exclude his early concepts of semantic and communicative translation. This new approach is based on a series of correlative statements, constituting a more obvious attempt to solve the conventional dualism of translation in order to reach what he calls a pure, universal culture and language to serve as a *tertium comparationis* between the source and the target language (Newmark, 1995):

> Translation is not simply a duality or a seesaw between the various factors related to two languages. On the contrary , it should encompass the medial forces that incline neither way: these are, indisputably , the material facts and the ideas which the two texts cover; the logic which is unrelated to context and culture that ensures that a text makes sense; the continuously increasing determination of universal human, animal and environmental rights, which leave their imprint on languages and are disseminated through translation, in particular through the reduction of sexist language, the elimination of words of prejudice, the decline of anthropomorphism and the rejection of opprobrious animal metaphors; the aesthetic principles of

writing, which ensure that within a framework of relevance, a translation is as economical, clear and agreeable as possible, whilst bad writing comes out as bad writing in any language, if it's faithfully translated; lastly, the move towards a pure universal language which covers every facet of feeling and fact.

It is in this sense that his statement 'I take translation very seriously. I don't think translation is a matter of fashion' should be interpreted, an attitude which may be considered the driving force of all his thinking on translation.

As a result of the broadening of Peter Newmark's theories, his publications have increased in number. His second book, *A Textbook of Translation*, was published in 1988 and, like his first book, was subsequently translated into several languages including Arabic, Spanish and Galician. In 1991, a selection of essays which had been published during the previous decade appeared as his third book entitled *About Translation*. Although concerned with a number of different topics in translation these essays share the common theme of a constantly growing attention to the ethical aspects of translation, in daily as well as academic practice. Next, in 1993, a collection of essays written for separate, individual issues of *The Linguist*, from 1988 until 1992, appeared in a single volume as *Paragraphs on Translation*, and this was followed by *More Paragraphs on Translation*, his most recent publication, which appeared in 1998.

From the relatively isolated position of his earlier years, Peter Newmark has gradually gained an international reputation as evidenced by his participation in large numbers of meetings and conferences throughout the world and his presence on numerous international examination boards. In 1984, he was invited by the *Hong Kong Baptist University* to design a four-year degree course in Translation Studies. Again, in 1991, he accepted the invitation from University Consultants Japan Ltd. to design and direct a course leading to a Diploma in Translation for Japanese students. During 1988–93, he was the President of the Institute of Linguists. Two years later, his contribution was instrumental in setting up a national policy on the role of languages and translation, not only within the UK, but also in relations with other countries throughout the world. His important contribution to the development of Translation Studies has also been acknowledged through the conferral of honorary degrees. In 1995, he received an honorary doctorate in Translation from the Scuola Superiore di Lingue Moderne per Interpreti e Traduttori of the University of Trieste and three years later he was awarded a second honorary doctorate, this time from the Hong Kong Baptist University.

Peter Newmark continues to be based in the Centre for Translation Studies in the School of Language and International Studies at the University of Surrey, preparing papers for conferences and meetings throughout the world and writing articles, mainly for *The Linguist*. Throwing some light on his life and his thinking will hopefully assist in a more comprehensive appreciation of the nature of his work and the significant contribution which he has made to the establishment and development of Translation Studies as a discipline in its own right in the UK as well as throughout the world.

Notes

1. In June 1997 Monica Pedrola of the Scuola Superiore di Lingue Moderne per Interpreti e Traduttori of the University of Trieste spent a month at the Centre for Translation Studies (CTS), Department of Linguistic and International Studies, School of Language and International Studies, University of Surrey, Guildford, engaged in research for a thesis on Peter Newmark and his work, which included interviews with Peter Newmark conducted during her period of study with CTS. This chapter is an English version of her text and interviews recorded.
2. Indented passages with no bibliographical reference are ideas expressed by Peter Newmark during the interviews.

References

Newmark, P.P. (1981) *Approaches to Translation*. Oxford: Pergamon.

Newmark, P.P. (1982) The English public schools: A reckoning. *New Universities Quarterly* 26(3), 263–79.

Newmark, P.P. (1988) *A Textbook of Translation*. Hemel Hempstead: Prentice-Hall International.

Newmark, P.P. (1991) *About Translation*. Clevedon: Multilingual Matters.

Newmark, P.P. (1993) *Paragraphs on Translation*. Clevedon: Multilingual Matters.

Newmark, P.P. (1995) A correlative approach to translation. In R. Martin-Gaitero (ed.) *V Encuentros Complutenses en torno a la traduccion* (pp. 33–41). Madrid: Editorial Complutense.

Newmark, P.P. (1998) *More Paragraphs on Translation*. Clevedon: Multilingual Matters.

Part 1 Word

Chapter 3

The Translator and the Word: The Pros and Cons of Dictionaries in Translation

Janet Fraser

The single word is getting swamped in the discourse, the individual in the mass of society — I am trying to reinstate them both, to redress the balance.

(Peter Newmark, 1988: xii)

Sometimes when I translate, I am hoping to release better words from my unconscious, my memory hold. I go on repeating the start of a sentence and stop, expecting something fresh to emerge, to pop out. Sometimes it does; it's a relief, and I start my smirk. More often, it doesn't, and I despair.

(Peter Newmark, 1991a: 32)

On occasions when I have been speaking about my research into the process of translation, I have been tackled by Peter Newmark about my claims regarding the extent to which professional translators use dictionaries and how this differs from the way in which students use them. I have claimed (typically in Fraser, 1993, 1994) that one of the key differences between student or trainee translators and practising freelance professionals lies in how they deal with unfamiliar words: while the former tend to rely heavily on dictionaries, and particularly bilingual dictionaries, the latter are more reluctant to do so and then use them more sparingly and, indeed, more sceptically, 'as a stimulus to the process of refining meaning and selecting an appropriate rendering' (1993: 135).

Newmark has always, however, taken the view that there is no good reason why professional translators should not use a bilingual dictionary as a first port of call (Newmark, 1998: 29):

> The bilingual dictionary is the translator's single, first and most important aid, and a translator who does not consult one when in doubt is arrogant or ignorant or both.

This mirrors earlier remarks in Newmark (1988: 174), where he specifies that:

> Multilingual dictionaries give few collocations and are therefore useful only as initial clues to a further source; bilingual dictionaries are indispensable but they normally require checking in at least two TL [target language] monolingual dictionaries and sometimes in SL [source language] monolingual dictionaries.

How, then, is the individual translator to deal with the single words in a text that cause difficulties, to avoid the despair described in the second quote at the beginning of this chapter? I want to demonstrate that there is a role both for the use of bilingual dictionaries and for what I shall call 'intelligent guessing' , not as a definitive solution but as a stage in a more efficient research process. I shall support my arguments with examples from a study of 21 practising professional translators. The methodology is described more fully in Fraser (1994). Briefly, the translators were given a French news item on reform in higher education in France and asked to translate it into English as though for publication in the *Times Higher Education Supplement*. As they translated, they gave a commentary on the processes in which they were engaging (a verbal or 'think-aloud' protocol, or TAP) which was subsequently analysed to identify and categorise these processes. In this contribution, I shall focus on how the translators in the study dealt with specific words and phrases from the text, which is reproduced at the end of this chapter (cf. Appendix). These are mostly items of educational jargon, with one idiom: *DEUG; les premiers cycles* and the related expression *des étudiants de maîtrise ou de troisième cycle; filière; se réorienter;* and *faire peau neuve*. The comments reproduced are taken verbatim from the TAPs.[1]

Scepticism about Bilingual Dictionaries

Before I outline the way the translators made use of the dictionaries they had available, I want to describe the general tone of scepticism about bilingual dictionaries that emerged in the translators' protocols. Two-thirds (14) of the 21 translators commented along these lines, and the following comments are fairly typical:

> 'I find quite a lot of the dictionaries these days are [pause] I would say useless';
> 'It is in here! Amazing! I'm always amazed when something I want is actually in [the dictionary]!';
> 'I hate words like this because almost certainly, my dictionary hasn't got it';
> 'I'll have to think about that one because that's the kind of thing you'd never be able to find in a dictionary';
> 'So we're going to try for *DEUG* which I'm not very hopeful of finding';
> 'I'm going to check that [pause] . . . and I find of course that it's not in the dictionary.'

Moreover, even when the translators found these words or phrases in a bilingual dictionary, they were often dissatisfied with the results:

> '[for *faire peau neuve*] "Turn over a new leaf" — that's complete cobblers, obviously';
> '[for *filière*] It doesn't help very much';
> '[for *premier cycle*] Not happy with the dictionary definition here.'

Even Newmark would agree on this point: 'Swearing at the dictionary must be any translator's favourite pastime' (1991b: 60).

Why were these translators so dissatisfied with their bilingual dictionaries[2] that, on the basis of past experience, they were often reluctant at all to use them or, when they did use them, found them wanting? I believe there are several reasons for this. Firstly, it is important to bear in mind that a bilingual dictionary, however good, can only ever give *a range* of possible TL equivalents for any SL term, not all the possible translations it can have, unless it is a purely technical term (and even then, the one-to-one equivalent is not as common as might generally be thought, cf. Rogers, this volume). This is so obvious that it should not need commenting on, yet it is easy for a translator to 'suspend disbelief' and treat the bilingual dictionary as the source of a comprehensive list of possible translations.

Secondly, in a linked point, the context of the SL text needs to be borne in mind if the translator is to make an informed choice from among the TL equivalents that are listed. For example, in the first and second editions of the *Collins-Robert*, the translations offered for *filière* (in education terms, a pathway, a route or a combination of subjects) include 'channels', '(administrative) procedures' and 'network', none of which fits within an overall context of educational reform (the third edition also offers, though some way down the list, 'new subjects' for the collocation *les nouvelles filières*); meanwhile, the *Harraps New Standard French and English Dictionary* (used by a few of the translators) had only 'official channels' alongside a number of highly technical equivalents. With a less imaginative translator, this had the effect of channelling the search for a good translation along unhelpful lines, as the first comment below shows, while a better translator, finding the dictionary wanting, drew on other resources, as the second sequence of comments shows:

> 'Let's see. Channels, official channels? Stock exchange — that's interesting. "This request must go through the usual channels"';
> 'Administrative procedures, channels, no. . . . Now, in the context, is it a department, is it a subject area, is it a section? Is it a facul-, no, it's not a faculty. . . . I'm going to use "strand" for now . . . I'd need to talk to someone working in a university and I'd ask them, do you talk about strands? What's your vocabulary?'

Similarly, [*se*] *réorienter* was given in all editions of the *Collins-Robert* as 'to restream, regroup according to ability' (neither of which, clearly, applies to higher education) and in the *Harraps* as 'to reorient, reorientate'. Again, the better translators were rightly sceptical about these translations:

> 'It gives "to restream", meaning "regroup according to ability"; is that *really* what it means here?';
> 'We need a bit of support here. "Restream" applies . . . more to schools, so I can't use that.'

Clearly, where the translation equivalents offered by a bilingual dictionary were unhelpful, translators were better off using other resources to find a helpful rendering: as one put it: 'Sometimes I will override the dictionary meaning and go by my instinct, by the context.'

Thirdly, account must be taken of how the word or phrase in question fits into the overall syntax of the section of the text under consideration. The text on which this particular study was based, for example, included the sentence *Les premiers cycles font peau neuve dans une partie des universités*. The *Harraps* gives 'to cast or slough a skin, to turn over a new leaf' as possible translations for *faire peau neuve* while the *Collins-Robert* (all editions) lists 'to adopt or find a new image (of a political party)' or 'to turn over a new leaf'; both these possibilities could, however, be used only with animate beings in English, whereas the TL idiom is clearly being applied to university courses and was therefore better rendered with a passive, such as 'are being completely overhauled' or 'have been given a new look'. The better translators used the dictionary translation as a starting point in the search for a better equivalent, as the first three comments below illustrate, while — as I comment above and illustrate in the remaining comment — less imaginative ones were unable to move beyond the words on the page:

> 'It's not actually the first- and second-year students who are adopting a new image, is it?';
> 'I think really "turning over a new leaf" is not, it implies that some*body* is, er, well, I suppose reforming their character, so I don't like that . . . I would say "undergoing a transformation" or something like that';
> '*Faire peau neuve*, "to adopt a new image, to change one's clothes, to turn over a new leaf". Right, er, now yes, um, *les premiers cycles* is talking about the stage in their education . . . Okay, I've got the feel . . . "are undergoing a metamorphosis" is a phrase that comes to mind . . . or "revised" but I don't particularly want to use "revised" again. [Consults computer thesaurus] Reviewed . . . "are being reviewed", "are being changed" . . . "modify" is better, "transfigure, transform". . . . "In some universities, the first- and second-year courses are being transformed"';
> '*Faire peau neuve*, it's obvious what it means but I'll see if the dictionary has a nice expression [pause] which I don't have in my head. . . . Um, "to turn over a new leaf" . . . "In some universities, first- and second-year courses are turning over a new leaf."'

'A poor translator', comments Newmark (1991c: 144), 'will translate the words as though they were isolated, will swallow any idiom or metaphor whole.' If there is a risk that an unimaginative, unconfident, lazy or just hard-pressed translator will opt for the easier solution of using what he or she finds in the dictionary rather than thinking beyond the dictionary, then a bilingual dictionary is more of a liability than a help for such phrases, as the translator needs to use it intelligently.

Similarly, the bilingual dictionaries used by the translators were less than helpful on the phrases *les premiers cycles* and *des étudiants de maîtrise ou de troisième cycle*. Here, however, the problem was not only finding the best translation but also rendering an idea that was a cultural concept and reflected a radically different organisation of higher education in France from that with which my (English-speaking British) translators were familiar. The *Harraps* gives 'first stage of secondary education' for *premiers cycles* and 'Master's' for *maîtrise* but has no entry for *troisième cycle*, while the translations offered in all three editions of the *Collins-Robert* are 'first and second year', 'research degree, ≈ Master's degree', and 'postgraduate *ou* [sic] PhD student' respectively. The problem for these translators was how to make these distinctions meaningful when the whole organisation of the higher education system was different. Some were satisfied with using the dictionary equivalents, even though they were signalled as being only approximate. Others were, however, rather more alert and demonstrated a healthy scepticism:

> 'It's a university degree taken after two years, um, something which doesn't have an equivalent [in the UK], so I'll explain it';
> 'It says that *premier cycle* is roughly equal to first and second year, but I think it's more specific than that *here*. I think a *DEUG* is a two-year diploma';
> 'The *maîtrise* is really the equivalent of our graduate, so *troisième cycle* would probably be "postgraduate"; we have the problem of the divergence of the French and British systems.'

Ladmiral is supportive of such scepticism, arguing that:

> [l]es mots n'ont pas de sens, ils n'ont que des emplois ... ce n'est pas à coups de dictionnaire que [le traducteur] arrive à briser la coquille qui renferme le sens des textes qu'il affronte [1979: 186].[3]

This was graphically illustrated by the translator who got fixated on the *Harraps* translation for *premier cycle* and commented:

> '*Cycle* ... um, 'first stage of secondary education, second stage of secondary education' ... but this is about primary education!'

The same translator translated *maîtrise* in accordance with the *Harraps* definition as 'Master's degree' but then rendered *étudiants de troisième cycle* as 'third-year students', demonstrating a complete lack of context for the translation of these terms. Malone (1988: 57) highlights the source of the problem:

> The entry:definition format ... [is chosen] in a standard bilingual dictionary because it is precisely the lack of any true lexical counterpart of the entry in the TL that necessitates the provision of a definition in lieu — a definition which, in a good dictionary, will reconstruct in spread out fashion the semantic features and relations implicit in the entry lexeme.

It was interesting, in fact, to note that while the term *premiers cycles* was generally expanded and explained in the body of the text (sometimes in conjunction with the French term), the phrase *des étudiants de maîtrise ou de troisième cycle* was, by contrast, generally telescoped into 'postgraduate students'. The translators were here reflecting the differences between the two systems in terms of the differing stages students go through (three distinct cycles, each with its own award(s), in France, compared with a basic distinction between undergraduate and post-graduate in the UK) and drawing on the assumptions they were making about the knowledge their TL readers already had about both systems. While it could be argued that the remit of a bilingual dictionary is not to educate its users, it is clear nonetheless that the *Harraps* here fails its users by providing only part of the story about higher education awards in France and by failing to 'recon-struct ... the semantic features' of the term *maîtrise*. My view is that although it looks 'translator-friendly' with its long lists of equivalents (the list for *filière* is particularly long), it is in fact of little help where a translator is faced with a cultural rather than just a lexical gap. The *Collins-Robert*, by contrast, shows a valuable progression through its three editions from mere expansion of the abbreviation to an explanation and contextualisation that is of real value to a translator. This alone is, of course, a crucial reason for translators keeping their working tools up to date.

'Intelligent Guessing'

While some of the translators showed a clear disregard for context, others used what I shall call a strategy of 'intelligent guessing' when confronted with words or phrases that were unfamiliar and, moreover, did not feature or were not adequately defined in a bilingual dictionary. *DEUG* (*diplôme d'études universitaires générales*, the lowest level of academic award, for which students qualify after successful completion of two years in higher education) came into this category. The acronym does not appear in the *Harraps* or in the first edition of the *Collins-Robert*; in the second edition of the *Collins-Robert*, it appears only in the abbreviations section, with its full French version but no translation or explanation, whereas in the third edition, *DEUG* appears in the main body of the dictionary with a cross-reference to *diplôme*, where it is defined as 'diploma taken after two years at university', a further illustration of the need for translators to keep dictionaries up to date! The strategy of 'intelligent guessing' was used by the translators in two ways, by some to work out what the individual letters might stand for so that they would be able to find them in another, more specialised, dictionary and by others, once they had established what the acronym referred to, to work out how it fitted into the context and, thus, how it might be best translated.

The context was, for example, used in the following sequences of comments to try to work out how to look up DEUG:

> 'Is it *diplôme d'éducation universitaire générale*, something like that? Because we're talking about reform in university education, we've got the E and U for *éducation* and *universitaire*, and I've just stuck *générale* on the end as a guess!';
> 'I see it comes from *Le Monde de l'Education*. Er, I think, um, for E, *éducation* is probably a reasonable guess. Er, I should say for the D, it would be something like *direction* or *directorat* . . . [But] it seems to be to do with *enseignement supérieur*, so I suppose [E]'s got to be *enseignement*, but what on earth U and G stand for . . . Now at this end of paragraph, I've been enlightened and I should probably have spent even more time reading the text before I started . . . It's now become clear the *DEUG* seems to be a qualification.'

In the first case, having done some preliminary guessing, the translator found the correct term in the current year's *Quid* (a yearbook giving a wide range of information and statistics about France, roughly equivalent to *Whitaker's Almanack*), while the second solved the problem by looking in the *Collins-Robert* under *diplôme* once she had 'guessed' what the D stood for.

Arriving at an Acceptable Translation

Rather than rely on the bilingual dictionary, then, the better translators in this study used a variety of resources to arrive at what they considered to be an acceptable translation. I have already commented on the inadequacies of bilingual dictionaries in some respects, and those translators who also, or instead, used a combination of monolingual SL resources, such as the *Petit Robert*, *Larousse* or *Quid*, fared better in finding a meaningful translation, albeit at the cost of more intellectual effort than merely finding a translation equivalent in a bilingual dictionary. *Quid*, for example, gave an explanation of the three *cycles* with their length and the award(s) given on completion of each, and also, as I comment above, defined *DEUG*, while the *Petit Robert*'s definition of *faire peau neuve* was a simple *changer complètement* which proved a better starting point in the search for a translation suitable for an inanimate subject than the bilingual equivalents. One translator summed up the advantages of monolingual resources: 'Filière. Now, as it's clearly specific, I think I'll go straight to the *Robert*.'

One reason for this was that, as I have already commented, bilingual dictionaries are not exhaustive, and the translators who expressed scepticism about their usefulness used them as a way of refining meaning rather than of establishing the best equivalent from those on offer. Typical comments in this vein included:

> 'I'll see which [of several possible renderings] the dictionary gives prominence to';
> 'The dictionary doesn't really help me there, but it sort of *pushes me along in the way I was thinking*' [emphasis added];
> 'I'll look in the dictionary to see if I can find anything that will *give me an idea* for that' [emphasis added].

This has been borne out by other studies too. Jääskeläinen (1989) found that fifth-year (postgraduate) students of translation in Finland had learned to exercise discretion with regard to their bilingual dictionaries:

> The fifth-year students never used the bilingual dictionary to solve a comprehension problem . . . They did use it for solving production problems, but . . . rather cautiously; in fact, they tended to use it as a source of inspiration when their own 'inner dictionary' suffered from a momentary malfunction [and] to confirm their spontaneous tentative variants. [1989: 188, 191–2]

'A dictionary is used more as an aide-mémoire and really, all you want is confirmation of what you are looking for', confirms Samuelsson-Brown (1993: 37).

Another reason for not consulting a bilingual dictionary as a first step is the willingness of many of these translators to tolerate uncertainty and let meaning emerge as they work their way through a text rather than needing, as students often do, to establish the exact meaning for a term before moving on:

> You have to get right to the end of the text to try and finalise some of the words that occur at the beginning. It seems like a laborious process but it's the only way to do it, to my mind.

The benefits of this approach included the fact that many terms do, as one translator commented, become clear or 'resolve themselves' over the full length of a text:

> 'Now that it's clear that *DEUG* is a qualification, I've now got a better translation of *filière*, "subject combination".'

Also relevant here is that professional translators tend to take a wider view of resources than merely dictionaries and are likely to use a variety not only of reference works but also of other sources of information: several translators referred to friends or relatives doing university courses in an attempt to retrieve educational terminology in English, and one, when confronted with *DEUG*, hunted for a prospectus he had for a French university.

Conclusions

Translators will always use bilingual dictionaries alongside other reference material, and therefore need to be aware of the limitations as well as the strengths of their bilingual dictionaries; they must know their way around them and how to use them efficiently, and need to keep them up to date. I believe, however, that in the training translators receive, learning to 'release words from [the] unconscious, [the] memory hold' plays a crucial part; as linguists, we have a capital of words, collocations and phrases that is often much larger and richer than we give ourselves credit for, and bilingual dictionaries need to be approached as tools in helping us to exploit this resource rather than as replacements for it. There could also be instances when the bilingual dictionary may not be the translator's best friend and 'intelligent guessing' may be a complementary or even an alternative, and better, strategy — not, clearly, where the bilingual dictionary has a good range of renderings but certainly where, for whatever reason, the equivalents on offer to the bilingual dictionary user are inadequate. With my tongue firmly in my cheek, then, I want to quote Newmark (1988: xii) once more: 'There are no absolutes in translation, everything is conditional, any principle . . . may be in opposition to another . . . or at least there may be tension between them.'

Henderson, whose work on the personality profiles of translators and interpreters is controversial but thought-provoking, found that when his profiles were weighted for experience, the contrasts between the two groups widened, with translators proving both 'more intelligent' and 'more self-sufficient' (1987: 97). Where there is a tension between the limited but easily accessible resources of a bilingual dictionary and the potentially richer mental resources an experienced translator has but will have to work harder to exploit, an intelligent translator will calculate the trade-off between the two approaches in terms of text-type and function, purpose of the translation, and deadlines to be met in order to reach a decision about the best way to resolve a lexical problem. Self-sufficiency means not only having extensive resources but also knowing where the limits of those resources lie, and a truly self-sufficient translator will, through instinct or good training, be eclectic in her/his choice of resources in any given task.

Appendix

Source language text

Les premiers cycles font peau neuve dans une partie des universités. En revanche, la loi adoptée par le Parlement au début juillet a été annulée par le Conseil constitutionnel.

Tutorat et modules sont les deux mots de la rénovation universitaire, lancée par Jack Lang en 1992, qui se met en place dans quelques universités à cette rentrée. Une trentaine d'établissements ont rénové certaines de leurs filières: Aix-Marseille–I et III, Amiens, Bordeaux-I et II, Chambéry, Clermont-Ferrand-II, Réunion, Lille-I, II et III, Limoges, Lyon-I et III, Marne-la-Vallée, Montpellier-I, Mulhouse, Nantes, Nancy-I, Nice, Pau, Perpignan, Paris-V, VII, VIII, IX, X, XII et XIII, Poitiers, Toulon, Toulouse-I et III, Valenciennes.

Ces DEUG nouvelle formule sont bâtis autour d'une discipline principale — la majeure — et de disciplines complémentaires — mineures — qui peuvent aider les jeunes étudiants à se réorienter en cours de DEUG. En début de première année, les étudiants recevront un enseignement sur les méthodes de travail et des informations sur les études. Des étudiants de maîtrise ou de troisième cycle leur serviront de tuteurs. Les unités de valeur (UV) sont remplacées par des modules, qui correspondent à une heure et demie ou deux heures d'enseignement par semaine. Il faut en acquérir de six à douze, selon les filières, pour obtenir le DEUG.

François Fillon, ministre de l'enseignement supérieur et de la recherche, avait envisagé de reporter cette rénovation. Le rapport qu'il a commandé à l'Inspection générale de l'administration l'en a dissuadé: les inspecteurs estiment que la réforme est applicable sans moyens supplémentaires; elle oblige néanmoins à une meilleure organisation des enseignements.

Par ailleurs, le Conseil constitutionnel a annulé le 28 juillet la loi qui autorisait les universités à déroger aux règles établies par la loi Savary de 1984. Le ministre avait donné son accord à ce texte présenté par plusieurs députés de la majorité et voté le 6 juillet. Il prévoyait que tous les établissements pouvaient déroger à la loi Savary, avec l'accord du ministère, pour « *expérimenter des formules nouvelles* ». Après l'annulation du Conseil constitutionnel, François Fillon a déclaré qu'une nouvelle loi serait présentée . . . après l'élection présidentielle de 1995.

Le Monde de l'Education no. 207 (September 1993)

Notes

1. The transcription of the TAPs was made possible by a grant from the Nuffield Foundation, whose support I gratefully acknowledge here.
2. Sometimes the *Harraps* but most commonly the *Collins-Robert*, usually first or second edition, with a few translators using the then new, third edition
3. 'Words do not have meanings, they have only usages . . . it is not by repeated use of a dictionary that [the translator] manages to penetrate the shell enclosing the meaning of the texts with which he is dealing' (my translation).

References

Collins-Robert French Dictionary (1978). HarperCollins/Dictionnaires Le Robert (2nd edn 1987; 3rd edn 1993).

Fraser, J.E. (1993) Public accounts: Using verbal protocols to investigate community translation. *Applied Linguistics* 14 (4), 325–43.

Fraser, J.E. (1994) Translating practice into theory: A practical study of quality in translator training. In Catriona Picken (ed.) *ITI Conference 7 Proceedings* (pp. 130–42). London: ITI.

Harraps New Standard French and English Dictionary (1971). Harrap (2nd edn 1981).

Henderson, J.A. (1987) *Personality and the Linguist*. Bradford: University of Bradford Press.

Jääskeläinen, R. (1989) The role of reference material in professional versus non-professional translation: A think-aloud study. In Sonja Tirkkonen-Condit and Stephen Condit (eds) *Empirical Studies in Translation and Linguistics*. Joensuu: University of Joensuu.

Ladmiral, J.-R. (1979) *Traduire: Théorèmes pour la Traduction*. Paris: Petite Bibliothèque Payot.

Malone, J. (1988) *The Science of Linguistics in the Art of Translation*. New York: State University of New York Press.

Newmark, P.P. (1988) *A Textbook of Translation*. London: Prentice Hall.

Newmark, P.P. (1991a) Paragraphs on Translation 11. *The Linguist* 30 (1), 28–32.

Newmark, P.P. (1991b) Paragraphs on Translation 12. *The Linguist* 30 (2), 60–4.

Newmark, P.P. (1991c) *About Translation*. Clevedon: Multilingual Matters.

Newmark, P.P. (1998) Paragraphs on Translation 53. *The Linguist* 37 (1), 29–31.

Samuelsson-Brown, G. (1993) *A Practical Guide for Translators* (1st edn). Clevedon: Multilingual Matters.

Chapter 4

On the Perils of Particle Translation

Gunilla Anderman

Normally, one translates ideas, on which the words act as constraints.
(Peter Newmark, 1982: 135)

Introduction

In translations into English, requests often emerge as overly strongly worded as in 'Do hear me out for God's sake', a proposed rendering of the Danish 'Hør mig dog til ende'. In this case, the cause of the translation problem is the presence of *dog* in the source text (ST) which has resulted in the somewhat over-emphatic English rendering of the plea 'Please, let me finish':

Hør mig dog til ende
Hear me/PART/[1] to (the) end[2]

The lexeme 'dog', described as 'an invariable word with pragmatic function' (Davidsen-Nielsen, 1993: 16), is commonly referred to as a particle.

In Danish, the particle 'dog' along with others such as *da, jo, nok*, 'sgu', *skam, vel*, and *vist* are well known for being 'notoriously difficult to translate' (Davidsen-Nielsen, 1993: 1). In addition to problems of over-emphasis, target text (TT) renderings may also fail to capture subtle nuances expressed by particles in the original; particles may simply go missing in translation and, with them, the modal element they were originally intended to convey in the ST. It has, for instance, been suggested that the failure to translate the numerous particles used in the conversational narrative used by the Danish writer Hans Christian Andersen has resulted in a more formal literary style in the English version of his famous fairy tales (Jones, 1992: 18). In what follows I shall first discuss particles from a linguistic perspective, synchronically as well as diachronically. This will be followed by an overview of the functions of particles in some European languages. The chapter will conclude with a discussion of corpus-based studies of particles in translation.

Particles in the Linguistic Literature

The translation of particles is not a problem confined to English. Just like Danish, 'German has its Füllworter or Flickworter (doch, eben, ja, wohl etc)' (Newmark, 1982: 148) And as any translator knows working between German, a language rich in particles, and French, generally acknowledged to be 'eine relativ partikelarme Sprache', a relatively particle poor language (Dalmas, 1989: 237), transferring the nuances conveyed by particles in the ST can be anything but an easy task. In addition to French, other Romance languages are similarly 'particle-poor' while the types of particle found in Danish and German also appear in Dutch and Frisian as well as in Swedish and Norwegian. English, on the other hand, has no defined grammatical category akin to this type of particle, so often used in the other Germanic languages, perhaps the reason why 'this is virtually a non-topic in the English-language linguistic tradition' (Abraham, 1991: 331). German linguistic research, however, following the seminal work by Weydt (1969),[3] boasts an extensive body of work on different aspects of particles. The subject has also been discussed with respect to a number of other languages ranging from Greek (cf. Tsohatzidis, 1989) to Russian (cf. van Schooneveld, 1989), Serbo-Croat (cf. Ličen, 1989) and Polish (cf. Tabakowska, 1989, Grochowski, 1989). In the case of the Germanic languages, considerable attention has been devoted to the subject (for Dutch cf. Abraham, 1981, for Danish cf. Davidsen-Nielsen, 1993, for Swedish, Aijmer, 1977, Andersson ,1976, Borgstam, 1977, for Swedish as spoken in Finland, Saari 1979 and for Norwegian cf. Askedal, 1989 and Fretheim, 1989). With the emergence of Translation Studies as an academic discipline, different aspects of particles have also increasingly been examined in contrastive, corpus-based studies and the problems related to their translation have been analysed (cf. Jakobsen, 1986 for English-Danish and Aijmer, 1996 for Swedish-English).

Classification and origin of particles

In discussions of particles in the linguistic literature, different proposals for their sub-classification have been put forward for greater ease of comparison and discussion. It is, however, acknowledged that the boundaries between different particle types are somewhat fuzzy. Palmer (1986: 45) does not for instance consider the so called modal particles — particles expressing modality — in German (*denn, doch, ja, schon, wohl*) to be specifically modal since they comment on a proposition rather than express an opinion about it. As my main concern here is with particles and how they fare in translation, less attention will be given to problems of subclassification and, as a result, the term 'particle' will simply be used throughout. Modal particles are, however, referred to as such when reflecting the terminology used in the research findings under discussion.

Particles may also be viewed in a dynamic perspective, another subject of considerable interest. This has been explained in terms of grammaticalisation involving a process of semantic 'bleaching', whereby grammatical and pragmatic functions develop from a lexical source (Abraham, 1991). Diachronically, the process of grammaticalisation tends to entail a move from lexis to syntax to morphology, as illustrated by the development of the future tense marker in the Romance languages from the post-positive verb 'habeo' in Vulgar Latin, for example *cantare habeo*, into a verbal inflection, for example French *chanterai*, Italian *cantero*, and Spanish *cantare* (Davidsen-Nielsen, 1993: 17). Or as in the case of Danish *sgu*, often used to signal that the speaker is emphatic, the particle is a derived and weakened version of 'så Gud (hjælpe mig)', 'so (help me) God'

(Davidsen-Nielsen, 1993: 17). In the case of Norwegian, the tag particle *da* is generally assumed to be diachronically derived from the adverbial *da*, meaning 'then', 'in that case' (Fretheim, 1989: 403). And in Swedish, the particle *nog*, which a speaker may use to signal that s/he is in possession of sufficient information to make an assertion, originates from the adverb *nog* with the lexical meaning of 'sufficient' (Borgstam, 1977: 219). The reason why the multitude of particles which are used in German, and other Germanic languages, are not found in English constitutes yet another important issue of obvious typological interest but one which falls beyond the scope of this chapter (cf. Abraham, 1991 for a more detailed discussion).

The Function of Particles

According to Nehls (1989: 282): 'German modal particles serve to express different kinds of emotional attitudes in interpersonal communication such as "astonishment", "doubt", "emphasis" "encouragement", "impatience", "reassurance", "reproach", "surprise", etc.' A further factor to be considered when determining the meaning of a particle is its association with sentence type. When, for instance, the German modal particle *denn* occurs in a yes/no question it conveys astonishment, as in:

Bist du denn schon in Japan gewesen?
Have you/P/already been to Japan?

When, on the other hand, the particle *denn* occurs in wh-questions as in:

Wie heisst du denn?
What is your name/P/?

the particle serves to convey a note of friendliness. In addition *denn* can also be found in exclamatory sentences such as:

Ist das denn nicht herrlich!
Is that/P/not wonderful!

Here the use of the particle serves to express an invitation to the addressee to share in the enthusiasm expressed by the speaker (Nehls, 1989: 283).

Modal particles may also be viewed as signalling 'gaps in the argumental configuration of a prior text portion and partly indicate how a missing argument is to be reconstructed by the hearer or reader' (Abraham, 1991: 333). This provides a further interpretation of the meaning of *denn*, in this case that of 'doubt', the speaker finding reason to believe that the person referred to will not come (1991: 333):

Kommt er denn?
Comes he/P/?
DOUBT

In addition to expressing doubt through the presence of the particle 'denn', speakers may also signal personal involvement through the use of *wohl*, another modal particle in German (1991: 336):

Kommt er denn wohl?
Comes he /P/ /P/?
DOUBT + PERSONAL INVOLVEMENT OF SPEAKER

The addition of *auch*, yet another particle, provides the information that the speaker wishes the proposition to come true (1991: 336):

Kommt er denn wohl auch?
Comes he /P/ /P/ /P/?
DOUBT + INVOLVEMENT + WISH FULFILMENT

Together with *doch*, *ja* ranks as 'the most frequent lexeme in the German language' (Abraham,1991: 367) and overall,'[m]odal particles are perhaps the most typical feature of colloquial German' (Nehls, 1989: 282). As suggested by Aijmer (1996), the use of particles may be explained in terms of relevance theory, which postulates that the relevance of an utterance is not unconstrained but must be set off against the effort of processing it (Sperber and Wilson, 1986). The use of particles is, as a result, particularly common in the interaction between speaker and addressee as 'a speaker who wants to help the hearer by reducing the processing effort therefore uses particles of different kinds. They serve as cues to the hearer by signalling the type of relevance conveyed by the new utterance' (Aijmer, 1996: 400). The sequence of the particles *da* and *vel* in Norwegian may, for instance, help to reinforce an expression of astonishment and incredulity (Askedal, 1989: 693):

Du kan da vel   ikke spise middag klokka åtte om morgonen?
You can /P/ /P/   not eat dinner o'clock eight in the morning?

Reflecting the attitude of the speaker to the addressee, particles may also develop interpersonal or polite functions as in the case of *ju* and *väl* in Swedish, two particles of high frequency use which may be used to signal uncertainty or weak commitment:

Det kan jag väl göra
It   can I   /P/ do
'I suppose I could do that'

The use of the particle *väl* may, however, also serve as a politeness strategy in indirect requests (Aijmer, 1996: 402):

Men du kan väl köpa lite köttfärs hos Märta . . .
But you can /P/ buy some mince at Martha's . . .

Here the presence of the particle *väl* makes it easier for the addressee to turn down the request, rendering it more polite by showing respect for his/her 'face needs'. (For a discussion of the abstract notion of 'face' cf. Brown and Levinson, 1987 and of the culture specific requirements of 'face' and their importance for dialogue in translation cf. Anderman, 1992). If, on the other hand, the speaker wishes to make it known to the addressee that there is some shared knowledge between them, the particle *ju* may be used in order to create a feeling of intimacy and rapport (Aijmer, 1996: 402):

Folk   kan tro   att du är smugglare ju
People may believe that you are smuggler /P/

In the case of Danish, it has been suggested that particles may be viewed as being predominantly either hearer- or speaker-oriented (Davidsen-Nielsen, 1993: 3–4). Particles considered primarily hearer-oriented are those describing the speaker's reaction to what s/he believes is the hearer's attitude to the state of affairs contained in the proposition and include *da, jo, nu* and *skam* (Davidsen-Nielsen, 1993: 3):

John er da/ jo nu/ skam en flink fyr
John is   /P/ /P/ /P/ /P   a nice guy

John er da   jo/ nu/ skam i London.
John is   /P/   /P/ /P/   /P/   in London.

While both *da* and *nu* signal potential disagreement, *jo* signals that the addressee is assumed to be aware of and accept the state of affairs referred to (Andersen, 1982: 90). The difference between *da* and *nu* on the other hand, has to do with the function of the former being pragmatically presupposing. By saying 'John er da i London' the speaker assumes that the addressee is in fact aware of the state of affairs referred to, in spite of the fact that, at the moment, s/he does not appear to accept it. Finally, *skam* is characteristically used to eliminate any doubts the addressee may have as to the truth of the proposition and is invested with a reassuring function (Harder, 1975: 107).

Speaker-oriented particles in Danish, on the other hand, reflecting the speaker's attitude to his/her own knowledge of the state of affairs referred to, include *nok, vel* and *vist* (Davidsen-Nielsen, 1993: 4):

John er nok/ vel/ vist/ en flink fyr
John is   /P/   /P/   /P/ a nice guy

John er nok/ vel/ vist/ i London
John is   /P/   /P/   /P/ in London

By selecting *nok*, 'the speaker informs the hearer that the evaluation of probability is made by himself alone' (Davidsen-Nielsen, 1993: 3). If, on the other hand, s/he is uncertain about the correctness of the state of affairs referred to, the speaker will select *vel*, if s/he wishes to include the addressee in the assessment of the situation by superimposing an inquiring element. Finally, by choosing *vist*, the speaker not only expresses his/her own lack of certainty but also informs the addressee that there are others besides him/herself who believe the situation to be true to which reference is made (cf. Galberg Jacobsen, 1992).

In the case of Swedish, the use of the particle *nog* similarly signals probability but with the added element of providing an assurance that the speaker is sufficiently well informed to be able to make an assertion (Borgstam, 1977). In sentences containing *nog* such as:

Otto kommer nog i morgon
Otto comes /P/ tomorrow

Borgstam views *nog* as the surface realisation of an underlying *jag vet* 'I know', an analysis she feels is similarly applicable to other Swedish particles such as *väl*, *ju* and *visst* (1977: 275).

In a comparative study of *jo, nog* and *väl*, Saari (1979) discusses the use of these particles in three different Swedish-speaking areas — in Borås, a town in the southern part of Sweden, in Tornedalen in the north and in Helsinki, the capital of Finland. Saari points to the possibility that *jo, nog* and *väl*, although different in lexical form, may be used interchangeably without difference in meaning. Thus, the preference on the part of a speaker for a particular particle to express a certain attitude may be regionally determined (1979: 239–42). A similar observation has been made by Burkhardt (1989) with respect to the use of the particles 'halt' and 'eben' in German. Burkhardt quotes an elderly Braunschweig informant who, without hesitation, ascribed *halt* to southern and *eben* to northern German usage (1989: 358). This would seem to lend further support to a picture emerging of particles as words 'of low semantic content' (Newmark, 1982: 148) presenting the translator with a context-bound rather than a lexically-based problem of interpretation.

The problems encountered in the translation of particles into languages where they are not used to encode modal functions are also directly or indirectly confirmed by the linguistic literature on the subject. According to Liefländer-Koistinen's study of the translation of the work by Heinrich Böll there seem to be 'special difficulties for Finns in capturing the right meaning of *doch* in Finnish translation' (1989: 185). In the case of Danish, Davidsen-Nielsen considers the use of particles to be 'a very characteristic feature of the grammar of Danish' and observes that they 'constitute a well-known stumbling block to foreign learners of Danish' (1993: 32).

Studies of Particles in Translation

Recently, the problems presented by particles in translation have been highlighted by corpus studies, specifically aimed at examining texts in translation, including the translation of particles. In an early study comparing English novels in Danish translation with novels written originally in Danish, Jakobsen (1986) observes that while *jo* ranked as the 58th most frequently used word in the Danish corpus this particle showed a much lower frequency of occurrence in the translated texts where it ranked as low as 114. As Jakobsen points out, the more limited occurrence of *jo* has a not insignificant bearing on the way in which modality is expressed in texts in translation (1986: 104). If, instead of using a particle like *jo*, modality is expressed by means of modal verbs or what Jakobsen calls 'heavy adverbials', the result is inevitably 'a distinct awkwardness of style' (1986: 104). As an example, Jakobsen points to the occurrence in the corpus of the verb *formoder*, 'presume' in English, and the adverb *formodentlig*, 'presumably', used 7 and 13 times respectively in the translated texts, while the texts originally written in Danish showed no instances of either (1986: 104). Instead the modality function of the English verb and adverb might have been rendered with greater stylistic ease in Danish through the use of appropriate particles, a more idiomatic means of achieving the intended meaning of the ST.

Jakobsen's findings for Danish are closely matched by Gellerstam's observations and conclusions drawn from his comparative corpus study of English novels in Swedish translation and novels originally written in Swedish (1996). In the translated texts, the word *förmoda*, 'presume', showed a frequency of occurrence of 62 while in the texts originally written in Swedish it only occurred 7 times (1996: 55). 'Speaker attitude', Gellerstam observes, 'is frequently expressed by adverbs like *väl*, *nog*, *ju* (notoriously difficult to translate out of context). In English, on the other hand, speaker attitude is frequently expressed by verbs, especially in dialogue [1998: 58].' Gellerstam quotes some examples from the corpus of translated texts, offering his own preferred, translation solutions. In the first case, he replaces verb and subject with the particle *väl*, in the second case a 'heavy adverb' with the particle *nog* (Gellerstam 1996: 58):

> Det är OK, antar jag
> It is OK, suppose I
> Det är väl OK
> It is /P/ OK

> Han är förmodligen ute
> He is presumably out
> Han är nog ute
> He is /P/ out

Gellerstam points out that it is not uncommon for English syntactic patterns to be found in the corpus in place of idiomatically more appropriate translation solutions, including instances of stylistically stilted attitudinal expressions such as *förmoda*, 'presume', and *anta*, the Swedish for 'suppose' and their related adverbs, i.e *förmodligen*, 'presumably', and *antagligen*, 'supposedly', or question tags such as *eller hur*, rather than more appropriate translation equivalents involving particles (Gellerstam, 1996: 58).

A need for a greater use of particles in translation into languages where they encode modal functions than appears, at present, to be the norm, manifests itself particularly strongly in the case of colloquial dialogue. Dalmas (1989) has examined the use of particles in the translation into German of the French detective stories by Georges Simenon, characterised by their frequent use of dialogue. Focusing on the ST words and phrases rendered by the particle *wohl* in the TT, Dalmas points to no less than 17 different ST variants including *bien*, not a frequently found choice in comparison with verbs such as *supposer* and *devoir* and adverbials such as *sans doute* and *probablement*. The corpus also shows instances of *peut-être* or questions in the ST resulting in the choice of *wohl* in the TT (Dalmas, 1989: 233). Further evidence of the presence of particles as a hallmark of idiomatic dialogue in German translation is provided by the study undertaken by O'Sullivan and Rösler, a comparison of English children's books, similarly characterised by their frequent use of dialogue, and their German translations (1989).

In a corpus-based study, consisting of Swedish fiction containing recurring passages of dialogue, Aijmer (1996) has examined the use of Swedish modal particles and their translation into English. The modal particles in the corpus were found to have varying frequency; *ju* emerged as the most frequently occurring particle, followed by *väl* with *nog* in third and *visst* in fourth position. In the case of *nog* which, according to Aijmer, 'signals that the speaker weighs the validity of the proposition against what he knows or what is generally known' (1996: 406), a number of different translation choices were represented. Most frequently, *nog* was rendered by an adverb such as 'probably', 'of course', 'certainly', while clauses such as 'I think' or 'I guess' occurred only on a few occasions. In addition to adverbs and clauses, other syntactic means are sometimes used in translation to convey the meaning of particles as observed by Nehls, according to whom 'the senses conveyed in German by modal particles have to be expressed by other linguistic devices' (1989: 284) in translation into English.

While the literature clearly points to the overall greater use of particles in the spoken language, they are also found in written language where they tend to occur in 'argumentative prose, for example, where the writer seeks to win over the reader to his own case or point of view' (Davidsen-Nielsen, 1993: 5–6). Particles are 'characteristic of linguistic interaction and serve to ensure that what is communicated is understood in the right way' (Harder, 1975). Particles may even have a role to play in poetry (Bornebusch, 1989: 284). In his study of the different functions of dialogical elements in the poems by Goethe, Kleist, Heine, Busch and Celan, Bornebusch shows how the use of particles, along with imperative and interrogative constructions, constitutes the most obvious indicator in the poems of the presence of dialogue.

When used in dialogue, particles are not infrequently linked to other features characteristic of conversational style such as stress and intonation. In Norwegian, one of the functions invested in the particle *da* appears to be its availability to the speaker to make use of two different intonation patterns: one pattern indicates that the speaker expects an affirmative answer while the other one signals anticipation of a negative response (Fretheim, 1989: 409). And a study of Hoffmannsthal's *Der Schwierige*, The Difficult Man, from German into Italian leads Burkhardt (1989: 368) to conclude that 'aufgrund der unterschiedenen Sprachstruktur die deutschen Partikeln häufig nicht übersetzt und nur durch Satzakzent oder Wortstellung zum Ausdruck gebracht werden können' (because of the difference in linguistic structure, the German particles are often not translated and can only be expressed through sentence stress or word order).

Particles in drama translation — a 'trilemma'

The conclusions to be drawn from the studies discussed would seem to point to the importance of preserving the intended meaning of particles in the translation of drama, a genre of translation almost exclusively concerned with dialogue. The question then arises as to what extent translators of plays appear to be successful in achieving this goal.

The language of drama translation is not a widely explored field of research but the limited evidence available does, regrettably, seem to suggest that there might be some lack of awareness of the problems presented by particles in translation.

In the case of translation from Norwegian of the plays of Henrik Ibsen it has been observed that '[t]he numerous Norwegian particles pose another problem . . . ' (Akerholt, 1980). Akerholt provides some examples to exemplify the problem as in the line below from *A Doll's House*:

De   har dog vel tid   et øyeblikk?
You have /P/ /P/ time   a   moment?

As a translation, Akerholt offers: 'You have perhaps time for a moment?' but she expresses her reservations, pointing out that '[h]ere the "dog vel" conveys a feeling of uncertainty and appeal, more so than the English "perhaps" can do' (Akerholt, 1980: 119).

In the case of the Swedish writer August Strindberg, Ibsen's Scandinavian compatriot, a corpus study of five translations of his well-known play, *Miss Julie*, shows *ju* to be, by far, the most frequently occurring particle with *nog* in second position closely followed by *väl* (Gustafsson, 1997). Attempted solutions to the problem presented by the translation of these three particles into English range from the use of an adverb to omission. The first translation following the gloss is by Elizabeth Sprigg (ES), the second by Kenneth McLeish (KM), followed by my own suggested version (GA):

Du är väl   inte svartsjuk på henne
You are /P/   not jealous   of her
'You're not jealous of her, surely' (ES, 1955: 103)
'You're jealous' (KM, 1995: 38)

Elizabeth Sprigge appears to have been looking for an appropriate adverb with which to replace *väl* in translation and found 'surely', listed as a translation equivalent in all the standard Swedish-English dictionaries. In this case, in a play set at the turn of the century, 'the dictionary approach' succeeds. In a contemporary play, however, it might be a less successful solution, risking perhaps the introduction of a supercillious note in what might have been intended as a more neutral exchange. Kenneth McLeish's omission of the particle, on the other hand, turning the negated statement into the affirmative in translation, certainly provides a more forceful and actable line. Instead it misses out on the potentially teasing note inherent in *väl* which might have been captured through the use of a tag question:

'(But) you're not jealous, are you?' (GA)

A brief passage from *Scenes from A Marriage*, the translated script of Ingmar Bergman's television series, provides a contemporary example, similarly showing particles to constitute problems in translation. Translated by Alan Blair, *Scenes from A Marriage* consists of six scenes, tracing the relationship between Johan, a research psychologist, and Marianne, a lawyer. In Scene Three, entitled *Paula*, John returns home to his wife to announce that he is leaving her for Paula. The verbal strategies of the couple in this scene have been analysed by Tannen (1994). Tannen shows that Marianne, naturally off balance and feeling anxious, attempts to seek her husband's involvement by asking a large number of questions, a total of 63 questions, almost twice as many as Johan's 37 (1994: 166). Tannen acknowledges, however, that objections may be raised because the text is accessible for the purpose of textual analysis 'only in translation' (1994: 172, footnote 2).

A closer examination of the ST shows Marianne exhibiting a considerably higher degree of anxiety than is already conveyed by the TT. A number of the particles she uses in Swedish clearly show that her hesitancy, lack of confidence, and concern to concede, frequently remain untranslated in the English version, confirming Aijmer's observation that 'modal particles tend to disappear in the translation process' (1996: 395). The STs by Ingmar Bergman (IB) are follwed by glosses, then translations by Alan Blair (AB) as well as my own versions (GA):

Du skulle ju inte komma   förrän i morgon   (IB, 1983: 77)
You were /P/ not come(ing) until to-morrow
'You were not coming until to-morrow'   (AB, 1983: 82)
'But I thought you weren't coming until to-morrow'   (GA)

Du måste vara hemskt trött och jag är   nog sömnig jag också (IB, 1983: 79)
You must be   terribly tired and I am /P/ sleepy I   too
'You must be awfully tired and I'm a bit drowsy too . . . ' (AB, 1973: 84)
'You must be awfully tired and (I think) I'm a bit sleepy too . . . ' (GA)

Translators working from source languages, where particles are used, into 'particle-poor' languages would seem to be facing a 'trilemma'. Firstly, matching a particle, i.e. an adverb, with another adverb, may, given the appropriate style and setting, be a successful solution but it may also result in stilted, at times over-emphatic TT versions. Here the strong pull towards finding a suitable one word equivalent constitutes a danger, perhaps a consequence of over-simplistic bilingual dictionaries or vocabulary lists of early learning, providing lexical items in isolation rather than in context (for further discussion of early modern language teaching and its later effects on vocabulary selection in translation cf. Anderman, 1998). Secondly, omission of the modality effect conveyed through the use of particles might, on the other hand, result in a dialogue lacking in nuance, less attractive to an actor or a director. Thirdly, full semantic interpretation of particles offers no panacea either, as modification in the form of paraphrasing might result in wordiness threatening the succinctness of the original ST dialogue.

Closer attention to the role and function of particles and to the means by which languages encode modal functions would seem to be the way forward. At this point in time, however, studies of the different ways cultural relativity is reflected in the modality systems of the languages of the world are not easily available (Aijmer, 1996: 423). Such studies would, however, put us in a position to gain a better understanding of the verbal means used by different cultures to encode modal functions including perhaps the case of the Crewe Indian, reported in Borgstam (1977: 217). Facing a Canadian Court of Justice, the Crewe Indian was asked to take the oath and 'to tell the truth, the whole truth and nothing but the truth'. 'I can't,' he answered, 'I can only tell what I know.'

Ensuring that doubts, surprise and hesitation as well as the whole range of human emotions expressed through the use of particles are appropriately conveyed and do not go missing in translation, would undoubtedly constitute a move towards a higher degree of cross-cultural understanding. A necessary step, perhaps, if translation is to be 'not merely a transmitter of culture, but also of the truth, a force for progress . . . ' (Newmark, 1988: 7).

Notes
1. PART, denoting particle will henceforth be abbreviated to /P/.
2. As is implicit in this chapter each particle has a number of different translation alternatives depending on context. Thus only glosses have been provided throughout except in cases where semantic interpretation is not self-evident
3. I am grateful to Peter R. Lutzeier for bringing to my attention the work of H. Weydt.

References
Abraham,W. (1981) Partikeln und Konjunktionen — Versuch einer kontrastiven Typologie Deutsch-Niederländisch. In H. Weydt (ed.) *Partikeln und Deutschunterricht* (pp. 168–88). Heidelberg: Julius Groos.
Abraham,W. (1991) The grammaticalization of the German modal particles. In E. Closs Traugott and B. Heine (eds) *Approaches to Grammaticalization* (pp. 331–80). Amsterdam: John Benjamins.
Aijmer, K. (1977) Partiklarna *ju* och *väl*. *Nysvenska studier* 57, 205–16.
Aijmer, K. (1996) Swedish modal particles in a contrastive perspective. *Language Sciences* 18 (1–2), 393–427.
Aijmer, K., Altenberg, B. and Johansson, M. (eds) (1996) *Languages in Contrast*. Papers from a Symposium on Text-based Cross-linguistic Studies, Lund, 4–5 March 1994. Lund: Studentlitteratur.
Akerholt, M.B. (1980) Henrik Ibsen in English translation. In O. Zuber (ed.) *The Languages of Theatre. Problems in the Translation and Transposition of Drama*. Oxford: Pergamon Press.
Anderman, G. (1992) Translation and speech acts. In Y. Gambier and J. Tommola (eds) *Translation and Knowledge. Scandinavian Symposium on Translation Theory IV*, Turku, 4–6.6.1992 (pp. 377–87). Turku: Turku University Press.
Anderman, G. (1998) Finding the right word. In K. Malmkjaer (ed.) *Translation and Language Teaching: Language Teaching and Translation* (pp. 39–48). Manchester: St Jerome Press.
Anderson, L.-G. (1976) Talaktsadverbial. *Nysvenska studier* 55–56, 25–47.
Askedal, J.O. (1989) Sprachtypologische aspekte norwegischer Partikelstrukturen. In H. Weydt (ed.) *Sprechen mit Partikeln* (pp. 691–702). Berlin: de Gruyter.
Bergman, I. (1973) *Scener ur ett äktenskap*. Stockholm: P.A. Norstedt & Söners Förlag.
Blair, A. (tr.) (1973) Scenes from a Marriage. In Ingmar Bergman: *The Marriage Scenarios* (pp. 7–202). New York: Random House.
Borgstam, S. (1977) Nog är tillräckligt. *Nysvenska studier* 57, 217–26.
Bornebusch, H. (1989) Abtönungspartikeln als Dialogizitätsindikatoren in lyrischen Texten. In H. Weydt (ed.) *Sprechen mit Partikeln* (pp. 477–87). Berlin: de Gruyter.
Brown, P. and Levenson, S. (1987) *Politeness: Some Universals in Language Usage*. Cambridge: Cambridge University Press.
Burkhardt, A. (1989) Partikelsemantik. In H. Weydt (ed.) *Sprechen mit Partikeln* (pp. 354–69). Berlin: de Gruyter.
Dalmas, M. (1989) Sprechachte vergleichen: ein Beitrag zur deutsch-französischen Partikelforschung. In H. Weydt (ed.) *Sprechen mit Partikeln* (pp. 228–39). Berlin: de Gruyter.
Davidsen-Nielsen, N. (1993) *Discourse Particles in Danish*. Prepublications of the English Department of Odense University, Vol. 69. Odense: Odense University.
Fretheim, T. (1989) The faces of the Norwegian inference particle *da*. In H. Weydt (ed.) *Sprechen mit Partikeln* (pp. 403–15). Berlin: de Gruyter.

Gellerstam, M. (1996) Translations as a source for cross-linguistic studies. In K. Aijmer, B., Altenberg and M. Johansson (eds) _Languages in Contrast_ (pp. 53–62). Papers from a Symposium on Text-based Cross-linguistic Studies, Lund: 4–5 March 1994. Lund: Lund University Press.

Grochowski, M. (1989) Preliminaries for semantic description of Polish particles. In H. Weydt (ed.) _Sprechen mit Partikeln_ (pp. 77–84). Berlin: de Gruyter.

Gustafsson, G. (1997) _Ju, nog_ and — _väl_ — Swedish Attitudinal Adverbs in English translation. A corpus study of five translations of _Miss Julie_ by August Strindberg. Unpublished MA dissertation, University of Surrey.

Harder, P. (1975) Praedikatstruktur og kommunikativ funktion. _Nydanske Studier og Almen Kommunikationsteori_ 8, 103–12.

Jacobsen, H. Galberg (1992) _Vist_ og _nok_. Om et par formodningsbiord i dansk. _Mal & Maele_ 2, 13–20.

Jakobsen, A.L. (1986) Lexical selection and creation in English. In I. Lindblad and M. Ljung (eds) _Proceedings from the Third Nordic Conference for English Studies_ (pp. 101–12). Stockholm: Almquist & Wiksell.

Jones, W.G. (1992) HC and PC. _Professional Translator & Interpreter_ 3, 18–20.

Ličen, M. (1989) Die serbokroatische Partikel PA und ihre deutschen Entsprechungen. In H. Weydt (ed.) _Sprechen mit Partikeln_ (pp. 171–84). Berlin: de Gruyter.

Liefländer-Koistinen, L. (1989) Zum deutschen _doch_ und finnischen _-han_. Beobachtungen zur Übersetzbarkeit der deutschen Abtonungspartikel. In H. Weydt (ed.) _Sprechen mit Partikeln_ (pp. 185–95). Berlin: de Gruyter.

McLeish, K. (tr.) (1995) _Miss Julie_ by August Strindberg. Calcutta: Seagull Books

Nehls, D. (1989) German modal particles rendered by English auxiliary verbs. In H. Weydt (ed.) _Sprechen mit Partikeln_ (pp. 282–92). Berlin: de Gruyter.

Newmark, P.P. (1982) _Approaches to Translation_. Oxford: Pergamon Press.

Newmark, P.P. (1988) _A Textbook of Translation_. Hemel Hempstead: Prentice Hall.

O'Sullivan, E. and Rösler, D. (1989) Wie kommen Abtönungspartikeln in deutsche Übersetzungen von Texten, deren Ausgangssprachen für diese keine direkten Äquivalente haben? In H. Weydt (ed.) _Sprechen mit Partikeln_ (pp. 204–16). Berlin: de Gruyter.

Palmer, F.R. (1986) _Mood and Modality_. Cambridge: Cambridge University Press.

Saari, M. (1979) Om adverben _ju, nog_ och _väl_. In _Festskrift till Björn Petterson 29.12.1979_. Skrifter utgivna av Institutionen för filologi II vid Tammerfors universitet, nordisk filologi. Tammerfors.

Sperber, D. and Wilson, D. (1986) _Relevance. Communication and Cognition_. Oxford: Blackwell.

Sprigge, E. (tr.) (1955) _Miss Julie_ by August Strindberg in _Twelve Plays_. London: Constable.

Tabakowska, E. (1989) On pragmatic functions of the particle TO in Polish. In H. Weydt (ed.) _Sprechen mit Partikeln_ (pp. 535–45). Berlin: de Gruyter.

Tannen, D. (1994) _Gender & Discourse_. Oxford: Oxford University Press.

Tsohatzidis, S. (1989) Particle distribution and pragmatic theory choice: A test case from Modern Greek. In H. Weydt (ed.) _Sprechen mit Partikeln_ (pp. 546–58). Berlin: de Gruyter.

van Schooneweld, C. (1989) On Russian modal particles. In H. Weydt (ed.) _Sprechen mit Partikeln_ (pp. 96–104). Berlin: de Gruyter.

Chapter 5

Accuracy in Translation

Viggo Hjørnager Pedersen

> ... *we do translate words, because there is nothing else to translate;*
> *there are only the words on the page; there is nothing else there*
>
> (Peter Newmark, 1988: 73)

Introduction

The above quotation is a salutary reminder that translators should stick to their text; however, the word of the text must of course be interpreted and rendered, as Cicero has it, *verbis ad nostrum consuetudinem aptis* — with such words as we are used to. If not, the result becomes impossible for a target language (TL) audience to cope with. This may be demonstrated by a very simple test: a word-for-word translation of the first three lines of the Anglo-Saxon poem *Beowulf*:

> Hwæt, we gar-dena in geardagum
> Theodcynninga   thrym gefrunon
> Hu tha æthelingas ellen fremedon (1–3)
>
> (Klaeber's edition, 1922)

> What! We spear-Danes' in yesterdays
> Folk-kings' power asked
> How those nobles valour promoted

The text that results from this experiment seems to me impossible — even though serious translations of this type have in fact been undertaken (cf. Thorpe (1855) and Schaldemose (1847), below). But the point of translating a literary text as literature must be to convey an idea of the appeal of the original, so that, even though 'equivalence' may not be achieved, the TL audience can still understand why the text in question is important. If we concede that this appeal, in a narrative poem like *Beowulf*, is dependent not only on the story, but also on the way the story is told, we must try to find ways of matching this appeal in a translation. In other words, although we must never forget the words of the original, we cannot just exchange them as counters and get the exact amount in our own currency.

Exactly how a match may be achieved depends on the circumstances of the case. Carne Ross (1961: 3) has suggested that if the languages and cultures involved are close to each other, you need not 'translate', but may 'transpose', rendering not only the content but also the form of the original. If that is not possible, however, an additional problem presents itself: how are we to decide whether a given solution is satisfactory or not?

A considerable time has passed since the appearance of House (1977), and the interest in evaluation of which *A Model for Translation Quality Assessment* bears evidence was soon to be replaced by the view of the so-called manipulative school — that translations should be described and not criticised. From a literary point of view, however, it seems to me fairly futile to discuss literary translations unless you are prepared to stick your neck out and say which, in your opinion, are good, and which are not. By all means let us describe the texts studied, and let us carefully state the reasons for our preferences. But in the final instance, the study of a literary text as literature must conclude in a value judgement unless we are willing to leave the description of translations to the computers.

The 'manipulators' seem to have two main objections to value judgements about translation:[1] they are arbitrary, and they tend always to consider translations as something second-rate compared with originals. However, the arbitrariness may be kept in check if the translation critic is under an obligation to carefully state the premises for such pronouncements; and the fact that translations do indeed often seem inferior to their originals need not prevent the critic from seeing that the translations may be excellent works of art in their own right, and should certainly not remove the obligation to look into what is possible in a given situation. A translation should not be assessed according to some general and abstract ideal, but seen as a result of work performed in a particular situation and from a specific language into another; and it is part of the critic's task, by comparing the translation studied with other original and translated texts in the TL, to see what may reasonably be expected in such a situation.

Bridging Translation Gulfs: The Example of *Beowulf*

In an earlier article (Hjørnager Pedersen, 1988: 61–71) I have tried to sum up all the difficulties that may beset a translator as being a question of *distance*: whichever scale you choose to apply — time, space, culture or language — the world of the TL reader may seem to be far away from that of the source language (SL) writer, and how do you bridge that gulf? In the following, I shall use some translations of *Beowulf* to exemplify some of the difficulties that a translator must come to terms with when embarking on such a project.

Summary of the poem

Beowulf celebrates a Scandinavian warrior hero, whom we meet on two occasions: as a young man, when he helps the Danish King Hrothgar by slaying two monsters — Grendel and his mother — who mar the peace of the King's hall and have a propensity to devour his warriors in their sleep. The second event described takes place fifty years later, when Beowulf, now an old king, slays a dragon, but subsequently dies of his wounds. Rather like Milton in *Paradise Lost*, the poet reflects on the events he describes, seeing them against the background of a mixture of Christianity and pre-Christian, stoical belief in *wyrd* ('fate').

Arousing interest in the text

The basic difficulty of all literary translation is to get it done: someone must be willing and able to study the original text and bring out a version in the TL, and there must be a publisher who believes that there is a TL audience willing to buy the translation. For centuries, *Beowulf*, like most literature from the early Middle Ages, was not considered to fulfill these criteria. The one existing manuscript led a very quiet life in the Cottonian collection (now in the British Library) until rediscovered in the late eighteenth century by the Copenhagen librarian Grim Johnson Thorkelin, and subsequently by the Danish romantic writer N.F.S. Grundtvig, the first major Beowulf scholar, who, as he expresses it, 'burnt like a volcano' to discover more stories from Scandinavian antiquity, and mastered the poem largely by learning it by heart, after which he 'made such a noise with [his] pen as if the heavens were about to fall' (Grundtvig, 1861: XVIII — my translation).

Since then, there has been no real difficulty in finding readers and translators; the very fact that the poem belonged to the Germanic past, which had made it unfashionable for centuries, made it extremely interesting in the Romantic period, and since then there has been continued interest in the story. But in contrast to its contents, the form of the poem has a limited appeal to modern readers, and, as a result, this century has seen many prose translations, and as it contains some obvious fairy tale elements there have also been a number of adaptations for children.

The form of the poem

This takes us to the question of form, i.e. the Anglo-Saxon long line with a varying number of stresses, a caesura and alliteration linking the two halves of the line — often with two words in the first half line alliterating with one in the second:

> Frommum *feohgiiftu*   on *fæder* bearme (21)

The text uses run-on lines and a syntax characterised less by neatly ordered sentences than by strings of words, many of which are appositions. Add to this the fact that the first half of a line is frequently an apposition to the first half of the preceding line, with the second half of that line wedged in as a parenthesis, and it becomes clear why the syntax may prove difficult to follow, as in the opening lines of the poem as shown below.

An additional problem is the use of compounds — more than a thousand of them in the 3182 lines of the poem, according to Klaeber (1922). Most of them are nouns, but adjectives (including participles) also occur, in which a whole phrase may be packed: *utfus*, 'eager to set out'; *Wiglaf*, 'the one left in battle'; *wyrmcyn*, 'race of serpents'; etc., and if you try to unpack the phrase, the translation tends to get longer than the original —something which Batteux among others warned against (cf. Batteux (1760: 3, 54) quoted and discussed in Hjørnager Pedersen, 1987: 22–3).

Exemplification

The extract from which most of the exemplification has been drawn may seem episodic in relation to the general story line, but is in fact crucial when we consider the main themes of the poem. Lines 1–52 tell the story of King Scyld (= Shield) who arrived mysteriously as a small child at a time when the Danes needed a king. His ability to rule and to subjugate neighbouring tribes is stressed. We next learn about his son, Beowulf, who grows up learning the virtues of a prince, especially generosity towards his retainers. Finally we hear about Scyld's funeral, when he is put back on board the ship that brought him, furnished with weapons and treasure, and set adrift.

This whole sequence obviously prefigures the poem at large, which starts with a state of chaos, because nobody can oppose the monster Grendel; but then a brave young warrior arrives to restore order; he is called Beowulf just like Scyld's son, and indeed behaves like a son towards the Danish king; and the poem, like the first episode, ends with the death and burial of a king, who is mourned by his retainers.

Establishing the text

In a poem like *Beowulf*, a number of details are debatable. There is no absolute certainty as to the nature of the words translated. Bits and pieces of the manuscript are missing, there are obvious scribal errors, whose correct emendation is less obvious, and there are ambiguities, where the translation depends on the interpretation of the original.[2]

Lines 20–1 constitute a good example of the consequences of translators working with different versions of *Beowulf* (. . . indicates a gap in the text):

> Swa sceal . . . uma   gode gewyrcean
> Frommum feohgiftum   on fæder . . . rme (*or* . . . ine?)

Which Klaeber (1922), following earlier editors, modifies to:

> Swa sceal (geong g)uma   gode gewyrcean
> Frommum feohgiftum   on fæder (bea)rme

The emendations are obviously conjectural, and there are other possibilities. However, in the first line we must look for a word starting with a 'g' to alliterate with *gode*. *Guthfruma* ('warrior prince') has been suggested. For the second line, Grundtvig suggested *fæder wine* ('the father's friend') and translated accordingly,[3] because he read the end of the line as ' . . . ine'; the meaning would be that the young prince should try to influence his father's friends to become his friends, too; a more tempting solution is *fæder feorme* ('the father's hospitality') meaning that the prince is munificent at his father's expense, but this solution yields four alliterating words in one line, which is above average.

Types of translation

It is a moot point, discussed by Apel (1983), among others, how far a translation from one evolutionary stage of a language to another constitutes interlingual rather than intralingual translation. Admittedly, modern English translations of Old English poetry can recycle a fair amount of the vocabulary of the original, as demonstrated by Ezra Pound's *Seafarer*, among others. However, linguistic differences between Old and Modern English are so great that it seems

natural to treat the modern English versions of *Beowulf* as translations in the
normal sense of the word.

A number of the translations considered here, such as those of Thorpe (1855)
and Schaldemose (1847), must be characterised in the words of Draskau (1978)
as 'translations of literature' rather than 'literary translations'. They are often
printed in parallel editions with one half-verse of Old English followed by one
of translation (cf. Thorpe (1855) and Schaldemose (1847), below).

For Germanic languages, the possibility of imitating the metre of the original
in literary translation is obviously there, although it has not been used very often.
For other languages, such as French, this is hardly the case. An alternative
approach is to try a different metre or metres, as did Grundtvig; most translators,
however, have chosen prose, which allows a translator to be fairly accurate, but
which on the other hand, for a gifted translator, is not incompatible with literary
quality.[4]

By way of example, below are the first lines of the poem, followed by
translations by Grundtvig (1820), Thorpe (1855), Bone (1945), Schaldemose (1847),
Hansen (1910), Haarder (1989) and Queval (1981) (Thorpe's and Schaldemose's
translations are accompanied by their own versions of the original text).

> *Hwæt, we gar-dena*   *in geardagum*
> *theodcynninga*   *thrym gefrunon*
> *hu tha æthelings*   *ellen fremedon*
>
> (Klaeber's edition, 1922)

> Fra ældgamle Dage,
> Det melder os Sage,
> Det toner I Sang.
> At Stol-kongesæder
> Beklædtes, med Hæder,
> I Old-Dane-Vang
> Af Høibaarne Helte
> Som Sværdet i Belte
> Ei bare omsonst
>
> (Grundtvig, 1820)

> *Hvæt! We Gár-Dena*   Ay, we the Gar-Danes'
> *in gear-dagum*   in days of yore
> *theód-cynninga*   the great kings'
> *thrym ge-frunon*   renown have heard of
> *hú tha æthelingas*   How those princes
> *ellen fremedon*   valour display'd
>
> (Thorpe, 1855)

We have heard the spear-Dane's [*sic!*] power, the force, in days gone, of
their kings — the acts of courage done of princes!

> (Bone, 1945)

> *Hvæt! We Gár-Dena*   Om Gar-Daners Vælde

in gear-dagum   I gamle Dage
theód-cynninga   de Folkenes Fyrsters
thrym ge-frunon   Frasagn vi hørde
hú tha æthelingas   Hvorlunde de Ædlinger
ellen fremedon   øvede Storværk

                                                (Schaldemose, 1847)

Om Spyd-Daners Færd i Fortids Dage,
Om Daad og Bedrift, af Drotterne øvet
Om Ædlingers Sejrsry Sagn har vi hørt!

                                                    (Hansen, 1910)

Ja, vi har spurgt til spyddaner før,
Folkekongers fylde i fortidens dage
hvordan heltene hentede hæder I kampen!

                                                   (Haarder, 1984)

Qu'on le sache!
De la gloire des rois des Danois à la lance, de l'heureuse
fortune des ces jours, de ces héros, de leurs prodiges et
prouesses, nous avons uoï parler.

                                                    (Queval, 1981)

What is striking about these translations is the fact that although 'there are only the words on the page' as Newmark observes, none of them — not even the so-called scholarly ones like Bone's or Haarder's — render the plain prose sense of the original, 'the words on the page', with reasonable accuracy. Bone, for instance, must of necessity use the archaic 'done *of* princes' rather than '*by* princes', although there is nothing archaic about the words translated; Haarder has *hentede hæder I kampen* — literally 'fetched glory in the fight' — for *ellen fremedon*, which means 'promoted valour'; Thorpe translates *theodcynninga* as 'great kings' renown' rather than 'folk-kings' renown'; and Schaldemose introduces the impossible and more or less incomprehensible *Gar-Daner* rather than using the straightforward *Spyddaner* — 'spear-Danes' — like Hansen.

This being the case, it is difficult not to prefer versions that do convey the fact that the original is a poem and not an academic treatise on old Germanic history and mythology. This may be accomplished — in Germanic languages, at least — by preserving as much as possible of the imagery, by using at least to some extent alliteration, and, if possible, by imitating the rhythm of the original. A third possibility is a free metrical rendering like Grundtvig's, which one easily forgives a few linguistic mistakes. More doubtful is the overall tone of this translation (cf. note 5).

It is impossible within the scope of a brief discussion to deal adequately with the many problems worthy of comment even in the relatively short passages selected for analysis here. In the following, therefore, we shall confine ourselves to looking at a few problem areas — metaphors, compounds, proper names and rhythm — which are indeed conveyed by the 'words on the page', but which are not easily transferred, once these words have been exchanged with words from the TL.

Metaphors

Old English poetry is rich in metaphor, and *Beowulf* is no exception. Most of these are stock metaphors, *kennings*, which are part of the highly ornate style of the poem. Many names are metaphorical, too, as we shall see. A close translation will render some of these *kennings* literally, as Newmark advocates,[5] a freer translation will not; but in some cases a literal rendering leads to a rather strange result, as in Morris and Wyatt's translation, where for instance *garsecg*, normally interpreted as '(hostile) ocean', is rendered literally as 'spearman', as in lines 48–9 *leton holm beran / geofon on garsecg* ('let the sea bear [the ship], gave it to the (hostile) ocean') rendered as 'let the holm bear him, gave all to the spearman'. Such a translation really cannot be understood without a note or gloss, and notes should be used sparingly in a literary translation.

Compounds

The real difficulty, however, is presented by the compounds, because so much meaning may be packed into them that a paraphrase is cumbersome in comparison, while a literal translation often sounds very strange. Thus the ship which is awaiting the dead Scyld is characterised as *utfus*, literally 'out-eager' or 'out-mad'. It is not difficult to render this idea; but in the languages I have been looking at it is rarely possible to do it in a way to match the terseness of the original. Grundtvig, who successfully paraphrases, has 'lå klar til at lette'; Thorpe 'eager to depart'; Bone — hopelessly — 'ready to wend'; Schaldemose and Hansen undertranslate by putting 'rede' (= ready); Haarder's 'med havdrift' is not bad[6] and Queval's 'avid d'horizon' is a stroke of genius, given that relative length matters less in a prose version like his than in a metrical version.

Proper nouns

Names are frequently metaphorical and/or allegorical, as in a mystery play or Restoration comedy. The very name of the hero, Beowulf, is now commonly believed to be a *kenning* signifying bee-wolf, i.e. one that behaves like a wolf to bees, i.e. a bear (which destroys their nest to get at the honey). But the point about this is that the word becomes opaque in translation, unless it is indeed rendered by 'bear', which is not normally the case. Bear is a good name for a king, be he a real king like Celtic Arthur (cf. Latin *arcturus*) or a tennis star like Swedish Björn Borg (Björn = bear). Beowulf is not recognisable as 'bear' in translations, however, any more than Scyld is easily interpreted as Shield, or Brecca as Breaker (applied to a wave). Likely solutions would be to choose literal translations whenever possible. In Danish, *Scyld* is normally translated literally as 'Skjold'; but his second name *Schaefing*, from sheaf (of corn), which suggests that he is associated with plenty, is normally left out. Here, as in other places where a direct translation is not possible, a note or gloss at the first mention of a name seems unavoidable.

Rhythm

A considerable part of the appeal of the poem rests on its rhythm and style: the sonorous sound of the line with its 4–6 beats divided in the middle by a ceasura. It seems to be difficult to imitate this pattern in modern English — at least there are no examples in my material — whereas it has been done with a fair amount of success by Hansen (1910) and Rytter (1929), and been attempted — with less success, because his lines tend to become too prolix — by Haarder (1984). Rytter's deliberately rustic Norwegian seems, in particular, to lend itself to transposition — the notorious *utfus* is simply kept in this translation — whereas Hansen's verse is late Victorian in quality, with echoes from the great Danish translator of Homer, Chr. Vilster.

If a translator cannot or will not transpose, the possibility of adopting an entirely different metre suggests iself.[7] However, although giving up verse definitely means losing a dimension, a lot of poetry may indeed survive in a good prose translation like that of Queval — which has been included to show that it is possible to translate *Beowulf* well into a non-Germanic language, even though it is hardly conceivable to imitate its form.

Conclusion

How, then, do we achieve an accurate translation? If the purpose of the text is to provide information about the content of the original, that is, if the aim is a translation of literature rather than a literary translation, the closest possible translation at phrase or even word level is the best; although even here I would prefer a readable translated text to a list of translated SL words. If on the other hand the purpose is to produce a literary text, the translation should above all be a work of art. It should also keep as closely as possible to the details of the original; but the degree of closeness must depend on the individual circumstances of the case. We may prefer Wilster's Homer to Pope's, because Wilster was able to use hexameters, which Pope could not possibly have done, and for the same reason we may prefer Hansen's *Beowulf* to Queval's, because it stays close to the metre of the original. But Pope and Queval did the best they could in their respective languages, and to me their translations are accurate in that they render a fair proportion of the content of the poems they translate, while at the same time being works of art in their own right and doing justice to the splendour of their originals.

Line 871 of *Beowulf, word other fand sothe gebunden*, celebrates the king's *scop*, whose job it is to give expression to the ideals of the whole court. Finding new words and combining them in the right way, so as to form a true poem, is also the task of the literary translator. And it is the task of the translation critic to describe the translation, its relation to the original, as well as to the TL culture, and to assess, among other things, its accuracy. In conclusion, therefore, I simply want to stress the fact that if the translator is to be both accurate and readable, a certain amount of freedom to rephrase the original message is necessary; but at the same time, a good translation will render as many details of the original as possible.

Notes
1. Cf. for instance Hermans (1985).

2. This is obviously not confined to medieval manuscripts, but indeed also applies to differences between printed texts. Many Shakespearean texts exist in two or more versions, just as modern writers frequently change their texts in subsequent editions, so that differences between two translations may simply be due to the fact that they render two different versions of the SL text.
3. Grundtvig admittedly paraphrases freely: Ei gik ham of Minde,/At Drotten, med Flid,/Skal Venner sig finde/I Ungdommens Tid (i.e. he remembered that a prince must take care to find friends while he is young).
4. The many shortened versions and adaptations for children will not be dealt with here.
5. Cf. Newmark (1981: 88) where the first procedure suggested for translating metaphor is 'reproducing the same image in the TL'. As Newmark adds, however, this presupposes that the image is transparent; but many images like *garsecg* or *Beowulf* are bound by convention: perfectly clear when you know the code, otherwise utterly incomprehensible.
6. The phrase is ambiguous, meaning both 'yearning for' and 'drifting towards' the open sea.
7. This is what Grundtvig did, and even his old enemy and rival, Thorpe (1855: XV), had to concede that it was a good metrical translation, although it sometimes introduces humour, that especially in the eyes of a hostile critic like Thorpe looks suspiciously like bathos. Thorpe instances Unferth's taunt to Beowulf about the swimming match with Brecca: 'Paa landed var I friske,/Men Vand kan slukke Ild,/I svømmed som to Fiske,/Ja snart som døde Sild'. Even as a taunt, comparing a hero to a dead herring does not tally with Thorpe's sense of decorum.

References

Apel, F. (1983) *Literarische Übersetzung*. Stuttgart: Metzler.
Arrowsmith, W. and Shattuck, R. (eds) (1961) *The Craft and Context of Translation*. Austin, Texas: University of Texas Press.
Batteux, C. (1760) *Principles of Translation*. Edinburgh.
Bone, G. (1945) *Beowulf. In Modern Verse*. Oxford: Blackwell.
Carne-Ross, D.S. (1961) Translation and transposition. In W. Arrowsmith and R. Shattuck (eds) *The Craft and Context of Translation* (pp. 3–28). Austin, Texas: University of Texas Press.
Draskau, J. (1978) Villon in English (unpublished MA thesis). Copenhagen University.
Grundtvig, N.F.S. (1820) *Bjowulfs Drapa*. Copenhagen: Seidelin.
Grundtvig, N.F.S. (1861) *Beowulfes Beorh eller Bjovulfs-Drapen, det old-angelske Heltedigt*. Copenhagen & London: Schönberg/John Russell Smith.
Grundtvig, N.F.S. (1865) *Bjovulfs-Drapen et høinordisk Heltedigt . . . fordansket af N.F.S. Grundtvig*, 2. Forbedrede udg. Copenhagen: Seidelin.
Haarder, A. (1975) *The Appeal of a Poem*. Copenhagen: Akademisk Forlag.
Haarder, A. (1984) *Sangen om Bjowulf*. Copenhagen: Gad.
Hansen, A. (1910) *Bjovulf*. Copenhagen: Gyldendal.
Hermans, T. (ed.) (1985) *The Manipulation of Literature*. London: Croom Helm.
Hjørnager Pedersen, V.H. (1987) *Oversættelseteori*. Copenhagen: Samfundlitteratur.
Hjørnager Pedersen, V.H. (1988) *Essays on Translation*. Copenhagen: Nyt Nordisk Forlag.
House, J. (1977) *A Model for Translation Quality Assessment*. Tübingen: Gunter Narr.
Klaeber, Fr. (1922) (ed.) *Beowulf and the Fight at Finnsburgh*. Boston: Heath and Company.
Morris, W. and Wyatt, A.J. (1895) *The Tale of Beowulf*. Hammersmith: Kelmscott Press.
Newmark, P.P. (1981) *Approaches to Translation*. Oxford: Pergamon.
Newmark, P.P. (1988) *A Textbook of Translation*. London: Prentice Hall International.
Queval, J. (1981) *Beowulf*. Paris: Gallimard.
Rytter, H. (1929) *Beowulf og Striden om Finnsborg*. Oslo: Det norske Samlaget.
Schaldemose, F. (1847) *Beo-Wulf og Scopes Widsith, 2 angelsaxiske Digte med Oversættelse og oplysende Anmærkninger*. Copenhagen: Stern Schubothe.
Thorpe, B. (1855) *The Anglo-Saxon Poems of Beowulf . . . With a Literal Translation*. Oxford: Parker.

Chapter 6

Friends, False Friends and Foes or Back to Basics in L1 to L2 Translation

John M. Dodds

> ... *brief translations from native to foreign language are useful in consolidation and testing of spoken and written foreign utterances* ...
>
> (Peter Newmark, 1981: 184)

Introduction

By way of introduction, certain premises have to be stated which will restrict the applicability of my remarks to a certain type of both text and translator. These premises will act as a brief but necessary word of warning to idealists in general and to all those hostile or indifferent to free market economy requirements being forced upon the profession and professional training. This contribution to the *Liber Amicorum* dedicated to Peter Newmark is designed to illustrate the teaching of translation between Italian and English. It will surely not appeal greatly to many deconstructionists, hermeneuticians and translatologists. It is not meant to, as the training situation referred to here is specifically that of professionals who have to learn how to translate out of their mother tongue into English in order to meet the needs of the market. Even though this particular mode of translation is often thought to be the anathema *par excellence* of the profession, it is a situation in which many translators outside the UK find themselves. In the present case, the discussion will focus on the situation in Italy and exclusive reference will be made to Italian to English translation, a relatively closely-related language pair, and to a class/examroom situation that would not normally involve highly specialised text types or an excessive degree of structural complexity.

Translator Training in Italy: Approaches and Methods

While the training focus may be on the professional requirements of the market, this does not mean, however, that translation trainees in Italy are not informed or taught about methodology, approaches, techniques and theories. Indeed, Peter Newmark's own *Approaches to Translation* (1981) was probably the very first *libro di testo* or set book on the subject ever to appear on compulsory reading lists at university level in Italy, whether in the traditional Humanities Faculties or in the two Schools of Modern Languages for Interpreters and Translators. In turn, Newmark's work leads, more often than not, to a wider discussion of theoretical propositions, mainly of linguistic models and text and discourse linguistics — particularly Arcaini (1986), Hatim and Mason (1990), Bell (1991) — but which would almost certainly include as well the hermeneutic approach, translatology and the theoretical assumptions of Translation Studies — most notably the works of George Steiner (1966, 1975), Seleskovitch and Lederer (1984), Mary Snell-Hornby (1988), Susan Bassnett (1991) — if not actual deconstruction theory.[1]

The point is that discussing theoretical problems and approaches is instructive as well as interesting to students who themselves generally say that they like knowing something about their profession, that even Horace, Cicero, and Catullus were not just great classical writers in their own right but that they were also great translators, that John Dryden too makes a distinction between metaphrase and paraphrase, as does Nida with his formal and dynamic equivalence and as indeed does Peter Newmark himself with his own semantic and communicative translation. Generally, students like to know that various approaches to translation exist, that there are text functions and text types, and that there are problems that go beyond the simple meaning of words. For example, Dante's *Divina Commedia* has been translated into English in more than ninety different ways with versions for the opening tercet of the first Canticle (*Nel mezzo del cammin di nostra vita*) as different as:

> When life had labour'd up her midmost stage
> Midway upon the journey of our life
> When I was thirty five

On the other hand, word-for-word translation may lead to amusing absurdities of the type *che cavolo vuoi* being translated as 'what the cabbage do you want?' Similarly, when ordering a *bitter* ('un amaro') in England, the poor Italian tourist would most likely end up with a pint of beer, or, even worse, should something strong to drink be required at the end of a meal, say a brandy or a grappa, ordering a *digestive* ('un digestivo') would probably result in the arrival of a crumbly biscuit.

However, when dealing with L1 to L2 translation, the main problem is and will always remain a question not so much of free or literal translation or Newmark's communicative or semantic approach, but simply a question of basics, of getting the language right, which in short means getting the grammar, the lexis and the idiom of the English language right (an ever-present and ever-increasing problem even when students translate into their mother tongue). Translation theory or discussions about methodology or theoretical problems certainly have their place in the classroom but they are not necessarily indispensable elements and tend to be ancillary to the main aim of the class, rather like the place of philology, philosophy of language or applied linguistics in a language-learning environment. The teachers/trainers themselves certainly need to have theoretical competence but it is a moot point, in the Italian context, as to just how much the student/trainee needs to know at a theoretical level.

Indeed, in Italy, it would be no exaggeration to claim that the teaching of translation and therefore the training of translators is *first and foremost* about the teaching of language, irrespective of whether the students are translating into their mother tongue or into their first or second foreign language. Here, language teaching is not the exclusive realm of the language teacher as, unfortunately, all too many translation/interpretation colleagues would conveniently wish us to believe. Taylor (1990: 1) is quite right when he states that 'translation or interpretation teachers may prefer to work on translation or interpreting skills as separate entities from language ability, considered as a *sine qua non* but taken for granted'. However, this is simply an unrealistic position of convenience assumed by those of us who would ideally delegate the laborious aspect of the job, i.e. teaching the language , and be left with the more interesting tasks, i.e. translation and interpretation.

This is by no means advocating a return to the 'almost universally condemned "Grammar-Translation Method" ' which, according to Catford (1965: viii), produced only 'bad grammar and bad translation' and which in any case is a language and not a translation teaching activity. But it may be noted that even in this totally different realm, translation is 'useful in consolidation and testing of spoken and written foreign utterances' (Newmark, 1981: 184), particularly important in what Corder (1973: 274) calls 'authoritative reconstruction', which is the students' ability to cope with target language (TL) problems that could be avoided in free expression exercises like composition and précis writing.

Errors in L1 to L2 Translation

In translation work, difficult expressions in the source text (ST) have to be dealt with, although more mistakes may be anticipated in restricted expression compared to free expression. Nevertheless, it still gives a good indication of how a learner is able to cope in a difficult linguistic situation. Translation indicates how well the more complex TL structures have been assimilated, since they cannot always be avoided, without resulting in textual impoverishment or omission. In fact, mistakes should be welcomed as they form part of the student's learning experience, suggesting that they are actively trying out and experimenting with linguistic structures in the foreign language, rather like a child during first language development. Again, Corder points out that 'no one expects a child learning his mother tongue to produce from the earliest stages only forms which in adult terms are correct or non-deviant. We interpret his "incorrect" utterances as being evidence that he is in the process of acquiring language' (1967: 8) and thus it is that mistakes often assume 'greater importance than correct forms used accidentally' (Nickel , 1973: 25). Simple, correct forms used safely in free composition may thus be seen to be less beneficial than the use of more complex, albeit erroneous, forms in translation. Indeed, the mistake is an extraordinarily useful indicator of students' progress and performance and, as such, has been regularly studied and analysed in Trieste over a period now well exceeding a decade. The interesting conclusions ensuing from this body of research have led to a general rethinking of the role of the translation trainer (and of the foreign language teacher[2]), particularly in relation to the L1 to L2 mode.

As Lado (1957: vii) indicated in the 1950s, one way of identifying areas of difficulty in the new language is through the application of contrastive analysis. The erroneous assumption of much contrastive analysis then was that the more complex the source language (SL) structure, the more likely it is that the TL form will be defective. Many errors were subsequently found to be psychological in origin and are thus not simply a question of linguistic complexity. For example, the apparently complex syntax of *fossi andato dal medico, oggi non sarei* . . . (3rd conditional with present consequence and suppression of the *se* 'if' particle) actually only rarely seems to pose problems for the advanced translation student in Italy — but how many times does s/he fall into the trap of *l'ho fatto ieri,* 'I have done it yesterday'.

Balanced against this is the fact that actual translation mistakes are few and far between, since translators working out of their mother tongue, unlike those working in the more accepted L2 to L1 mode, are better able to understand the original ST. Therefore, convoluted, stiff, pompous, recherché and syntactically complex written Italian does not create comprehension problems or textual re-elaboration problems for Italian native speakers with advanced English-language competence. Indeed, according to a dissertation containing statistical research carried out some years ago (Carbone, 1991), there was a less than 5 per cent error rate in ST comprehension in exam papers that students had sat over a five-year period (1986–90).

In fact, in all the error analysis studies carried out in Trieste over the last ten years or so, the figures themselves are more than eloquent in pointing to where translation students' problems lie, and, consequently, in pointing to those areas where repeated errors are likely to recur and where teaching strategies should be developed in order to combat their causes. Two elaborated sets of data are already available and have been published (Dodds, 1994) for the 1986–90 period, while results for 1991–5 are still being evaluated but suggest little change. However, errors have been further subdivided into 'interlingual' and 'intralingual' categories, i.e. whether or not the error is due to influence of the L1 on the L2, or has to do with the system of the L2 alone, such as when an irregular verb is inappropriately given a regular ending. Thus the regular past form *walked* might, by analogy, generate the form *swimmed* (found in American dialects but not in standard British English) or the incorrect *runned*. At a lexical level, this sort of intralingual error manifests itself especially when students mistakenly opt for an inappropriate term on those frequent occasions when non-equivalent cognate pairs exist for just one SL term such as *politica* ('policy' or 'politics'), *economico* ('economic' or 'economical'), *ultimo* ('last' or 'latest').

However, the frequency of intralingual errors seems to be more or less insignificant in terms of communiction, especially when compared to interlingual interference, or the influence of the SL on the TL grammar, lexis or idiom. For instance, students often produce syntactic errors of the following type:

L1 source	*non soltanto mi ha accusato di*
L2 error	'not only he accused me of'
L2 target	'not only did he . . . '

L1 source	*assolutamente non devi*
L2 error	'you absolutely don't have to'
L2 target	'you absolutely mustn't'

In another common error, the student's L2 formulation mimicks the SL structure, even though the student is usually quite aware that a different structure is

Table 6.1 Common interlingual (Italian to English) lexical errors

Italian source	L2 error	L2 target
beni durevoli	'durevols' or 'durevol goods'	'durables'
già candidato	'already candidate'	'former candidate'
elettrodomestici	'electro-domestics'	'electrical appliances' or 'household appliances'
concorrenziali	'concorrential'	'competitive'
congiuntura	'conjuncture'	'situation'

required in the TL. For example, students usually know that conjecture or hearsay in English is not usually grammatically marked as it often is in Italian ('according to' being the only indicator necessary) or, if it is marked, that it is most commonly expressed not with the conditional tense but with the verbal locution 'to be said to', which produces a more acceptable TL version. Nevertheless, structural errors still occur:

L1 source	*secondo fonti attendibili gli Stati Uniti avrebbero già accettato . . .*
L2 error	'according to reliable sources, the United States would have agreed to . . . '
L2 target	'according to reliable sources, the US is said to have already agreed to . . . '
	'according to reliable sources, the US has already agreed to . . .'

At a lexical level, students experience even more difficulties. In their attempts to play safe, they frequently gamble their exam results away by opting for non-existant cognates. If they do not know the TL term, they will simply anglicise the Italian with some odd results, especially when they only make use of poor monolingual learners' dictionaries or when dictionaries are not allowed as is very often the case in Italy. Some typical errors are shown in Table 6.1.

The Study

Two error corpora were compiled on the basis of the translation examination papers of intermediate-level students with English as their second foreign language or L3 (123 subjects) and of advanced students with English as their first foreign language or L2 (135 subjects). All the subjects were Italian native speakers, all but two of whom were in the 18–24 age bracket; 92 per cent were female. The papers consisted of two texts, literary and current affairs reporting. The results of the error analysis are presented in Table 6.2.

Table 6.2 shows that lexical errors are the most frequent type, but that other L2 errors also occur, indicating inadequate mastery of what could be called the 'basics' of the L2, in this case the TL. These figures suggest that translation teachers running courses in L1 to L2 translation in Italy (and there are many) are faced with many problems which have to do with L2 competence rather than translation competence.

Table 6.2 Error distribution for two Italian to English translation tasks: for intermediate L3 students and advanced L2 students with Italian as L1

Error category	Intermediates (English as L3)		Advanced (English as L2)	
	f	*f*/N (%)	*f*	*f*/N (%)
Lexis	1433	47.3	902	50.5
Grammar	992	32.7	777	43.5
Spelling	396	13.1	62	3.5
Punctuation	108	3.6	12	0.7
Word Order	101	3.3	32	1.8
N	3030	100.00	1785	100.00

Literal versus Non-literal Translation

Newmark has argued that the most constructive theory in translation, i.e. that which is about translation problems, 'is inevitably about non-literal translation. If all translation were literal, there would be little to write about' (1993: 223). He is also often the first to applaud outstanding instances of non-literal translation, thus giving the lie to those who accuse him of being a proponent of literalism, usually through an interpretation of his claim that 'literal word-for-word translation is not only the best, it is the only valid method of translation' (1981: 39), which ignores the accompanying strict proviso that says 'provided equivalent effect is secured'. His claim is also in total contrast to Danica Seleskovitch and Marianne Lederer who 'persistently identify interpretation with translation and regard themselves as translatologists', advise students 'never to repeat the same words' since 'however similar they are in English and French, they are always [*sic*] so subtly different that it is preferable to avoid their use if one does not want to run the risk of saying something different when one wants to say the same thing. It is preferable to mistrust all friends as one cannot hope to know all false friends' (Newmark, 1996: 185, quoting from Seleskovitch and Lederer).

A pretty sad concept of friendship this, one which implies that the teacher should not show the students when and where to trust their 'friends', their SL/TL cognate equivalents, nor to show them how to tell them apart from their 'false friends' and their 'foes', but rather to change everything on the assumption that equivalence never actually exists — a sort of creative writing class for translators. In a very recent number of *The Linguist*, Ross Smith, a highly- experienced professional, asks: 'what effect could the witless advice not to use "the same words" have on gullible young translators yet to start earning a living in this tough profession?' (1997: 114). The consequences could also be particularly dire in L1 to L2 translation, as little time and effort would be spent on other error sources and because errors of the following kind — where a potentially offensive alternative is offered — may be introduced if literal translation is avoided:

L1 source	*non ha assolutamente senso . . .*
L2 error	'it is utter nonsense to . . . '
L2 target	'it makes absolutely no sense to . . . '

Newmark's own and not by any means infrequent applause for many laudable, non-literal brainwaves is ample evidence that translation is a creative process but his insistence on the basics — on everyday and every-minute-of-the-day literal translation — should not be forgotten in our admiration of the sublime. His praise, for instance, *inter* alia of Patrick Creagh's translation of Claudio Magris' *Danubio* (1986) when he simply lists examples of 'happy translations' which may serve as an inspiration for identifying and creatively dealing with false friends (Newmark, 1993: 219): 'in the swim of things' (382) for *nel giro* (410); 'the world is humdrum' (16) for *la prosa del mondo* (12); 'taken on a new lease of life' (307) for *ha ripreso vigore* (327); 'in the swim' (brilliant) (373) for *aggiornato* (401). The futile search for non-existent cognates is thus contained through inventiveness in the face of lexical adversity and not just through rash guesswork — one of the most important pieces of advice being 'if you don't know, don't guess', especially if you are not armed with reliable dictionaries. Thus it is that the student's attempt at *beni durevoli* might well have become 'long-lasting' rather than 'durevol', *prezzi concorrenziali*, 'cheaper/lower' rather than 'concorrential prices' and *elettrodomestici* 'radios, TVs, dishwashers, washing machines and the like' rather than 'electro-domestics'. It is in this way that convoluted, long-winded SL expressions may be streamlined (concision being so congenial to English) so that *delle jeep con la stella di Davide* simply becomes 'Israeli jeeps' and *il clima psicologico positivo delle famiglie italiane* might be smoothly rendered as 'the feelgood factor in Italy' (both student versions). Here, as well as on many more occasions, the approach advocated by Seleskovitch and Lederer proves right, but their absolutist advice must surely be invalidated by the very relativist nature of the translation process in which the exception may often prove the rule but should never become the rule.

So what can be learnt from this apparent swinging from one extreme to the other — from first advocating a literal approach to translation to then listing and singing the praises of non-literal translation? Firstly, it must be said that there is no contradiction here, for translation as a creative, pragmatic process is bound to require all the approaches at the disposal of the translator who can ill afford to exclude anything from his or her repertoire. There is no contradiction when Newmark applauds Patrick Creagh's 'happy', non-literal translations and then states that 'literal word-for-word translation' is the best approach 'provided equivalent effect is secured', as on countless occasions in the translator's working week the literal approach will be resorted to and equivalent effect will be achieved, albeit subjectively (but then again all translation is subjective by its very nature). Simply, it should not be forgotten that there would not have been a great deal of point in listing and applauding the countless occasions on which Creagh successfully opted for close, literal translation if 'literal word-for-word translation' was not the best approach, subject to achieving equivalent effect. The basics are always there, i.e. 'friendly' SL items, whether in the syntax or the lexis, just waiting to be translated literally into the TL — otherwise it is doubtful that deadlines would ever be met. For example, in the examination paper which contained *il clima psicologico*, due credit was given to those students who avoided the 'unfriendly' TL cognates, but no mention was made of the rest of the paragraph which, generally speaking (apart from the proper noun *Isco* and the ever-present *faux-amis* and *passato prossimo*), is 'translator friendly':

> *Nel mese di febbraio il clima psicologico delle famiglie italiane ha continuato a migliorare. Lo conferma l'ultima indagine Isco condotta nella prima decade di febbraio '96 su un campione di 2 mila famiglie in tutta l'Italia.*

Imaginative translations such as 'feelgood factor' and 'psychological climate' lose their positive impact when they appear in a context where basic errors are made, as in the following version:

> In february, the feelgood factor of the italians has continued to get better which confirms the last Isco survey of the first decade of the month on 2 thousand families in Italy.

The effectiveness of such translations only emerges when the surrounding context allows it:

> In the month of February, the psychological climate of Italian families continued to improve. This was confirmed by the latest survey of an Italian Statistical Office (ISCO) carried out in the first ten days of February on a two thousand family sample throughout Italy.

While neither version is that of a native speaker of English, there can be little doubt that in the first version, the student has merely created a distortion of the English language in his failure to render tense, voice, lexis and even definite articles and capital letters according to the English norm. The second, more appropriate version has a rather Italian sentence structure but the basics are there: it is correct and comprehensible — and, as interpreters say, the message gets across. Had the student in good faith followed that unfortunate piece of advice offered by the translatologists to the effect that using 'the same word' is unwise and should be avoided, the result would have been quite different. As Gérard Ilg so wisely puts it with reference to interpreters, and one might argue also to translators, 's'abstraire du mot est un excellent antidote qui permet d'arracher les étudiants à leurs habitudes thème et version, mais ce n'est pas une raison de condamner sans appel le mot' (1980: 118). In other words, the whole process of translation is one of fine tension and balance. It is not wise to ask young trainees to walk the high wire before learning how to walk and run on the ground, and when they do start to be adventurous and take their first steps on that wire, they must know who their friends are and who they can trust. It is not preferable to mistrust all friends for, just as in human psychology, the translated text too will assume a very distorted personality. David Snelling, another conference interpreter, sums up very nicely what the L1 to L2 interpreter (and again by extension the translator) should set out to do and why:

> Aware, then, of the perils involved in foreign-language target-text formu-lation, with his imperfect mastery of language register and of judging the impact intensity of his expression, the young interpreter will adopt a humbler approach and neither cast his net so wide nor set his sights so high. All of our lives have been plagued by the zealous determination of some young colleagues to use simultaneous interpretation as a pretext for a

firework display of language, never resorting to a simple term when a complex, ill-digested, obsolete one, preferably with a slightly different meaning, can be used instead. [1992: 2]

Conclusion

Whether the analogy be with the high wire or fireworks, the perils of translation are well known to the experienced teacher who is or should be the young, inexperienced trainee's first friend and guide, even though the trainer/trainee relationship does not always seem to be one of friendship. But it is within this relationship that the inexperienced learn the basics of their profession, they learn safety first and only then start thinking about possibly facing the hazards of changing the words and why and when and how to do so. It should not be forgotten either that professional translators have a job to do, they have to be taught how to do it well, quickly and efficiently with minimum risk for maximum output. The 'firework display of language' can be left to the a posteriori hypotheses of the translation critic, the theorist and the Ph.D. student in translation studies or translatology who, in the luxury of their academic research, can in Thomas Paine's words willfully ignore everyday basics in favour of 'the sublime and the ridiculous which are often so nearly related, that it is difficult to class them separately'.[3]

Notes
1. For a much more complete description of the multi-disciplinary nature of translation theory as taught in Italy, cf. Ulrych (1997).
2. The results obtained have also led to some interesting developments for EFL teachers, cf. Taylor (1990).
3. The full quotation on the sublime and the ridiculous taken from Thomas Paine's *Age of Reason* (1794) is often forgotten but here seemingly most appropriate.

References

Arcaini, E. (1986) *Analisi linguistica e traduzione*. Bologna: Patron Editore.
Bassnett, S. (1991) *Translation Studies*. 2nd edition. London and New York: Methuen.
Bell, R.(1991) *Translation and Translating*. London: Longman.
Carbone, A. (1991) Error analysis and its application to the teaching of translation. Unpublished degree dissertation, University of Trieste.
Catford, J.C. (1965) *A Linguistic Theory of Translation*. London: Oxford University Press.
Corder, S.P. (1967) The significance of learner's errors. *International Review of Applied Linguistics*. V/4, 3–17.
Corder, S.P. (1973) *Introducing Applied Linguistics*. Harmondsworth: Pelican Books.
Dodds, J.M. (1994) Training the translation teacher II. In C. Picken (ed.) *Translation — The Vital Link* (pp. 234–43). London: Chamelon Press.
Hatim, B. and Mason, I. (1990) *Discourse and The Translator*. London: Longman.
Ilg, G. (1980) L'interprétation consécutive — les fondmants. *Parallèles — Cahiers de l'ETI*, 3, 109–36.
Lado, R. (1957) *Linguistics across Cultures*. Michigan: University of Michigan Press.
Magris, C. (1986) *Danubio*. Milan: Garzanti.
Magris, C. (1989) *Danube* (trans. by P. Creagh). London: Collins Harvill.
Newmark, P.P. (1981) *Approaches to Translation*. Oxford: Pergamon Press.
Newmark, P.P. (1993) Translation as a weapon. In L. Avirovic and J.M. Dodds (eds) *Umberto Eco, Claudio Magris — autori e traduttori a confronto*. Udine: Campanotto editore.
Newmark, P.P. (1996) Paragraphs on translation. *The Linguist* 35(6), 184–6.

Nickel, G. (1973) Aspects of error evaluation and grading. In J. Svartvik (ed.) *Errata —* *Papers in Error Analysis* (pp. 24–49). Lund: CWK Gleerup Bokförlag.

Seleskovitch, D. and Lederer, M. (1984) *Interpréter pour traduire*. Paris: Didier.

Smith, R. (1997) The merits of literal translation. *The Linguist* 36/4, 114–15.

Snell-Hornby, M. (1988) *Translation Studies: An Integrated Approach*. Amsterdam: John Benjamins.

Snelling, D. (1992) *Strategies for Simultaneous Interpreting*. Udine: Campanotto Editore.

Steiner, G. (1966) Introduction. In *The Penguin Book of Modern Verse Translation*. Harmondsworth: Penguin Books.

Steiner, G. (1975) *After Babel: Aspects of Language and Translation*. London: Oxford University Press.

Taylor, C.J. (1990) *The Error Analysis of Translation and its Application to Language Teaching*. Trieste: SSLMIT, University of Trieste.

Ulrych, M. (ed.) (1977) *Tradurre: un approccio multidisciplinare*. Turin: Utet.

Chapter 7

Training Translators in a 'Third Language' — A New Approach

> *In general, there are more faithful friends than faux amis,*
> *and we must not hesitate to use them . . .*
>
> (Peter Newmark, 1988: 72)

The Role of the 'Third Language' in the Training of Translators

In recent years the training of translators at university level has made considerable progress in many parts of the world. The number of universities that have introduced courses of this kind has greatly increased; at the same time Translation Studies, as the curricula show, has gained more and more a profile as a separate academic discipline, and the innovative works of Peter Newmark have made a decisive contribution to this happy development. The continuing consolidation of the discipline over the years can be traced (for instance) in the training of translators at universities in the German-speaking world (cf. Arntz, 1989). As late as the 1960s, this offered if anything an unclear picture: at the centre of things in those days were general language and translation classes, yet the influence of the traditional philological disciplines, with their strong orientation towards literary studies, was very evident. But even then there were noticeable efforts to create a distinct and unmistakable profile, leading for example to the introduction of non-linguistic subsidiary subjects such as Principles of Law or Introduction to Economics. In the 1970s Linguistics, including the fledgling discipline of Translation Studies, took up a more central position in the curriculum, while at the same time courses to improve the students' command of their own native language were introduced. Since the 1980s Information Technology has gained increasingly in significance, so that step by step appropriate course elements have been integrated into the curriculum. In addition, the non-linguistic subsidiary subjects and technical translation classes closely linked to these courses acquired a stronger position. In the 1990s came further subject areas with an interdisciplinary orientation — Psycholinguistics, for example, or the Linguistics of Specialised Texts.

Simultaneous with this continuous expansion of the academic horizon, research came to play an ever more important role at many universities. By this means, many individual departments and institutes were able to specialise, allowing a certain division of labour between them. The multifaceted nature of

Translation Studies has always undermined the idea of an undifferentiated, monolithic training course. Beyond the core of essential, obligatory subjects, it seems far more sensible to allow students the opportunity to establish their own emphasis by means of course specialisation. The University of Hildesheim now offers two distinctly separate and different language/translation degree courses: the Diploma programme in Technical Translation, and an MA in International Information Management. In the spirit of the above-mentioned division of labour, no effort is currently made to provide for the specialised training of interpreters.

Fortunately, the growing importance attached to theory has not led to the situation of which critical voices have always warned: that one would end up talking *about* foreign languages and not *in* them. It would indeed be fatal for the vocational prospects of graduates if the practical command of foreign languages came to be seen in university degree programmes as being of only secondary importance. In fact, reflecting on language should provide an additional motivation to learn languages, and, seen methodologically, it should make the learning easier. More and more advanced students of translation are deciding to learn one or more languages in addition to their (generally two) compulsory foreign languages. For many, it is not simply a matter of improving their job prospects; they also want to test whether the knowledge of language and language methodology acquired earlier in their studies can be used to help them learn a further foreign language.

The challenge to the teacher is to activate in an appropriate way the considerable knowledge that these learners have already gained, intensifying the learning process so that the learner can with a relatively modest investment of time achieve an acceptable level of linguistic and translatory competence. One interesting approach is offered by methods that initially restrict the learning goal to individual skills, for example reading and/or listening comprehension. However, up to now there has been very little by way of teaching materials suitable for a modified approach of this kind (Arntz, 1997: 71ff.). Most of the language learning textbooks that are available aim at a general command of the language, i.e. at the more or less simultaneous learning of skills in speaking, listening, reading and writing. This is especially true for the more rarely learnt languages; here in particular the attempt is made to reach the largest possible target group, which rules out any possibility of greater differentiation. The development of suitable teaching materials is thus absolutely essential.

The Hildesheim Third Language Model

On the basis of these considerations, advanced language students at the University of Hildesheim are offered a number of course cycles over (in each case) three semesters: in each, in the first course module, the students acquire knowledge of the language; this is followed up by a second course module to give the students a more active command; and in the third and final module, non-fictional texts are translated out of the foreign into the native language. This three-part cycle is given a theoretical foundation by a specific Linguistics course that runs parallel to the first course module and in which questions of foreign language teaching method play an important role. The languages in question are (for the moment) lesser used Germanic and Romance languages (Dutch, Danish; Italian, Portuguese). Given the close co-operation within Europe, solid, basic knowledge in these languages — that can be built on later as required — constitutes a valuable additional qualification.

The teaching materials are based on a contrastive approach: the point is to use language knowledge that the students have already gained to help them in learning a 'new' language; in the case of Dutch, for example, this would be their existing knowledge of German and English. Equally important is the modular structure of the programme: each module is self-contained, so that the participants can restrict themselves to module one or go on to take module two, which aims at an active command of the language. Working with the materials has clearly shown that, for learners used to language work, it is motivating and time saving to concentrate first on getting a comprehensive survey of the structures of the language before then obtaining active language ability.

Now that the scheme outlined above has been successfully tested for Dutch and Italian (Arntz 1996: 111ff.), it will be discussed below on the basis of these two languages.

Module one — receptive competence

For Dutch, this module is designed to give students the knowledge of Dutch that they will need to read Dutch non-fictional and technical texts.

The teaching materials are divided into ten lessons. At the core of each lesson is a Dutch text, in each case a non-fictional text covering some aspect of Dutch or Flemish life. The first texts are about the particular characteristics of the Dutch language and its relationship to the other Germanic languages, especially German and English. A further series of texts deals with the social and economic situation of The Netherlands and Belgium. Finally, there are texts concerned with the recent history of the two countries and their role in Europe.

While in the course of the ten lessons all necessary Dutch grammar is covered, the focus is on linguistic phenomena that occur frequently in written language, and especially in non-fictional texts. For this reason, these phenomena are presented not as in everyday teaching materials but in a different order and with different emphasis. The contrastive approach is apparent in the way that, especially when working with the texts, numerous implicit and explicit comparisons with German and English are established before being treated in more detail in the exercises.

In these efforts to trace and take pedagogical advantage of similarities and differences on all levels between Dutch and its powerful neighbouring languages, the so-called 'false friends' have a major role to play (Südhölter, 1989: 330). These are cases in which lexical items in two languages are similar or identical in form yet partially or even wholly different in meaning. They offer an inexhaustible supply of potential errors for the Dutch learner of German or the German learner of Dutch. That 'false friends' should prove to be so treacherous with respect to two closely-related languages has paradoxically to do with the fact that there are so many 'faithful friends' here, i.e. items that are identical in form and content, the learner thus often failing to take into account the (likewise very frequent) hidden differences. This particular problem is presented explicitly during the first part of the course, with numerous examples. A pragmatic systematic method is developed, which distinguishes between 'faithful friends', 'distant acquaintances' and 'false friends'.

The reason why the group of 'false friends' is so substantial is that, because of their close relatedness, over the years two languages have a large lexical common ground, elements of which have developed, in form and/or content, in different directions — the changes in content, including those that at first glance seem harmless, having particularly severe consequences. Often it is sufficient for just one component to be changed or added for vital changes in meaning to occur. Thus *uur* in Dutch (henceforth nl) is not *Uhr*, but *Stunde* in German (henceforth de), and *gemakkelijk* nl is not *gemächlich* de, but *leicht*.

But even 'good friends' and 'distant acquaintances' can cause the learner problems. 'Good friends' in the present context is taken to mean all those lexical items which have identical, or at least broadly identical, meaning in the two languages, and which resemble each other in form so closely that they can be taken straightforwardly to be equivalent. This produces a wide range, from cases in which the root of the word is identical and there are only minor differences in form, pronunciation and grammatical indicator (for example, *das Kind* de *het kind* nl; *die Stadt* de *de stad* nl) to those in which the root is different but there is agreement as to the 'inner form of the word' (for example, *die Krankenkasse* de *het ziekenfonds* nl; *eindrucksvoll* de *indrukwekkend* nl).

Finally, with 'distant acquaintances' the meaning is similarly identical or near identical in the two languages, and they reveal a certain formal similarity as well, and yet the content connections can only be reconstructed with difficulty. Here too there is a wide spectrum: on the one hand, those cases in which the meaning of a word can be found out with the help of elements that the two languages have in common: *opvoeden* nl — *erziehen* de (cf. *voeden* nl — *füttern* de — *to feed* in English (henceforth en), and on the other, cases in which the meaning can be discovered on the basis of etymology or through comparison with other Germanic languages: *taal* nl ('language'), cf. *tell/tale* en — *zählen/erzählen* de; *spelling* nl, cf. *spelling* en; *trein* nl, cf. train en.

How far the limits of the circle of 'distant acquaintances' should be drawn and where the 'completely different' one begins depends in the final analysis on how much additional knowledge the learners bring to the classroom. Here the lecturer will have to choose the appropriate emphasis, depending on the target group in question in each case.

So far, we have only been concerned with acquiring a passive mastery of a language. If, on the other hand, an active command is required, then some of the examples given here could quickly transform themselves from 'faithful' to 'false' friends'. Experience has shown that, precisely when it is a matter of languages that are so closely related, most learners tend to take elements and structures of languages with which they are already familiar and apply them to 'new' languages. In order to counteract this tendency, learners, including those in module one, are constantly encouraged to register not only the clear differences between the two language systems but also similarities and trivial differences. By this means, the groundwork is also laid for a successful transition to the active command of the language that is to be acquired in the next module.

Module two — active competence

By the time that they begin this module, the students have become fairly well acquainted with the structures of Dutch and can now concentrate principally on acquiring oral fluency and broadening their knowledge of lexis and phraseology. Since the learners have had a good grounding in methodology, the transition from module one to module two is not a difficult one. It must be pointed out, however, that the teaching materials for this module are still in preparation, at present the students are working with materials that were not created specifically with these ends in mind. There is no doubt that materials following on more closely from module one would lead to even better results.

Module three — translatory competence

In this third and final module, non-fictional texts of varying degrees of difficulty and from different subject areas are read, analysed and translated. (The choice of texts can be made to reflect the participants' own range of interests.) Here, too, the contrastive approach involving a systematic comparison of language structures plays an important role, and multi-stage translations based on the interlinear approach are particularly suitable.

This may be illustrated by means of the following example:

STRESS, ONGEDULD EN AMBITIE VORMEN ONGEZOND GEZELSCHAP
Streß,   Ungeduld und Ehrgeiz   bilden   ungesunde   Gesellschaft

Stress draagt bij op de ene   of andere manier aan het mechanisme   dat
Streß trägt   bei auf die eine   oder andere Weise zu dem Mechanismus, der

tot het hartinfarct leidt. Als men   stress beschouwt als een
zum   Herzinfarkt führt. Wenn man Streß betrachtet   als einen

milieufactor die van buitenaf op het individu inwerkt,   dan moet
Umweltfaktor, der von außen auf das Inviduum   einwirkt,   dann muß

die   individu   daar wel gevoelig voor zijn. Niet iedereen immers
dieses Individuum da   wohl sensibel für sein. Nicht jeder   ja

reageert op dezelfde wijze op stress.   De milieufactor vertoont
reagiert auf dieselbe   Weise auf Streß.   Der Umweltfaktor zeigt

kennelijk een wisselwerking met de persoonlijkheidsstructuur van de
offenbar   eine Wechselwirkung mit der Persönlichkeitsstruktur   des

betrokkene: pas dan   is sprake van een   risikofactor.
Betreffenden; erst dann   ist Rede   von einem Risikofaktor.

Source: *NRC Handelsblad*, 10. 9. 1992

Revised translation

STRESS, UNGEDULD UND EHRGEIZ SIND EINE UNGESUNDE GESELL-SCHAFT

Streß ist in irgendeiner Form an dem Mechanismus beteiligt, der zum Herzinfarkt führt. Wenn man Streß als einen Umweltfaktor betrachtet, der von außen auf einen

Menschen einwirkt, dann muß dieser Mensch dafür auch empfänglich sein. Nicht jeder reagiert ja in gleicher Weise auf Streß. Zwischen dem Umweltfaktor und der Persönlichkeitsstruktur des Betroffenen besteht offenbar eine deutliche Wechselwirkung: erst dann kann man von einem Risikofaktor sprechen.

While 'false friends' play no significant role here (an example would be *immers* nl, which is not at all the same as *immer* de), the text is nevertheless syntactically and stylistically far from harmless. The interlinear translation of the sentence *Stress draagt bij op de ene of andere manier aan het mechanisme dat tot hartinfarct leidt* is not grammatically correct, but the corrected version, *Streß trägt auf die eine oder andere Weise zu dem Mechanismus bei, der . . .*, while now grammatically correct, is still not fully acceptable for stylistic reasons. A stylistically acceptable version is given above in the revised translation. On the other hand, the interlinear translation of the sentence *De milieufactor vertoont kennelijk een wisselwerking met de persoonlijkheidsstructuur van de betrokkene* is already grammatically correct, but likewise requires (as the revised translation shows) stylistic emendation.

It is clear that a contrastive way of looking at things, as shown in the examples given above, also helps to consolidate the learners' active command of the language.

The Linguistics course

Parallel to module one, which serves to develop practical skills in reading, a theoretically-oriented course is offered that, taking the chosen foreign language as a starting point, introduces the students to methods and problems in Comparative and Contrastive Linguistics. At the same time, it provides a survey of language learning and teaching methodology. The key features of this course will be illustrated below with reference to Italian.

Italian as a Romance language

First, Italian is introduced as a member of the Indo-European language family and as a Romance language. Then the development from Latin to Italian is traced; this gives an opportunity to demonstrate the different perspectives of the diachronic and synchronic approaches to languages. Specific text examples illustrate the development from Vulgar Latin to Italian on the lexical, morphological and syntactic levels (cf. Dardano, 1995: 70ff.). A comparison with French and Spanish, through the use of parallel texts, reveals the varying degrees of distance to Latin of Romance languages today, with French the furthest away, Italian the closest, and Spanish in a position midway between them. This multilateral diachronic and synchronic comparison of languages is reinforced using appropriate examples such as the development of future forms in different Romance languages.

Typology of Romance languages

The application of the traditional typological classification to Latin and Romance languages brings a basic difference to light (cf. Dardano, 1995: 84ff.): Latin declension and conjugation are achieved mostly by means of morphemes that merge into the root word (for example *pater — patris; habere — habueram*), whereas modern Romance languages use unattached morphemes to a much greater extent, notably prepositions for declension (for example *il padre — del padre* in Italian (it) and auxiliary verbs in numerous types of conjugation (for example *avere — avevo avuto* it).

An analysis of further typological approaches shows that besides morphology there are a number of other criteria, supporting the idea of the relativity of typologies. Finally, starting out from the traditional viewpoint of Structural Linguistics, the levels of language description and the linguistic disciplines assigned to them — from Phonetics through to Pragmatics — are subjected to systematic review, laying the methodological foundation for the (in the strict sense) contrastive part of the course.

Comparison of terminology and texts

The starting point is the onomasiological method routinely used in terminological studies: the two systems to be compared with each other are first considered and analysed in isolation before being brought together. This is done first of all by means of examples taken from a specific subject area that is not related to any particular language (drawn, for instance, from technical or scientific disciplines). Distinct differences between languages are encountered, on the other hand, in legal terminologies. In contrast to technical ones, these have no concrete point of reference in the world beyond language; they refer instead to an abstract idea, i.e. to a particular system of laws which differs *per definitionem* from other systems of laws. This too can be demonstrated, using terminological examples taken from the German and Italian legal systems. Far more complex problems are posed by the comparison of texts across languages. A particularly clear example is provided by the text type 'verdict', as is shown by the comparison of textual and syntactic structures in the verdicts of a German and an Italian district court in civil law cases.

Comparison of translations

This raises the question of what criteria there are for evaluating the degree of equivalence between linguistic elements, a fundamental problem in language comparison that is also relevant when judging the quality of translations. The most important theories in Linguistics and Translation Studies relating to synonymy and equivalence are therefore first presented and then tested to establish their relevance and applicability. It may be appropriate here to give a specific example, and so one or two aspects of Comparative Translation (Italian to German) will now be pointed out with the help of an excerpt from the classic children's book *Le avventure di Pinocchio* (Collodi, 1993: 22). Since its initial publication in 1883, this book has appeared in numerous German translations, which sometimes vary from each other quite considerably (cf. Marx, 1990: 33ff.):

> Appena Maestro Ciliegia riebbe l'uso della parola,   cominciò
> When   master   Cherry   had regained the use of language, he began
> a dire tremando e balbettando dallo spavento:
> to speak trembling and stuttering with fear:
>
> — Ma di   dove sarà uscita questa vocina che ha detto ohi? . . .
> But where did the little voice that said ow come from? . . .

Eppure qui non c'è anima viva. Che sia per caso questo pezzo di legno che
There isn't a living soul here.   Could it be that this piece of wood

abbia imparato a piangere e a lamentarsi come un bambino? Io non lo
has learnt to cry and moan like a child?   I cannot

posso credere.
believe it.

Questo legno eccolo qui; è un pezzo di legno da caminetto, come tutti
This wood here; it is   a piece of wood from a fireplace, like all

gli altri, e a buttarlo sul fuoco, c'è da far bollire una pentola di fagioli . . .
other pieces, to be thrown on the fire to boil a pot of beans . . .

O dunque? Che ci sia nascosto dentro qualcuno?   Se c'è nascosto
Or what?   Could there be someone hidden inside? If there is someone

qualcuno tanto peggio per lui.   Ora l'accomodo io!
hidden so much the worse for him. Now I'll fix him

T 1	T 2	T 3
Als Meister Kirsch seine Sprache wiedergefunden hatte, begann er zitternd und stammelnd vor Schreck:	Als Meister Kirsche endlich der Sprache wieder mächtig war, fing er, noch vor Schreck zitternd, an zu stammeln:	Nach einiger Zeit fand Meister Pflaum die Sprache wieder; aber er zitterte immer noch entsetzlich und fragte stotternd:
'Wo mag nur dieses Stimmchen hergekommen sein, das da "au" gesagt hat? Hier ist doch keine Menschenseele. Sollte etwa dieses Hozscheit gelernt haben, zu weinen und zu jammern wie ein Kind?	'Wober mag nur das Stimmchen gekommen sein, das "au" gesagt hat . . .? Hier ist doch keine Menschenseele! Oder sollte etwa das Stck Holz weinen und jammern können wie ein Kind?	'Wo mag denn nur dies Jammerstimmchen hergekommen sein? Das Holz da wird doch nicht weinen und klagen können wie ein kleines Kind! —
Das kann ich nicht glauben! Hier ist das Holz. Es ist ein Holzscheit für den Kamin wie alle anderen auch, und wenn man es ins Feuer wirft, kann man sich damit einen Topf Bohnen kochen. Was also? Sollte sich jemand darin versteckt haben? Wenn es so ist, um so schlimmer für ihn. Jetzt zeige ich es ihm!'	Das kann ich einfach nicht glauben! Dieses Holz hier, seht nur! Es ist ein Stück Feuerholz wie alle anderen, es bringt auch einen Topf Bohnen zum Kochen, wenn man es in den Herd wirft . . . was also? Oder — ob jemand sich darin verkrochen hat . . .? Und wenn tatsächlich — um so schlimmer für ihn! Dem werd' ich's geben!'	Unmöglich! — Schau mir's nur einer an: ist es nicht ein Scheit wie jedes andere? Hätte man es gesägt und gespalten, so wäre es vielleicht längst zu Asche verbrannt. — Nanu!? — Oder . . . wirklich! es könnte sein? — Einer versteckt in dem Holze? — Na! Der hätte sich einen ungeschickten Platz gesucht! Wart, dir will ich's bequemer machen; gleich helf' ich dir heraus.'
(C. Collodi (1967) *Die Abenteuer des Pinocchio*)	(C. Collodi (1983) *Pinocchio zieht in die Welt*)	(C. Collodi (1953) *Die Geschichte vom hölzernen Bengele*)

The different German names chosen for the carpenter Maestro Ciliegia are indicative of the different approaches adopted by the three translators: *Meister Kirsch* (T1), *Meister Kirsche* (T2), *Meister Pflaum* (T3). A number of the solutions offered in T3 are distinctly unusual, and difficult to justify. Parts of the original text are left out (cf. *c'è da far bollire una pentola* . . .), while others are extended considerably (*Einer versteckt in dem Holze* . . .). By comparison, T1 and T2 keep much more closely to the original. These examples thus provide excellent material for a discussion of one of the key questions of translation criticism: to what extent are deviations from the original necessary or useful? And this is a question which in turn is closely linked to basic problems in Translation Studies.

The text allows considerable leeway for differences in style, and yet particular solutions are to a large degree predetermined by the language into which the text is being translated. This is true, for instance, of modal particles, which are far more important in German than they are in the Romance languages (cf. Anderman in this volume). Thus all three translators insert a modal particle into the translation of *Ma di dove sarà uscita questa vocina* . . .?: (But where did the little voice . . .) *Wo mag nur/denn nur das/dieses Jammerstimmchen/Stimmchen hergekommen sein* . . .?

The methods of Contrastive Linguistics

The methods applied in Contrastive Linguistics with the two languages Italian and German can be clearly illustrated using modal particles. Unlike Translation Studies, which tends to concern itself with the level of 'parole', Contrastive Linguistics analyses corresponding and divergent structures on the level of 'langue' and, where it resorts to translations, takes these merely as the starting point; the intention is to find the most neutral 'common denominator' possible while eliminating as far as possible any elements of individual style (cf. Coseriu, 1981: 194). It is interesting to note that Contrastive Linguistics (in contrast to Translation Studies) is interested in all levels of language, including Phonology and Phonetics.

Precisely because modal particles play such different roles in Italian and German, the systematic comparison of the phenomenon in the two languages is of great methodological and pedagogical interest. It reveals that the German modal particle is rendered in Italian in very different ways (cf. Held, 1988). Although it can be achieved on the lexical, syntactic, phraseological or prosodic levels, it often happens that the information given by the German modal particle is only implicitly present in Italian, so that here in particular the text needs to be considered as a whole.

Finally, attention is paid to the practical applications of Contrastive Linguistics, which tend to be located in the area of teaching. The essential motivating force in the development of Contrastive Linguistics was the intention to apply the results in foreign language teaching — which at least in part was what indeed happened. With these thoughts in mind we progress to the final topic.

Comparative language studies and foreign language teaching

An obvious starting point is the language module that runs parallel to the Linguistics course and is an important factor in the comparative approach (cf.

Cavagnoli and Veronesi, 1996). Of special interest in this context are the tests that were carried out in connection with the evaluation of the Italian teaching materials. One test consisted of various subjects — in a group, but without the help of the teacher — making themselves familiar with Italian practice texts. Their conversation was recorded, transcribed, and systematically analysed. The subjects' learning behaviour was then compared with that of subjects who were confronted with the same materials in a traditional type of lesson. This comparison produced interesting results in connection with the strengths and weaknesses of the materials being tested and their possible range of application. In a further test the attempt was made to describe all the individual steps taken by someone working with self-instructional programmes in foreign languages. On the basis of practical applications like these, the chances are good for research projects in innovative foreign language teaching based on the comparative approach.

Conclusions

The experience gained so far shows that with the help of the method described it is possible to provide advanced students within a relatively short time with a solid grounding in an additional foreign language. The pragmatic link-up between theory and practice meets with the learners' approval. It is useful here that the theoretical components in particular can be rearranged as required: in choosing what to focus on, the characteristics of the language in question can be taken fully into account. Thus, in the case of Italian, it was better (as was shown) to deal with the contrasting diachrony/synchrony more intensively than with phonology and phonetics; on the other hand, the latter topic would be much more to the fore in a comparable course in Portuguese.

Clearly this innovative concept still requires further tests, modifications and improvements. However, one can already say that course materials of the kind outlined above have the potential to awaken interest in languages, and especially the 'lesser used'of Europe. And that is an aim that is well worth the trouble.

References
Arntz, R. (1989) Neuere Entwicklungen in der Übersetzer- und Dolmetscherausbildung in der Bundesrepublik Deutschland. Das Beispiel Hildesheim. *Interface, Journal of Applied Linguistics* 1/1989, 3–13.
Arntz, R. (1996), Language description and LSP teaching. In H. Somers (ed.) *Terminology, LSP and Translation. Studies in Language Engineering in Honour of Juan C. Sager* (pp.109–24). Amsterdam/Philadelphia: Benjamins.
Arntz, R. (1997) Passive Mehrsprachigkeit — eine Chance für die 'kleinen' Sprachen Europas. In A. Grinsted (ed.) *Language and Business Life. XXII International Association Language & Business Conference 1996* (pp.71–89). Kolding: Handelshøjskole Syd.
Cavagnoli, S. and Veronesi, D. (1996) Fachsprachliche Lesekompetenz für Juristen und Wirtschaftler. *Fachsprache — International Journal of LSP* 3–4/1996, 150–9.
Collodi, C. (1993) *Le avventure di Pinocchio.*
Coseriu, E. (1981) Kontrastive Linguistik und Übersetzung: Ihr Verhältnis zueinander. In W. Kühlwein and G. Thone (eds) *Kontrastive Linguistik und Übersetzungswissenschaft.* Akten des Internationalen Kolloquiums Trier/Saarbrücken. 25–30.09.1978. München: Fink.
Dardano, M. (1995) *Manualetto di linguistica italiana.* Bologna: Zanichelli.

Held, G. (1988) Italienisch: Modalpartikelforschung. In G. Holtus (ed.) *Lexikon der romanistischen Linguistik* (LRL). Bd. IV (pp. 316–36). Tübingen: Niemeyer.

Marx, S.(1990) *Le avventure tedesche di Pinocchio.* Firenze: La Nuova Italia.

Südhölter, J. (1989) Niederländisch. In K-R. Bausch (ed.) *Handbuch Fremdsprachenunterricht* (pp. 327–30). Tübingen: Francke.

Part 2 Context

Chapter 8

The Role of Contexts in Translating

Eugene A. Nida

> *Visibly and linguistically, words are put into context by their*
> *collocations, their grammatical functions and their position in the word order*
> *of a sentence. Outside language, invisibly and referentially they are within a*
> *context of a real or imagined situation, a cultural background, a topic and a*
> *shared experience with the reader.*
>
> (Peter Newmark, 1991: 87)

It is a pleasure to help celebrate the many contributions that Peter Newmark has made to Translation Studies. No one has been so outspoken and so generally right as Newmark, who has never been known to put up with nonsense. We have not always agreed, but at conferences some persons have accused us of planning joint tactics in advance. I am personally much indebted to him for so much that I have learned from his books and articles and from our sharing in conferences. But here I wish to continue to deal with an issue that we have previously discussed, namely, the multidimensional role of contexts in translating.

No translator can afford to overlook the role of contexts in translating because they are crucial for so many decisions, whether in the choice of particular words or in the organisation of an entire discourse. The most obvious relevance of contexts occurs in the choice of words in the immediate syntagmatic context of a single sentence or in the subtle connections between different words within the same semantic field or domain, as an extension of paradigmatic contexts. For example, in translating from Spanish into English it is difficult to know precisely how to speak of the leader of the dominant party in power in Spain. Technically, he is simply the president of the party, but is often referred to simply as 'President', because he presides over the governing party. His function, however, parallels more closely the role of a prime minister in most countries having a parliamentary system.

Whether 'President' or 'Prime Minister' is used in an English translation of a Spanish text depends on factors that go far beyond a coin-tossing solution. If a translator employs 'President', readers of the English translation will wrongly assume that the leader of the government has powers comparable to those of the President of the United States. If, however, he is called 'Prime Minister', which is closer to his actual function, the designation will appear completely contrary to usage in Spain. Regardless of the alternative designation, some supplementary information in the text or in footnotes is essential.

For the proper choice of terminology in any text it is essential to consider how key terms are treated in other texts written by the same author or by other authors on the same or similar themes, and it is often very useful to determine how other translators have dealt with the same problems. All of these contextual elements are part of the complex of contexts that is relevant for translators, especially in cases in which diverse terms are used in different countries employing the same language. For example, terminology for certain computer functions differs between mainland China and Taiwan, and accordingly texts being addressed to people in both areas must reckon with these differences.

A translator must be aware of usage in published texts as well as in everyday usage in different parts of a language area. Consider, for example, the diversities in the Spanish language between Latin America and Spain, especially for semantic areas in which Latin Americans tend to borrow more from American English than from the Spanish of Spain.

The syntagmatic contexts of actual texts are of primary consideration, but frequently paradigmatic factors are also crucial. The choice of a proper term depends so much on other semantically-related terms, for example, for English 'friendly' there are several possible semantic equivalents in Spanish: 'amigable', 'amistoso', 'amable', 'simpatico', 'cordial', listed in some Spanish dictionaries as synonyms, but differing significantly in both designative and associative meanings. For example, 'amigable' is an almost unknown term in most of the Spanish-speaking world; 'amistoso' occurs usually in contexts referring to states or events; while 'amable' suggests intimacy and someone who is lovable. The adjective 'simpático' is certainly the most common equivalent for the English 'friendly', while 'cordial' represents a somewhat higher register and a more impersonal setting. The choice of one or another of these Spanish terms depends primarily on both the Spanish and the English contexts of coresponding texts.

In addition to the immediate or remote syntagmatic and paradigmatic contexts, a translator must always consider the contexts that are prior to the formation of the source text (ST). Information about the author, the circumstances that prompted the writing of a text, and peculiarities of the author's style or special interests and knowledge can all figure significantly in translating. Even the sympathy that translators may have for the contents and style of STs almost inevitably becomes part of the relevant set of contexts. In fact, some outstanding translators simply refuse to translate texts that they cannot relate to in a positive manner, because they do not believe that they can do justice to something that is contrary to their standard of values.

If a text has already been translated, whether into some other target language or into the same language that a translator is to employ, these existing translations constitute particularly important contexts because many receptors will undoubtedly be influenced by what they already know about the ST through the existing translations. This is a very important aspect in translating Classical texts of high literary quality because so often outstanding translators have already had a hand in establishing a model for rendering many key terms or well-known expressions. Such prior translations become especially important in translating religious texts, in which various ideas about divine inspiration can constitute real barriers to new and/or more correct renderings.

Prior contexts may be so sociologically and theologically dominant as to preclude changes, even when the existing tradition is unintelligible. Perhaps the most obvious example of this force of a prior context is the first line in the Lord's Prayer, 'Hallowed be thy name'. People who know only English normally have no knowledge of the meaning of 'hallowed', especially when it is pronounced as three syllables (this word occurs as three syllables only in this context). Modern English has no real passive imperatives, and even if 'Hallowed be' is understood as a passive imperative, the statement is meaningless when applied to God, who is regarded as the essence of holiness.

Furthermore, the use of 'thy name' as a reference to God is likewise misleading for most persons, because they do not recognise this use of 'name' instead of 'God' as a matter of 'positive taboo' or 'divine avoidance'.

When prior translations of a text exist, translators should force themselves to translate without following an existing translation. Paying constant attention to what other translators have done with the text will greatly impair the creativity of the translating process and is likely to end up as merely a revision of an existing translation.

There may, however, be considerable advantages in reading academic and popular reviews of STs, because these often contain important information about problems of comprehension and the difficulties encountered because of particular words. They may also contain perceptive records about the levels of style and the appropriateness of the vocabulary for particular audiences.

For a translator, however, the most important factors are the subject matter of a text and the level of language required to prepare a text that will be adequately understood by the prospective audience.

In general, texts that deal with technical subjects are better translated than novels, detective stories, and newspaper reports, since publishers apparently realise that technical content requires greater knowledge and interlingual competence. Unfortunately, however, this is not always the case. For example, a volume in French about textual problems in biblical Hebrew was given to an American who was both fluent in French and an editor of an academic journal dealing primarily with such matters. The results, however, were totally disappointing because the translation was so literal that even scholars in the same discipline found it difficult to understand the translation correctly. The translator accurately understood the subject matter but totally misunderstood the nature of translating.

The style of some texts provides special problems for translators. Octavio Paz's Spanish volume *El Laborinto de Soledad* (*The Labyrinth of Solitude*) is particularly difficult to translate because of the many long sentences, the highly generic vocabulary, the numerous intricate parentheses, and the extended figurative expressions that are both illuminating and subtle. The remarkable style of this and other books and of his insightful poetry won Paz the 1990 Nobel prize for literature, but his writing would never win a prize among translators for ease in translation.

Consider for example the following literal translation of a sentence of forty-eight words in Spanish: 'I believed, as does Samuel Ramos, that the feeling of inferiority influences our preference for analysis and that the lack of our creations can be explained, not so much by the growth of our critical faculties at the expense of our creations, but as an instinctive lack of confidence in our own capacities.' Or consider the way in which a combination of prose and poetry combine in the following description of Mexican life: 'It floats without opposing anything, it hovers, blown by the wind, at times breaking up like a cloud and sometimes shooting up like a skyrocket. It creeps, folds, expands, contracts, sleeps or dreams, a beautiful rag.'

The context of translating also includes the publisher and any editor, paid by the publisher or by a translation agency. Most publishers target a particular audience and they usually try to satisfy the tastes and interests of such people. But their decisions about translation may at times seem strange. For example, one publisher refused to hire theologians to translate books on theology, since, as the publisher explained, 'Theologians are too anxious to show that they know Greek and Hebrew.' This type of reasoning might seem to be completely unjustified, but it was based on years of experience in trying to get translators to do justice to the ST without showing off their own expertise.

Most competent publishers do, however, look to people experienced in a particular discipline and in effective translating so as to guarantee translations that will hold up to criticism and be acceptable for a number of years.

In some instances translators unfortunately run into real problems with editors who do not understand the nature of translating. An editor's knowledge of foreign languages is often limited and, accordingly, his/her examination of translations depends on two techniques: studying a translation for verbal correspondences and for consistency in grammatical constructions. But consistency of rendering is no guarantee of adequacy, because translators can be consistently wrong as well as right. What editors with limited knowledge of foreign languages should look for is consistent inconsistencies, because no two languages are ever completely consistent in every aspect of their correspondences.

The context of the intended audience is particularly important in selecting terminology and in building in redundancy so as to match the channel capacity of prospective readers. An article on some important scientific discovery may require three distinct levels of translating depending on the prospective readers: high school students, university students, and professional scientists. But the manner in which the translated texts are used is also relevant. For example, the translation of a drama for personal reading may always employ footnotes to explain particular meanings and stage directions, but a text to be used in a dramatic performance has no place for such notes. Also the translation of a technical text to be used as a basis for scholarly discussion is very likely to differ from one that is intended to promote the use of some new invention.

Some of the most extensive modifications in translation occur when supplementary codes are involved, for example, in translating songs, which require close attention to rhythm and singable vowels. In opera the problems are compounded by the singing quality of the vowels in arias, the placement of stress, and the timing of the action. Subtitling becomes a serious problem in condensing dialogue, and facial movements (especially the lips) are crucial for cinema and television performances.

All of these contextual elements have important implications for translating, but probably the most important components are the translators themselves, first, in terms of knowledge and competence in interlingual communication, but second, and even more importantly, their personal integrity. R.W. Jumpelt, an important translator of documents on aviation during World War II, explained his principle of translating by saying, 'I want to make sure that no one ever misunderstands what I have translated.'

References

Newmark, P.P. (1991) *About Translation*. Clevedon: Multilingual Matters.
Paz, Octavio (1950) *El Laborinto de Soledad*. Mexico-Buenos Aires: Fondo de Cultura Económica.

Chapter 9

Translation Theory, Translating Theory and the Sentence

Candace Séguinot

There is at present a confusing tendency for translation theorists to regard the whole text,the basis of discourse analysis, as the unit of translation (UT), which is the opposite of Vinay's and Darbelnet's original concept.

(Peter Newmark, 1988: 54)

Introduction

Like many people, I remember learning in secondary school that a sentence is a complete thought. As I recall, the definition usually came up in the context of correcting punctuation. It went something like this: 'That's a sentence — it expresses a complete thought — so you need a period there.' As I got older and less respectful of received wisdom, I began to ask certain questions, of myself, mainly (I was not entirely disrespectful), and as I began to study language more closely, of the material I saw around me. For example, if a sentence is a complete thought, what would an incomplete thought look like? And when I heard someone say that a string of words was grammatically incomplete, I wondered what the relationship was between this grammatical level and the other level, the level of thoughts.

Of course, as soon as we look at the difference between a sentence in isolation and a sentence embedded in a text it becomes clear that the opposite is not only possible, but commonplace: sentences which are marked as complete by their punctuation are not really complete on the level of meaning. Take the example of sentences like, 'He came today' or 'The latter has been revised' and 'The separatist-turned-federalist has vowed to continue the fight', in the context of the pair of statements, 'Guy Bertrand has lost his court case to obtain an injunction on a future referendum in Quebec. The separatist-turned-federalist has vowed to continue the fight.' What these sentences have in common is that they require a knowledge of a referent for their interpretation, information available in the text, but not in the sentence itself. Sometimes that extra information is not actually available in a text, but it can be understood through intertextuality, i.e. references to other texts, or through familiarity with the particular field of discourse. For example the sentence 'No means no' depends for its meaning on its opposite, 'No (really) means yes.' In North America 'No means no' is a slogan associated with campaigns to end violence against women.

84

In addition, the context itself can help the process of understanding. When you rush out and leave a note like 'Clean dishes' in the kitchen, the actual state of the dishes will allow your partner to disambiguate the two potential meanings and presumably either wash them or put them away.

What this is leading to is a discussion of some of the same difficulties in the teaching of translation with regard to the status of the sentence and its relationship to meaning. The notion that text or context, in terms of the last example, help clarify meaning for translation refers to a different process of checking reality than the state of dishes. The sentence-level issue of potentially ambiguous words or structures is less important in understanding how meaning is conveyed in translation than understanding the process of understanding itself. As is the case in general processes of communication, contextualisation leads to inferencing based on probabilities and personal experience and so helps determine the pragmatic consequences of interpreting the force of a sentence or utterance. The mode and manner of delivery will influence the interpretation. If I write the sentence, 'I smell smoke', and you read it at some later time, when you and I are not in the same room, you will probably not have the same 'thought' as if I _say_ the same words when we _are_ in the same room together.

Meaning and Context

Some genres and discourse types depend more on localising an event than others, and the interpretation of meaning becomes problematic with a change in intended audience. News reporting is a case in point. Since local colour is useful to hook the reader into a story, the details of the story will vary according to the place of publication. When an oil tanker foundered off the coast of the Shetland Islands, the lead-in to the story in the _Globe and Mail_, Canada's national newspaper, referred to it thus:

> Pounded by ferocious winds, a Canada-bound oil tanker carrying twice as much crude as the Exxon Valdez spilled was breaking up off the Shetlands early today.

And here, translated into English, is the lead-in in one of the major Quebec papers:

> An ecological disaster threatens the Shetland Islands north of Scotland where an oil tanker carrying 90 million litres of crude oil (twice the load of the Exxon Valdez in Alaska) went down yesterday when its engines failed during a severe storm.

Comparing the two, we see that the article published in Quebec assumes that the target language (TL) audience needs extra information to understand where the Shetland Islands are and where the Exxon Valdez accident took place.[1] The _Globe_ has a national distribution of English readers whereas the Quebec paper is published far from where the accident took place and serves a francophone population who may be less familiar with British geography. Another problem also familiar in translation is the non-simultaneity of the production of texts: one paper may have direct reporting, another depends on a wire service. Just as with translation, then, context-dependent time references need to be changed. For one paper the event is 'today,' for the second, 'yesterday'.

Of course, context includes more than the physical and temporal situation. There is a reason why all four major papers in the province of Quebec described the tanker as heading for the Ultramar refinery at St Romuald in Quebec beyond the knowledge of geography. The French newspaper *Le Monde* also described the tanker as heading for Quebec, a fact which points to more than the use of local colour, while *The Times* and the *New York Times* omitted any mention of Quebec, but said near the end of the articles that the tanker was *en route* to Canada.

The terms chosen to localise the destination of the tanker are just one example of subjectivity in the selection of information. And just as terms of reference are not a given in the conveying of information but vary according to the knowledge level or expectation of the audience, their interpretation in translation depends on the target audience. Communication, above all, is between and about people, and not just about their need to sell refrigerators and make hotel reservations. It is the way we establish a sense of ourselves and our relationships to others and to the universe in which we live. That means that we bring certain needs and expectations to the act of understanding, and filter and interpret meaning from our individual perspectives.

Meaning and the Sentence

As we try to understand the relationship between meaning, the sentence, and translation, it is clear that subjectivity is coded in language in many different ways. Take the example of someone introducing their child to an acquaintance. Any of the following sentences would do in terms of performing the function:

(1) I would like to introduce you to my son.
(2) I would like you to meet my son.
(3) I would like you to meet my pride and joy.
(4) I would like you to meet the source of my grey hairs.

Each of these sentences could accomplish the task, yet there are differences in the way that the acquaintance — and the son — would interpret the form of the introduction. Though the metaphors in sentences (3) and (4) both refer to the same person, the form of enunciation tells the hearer just as much, if not more, about the speaker than about the child. As for the difficulties of translating these differences, it might seem at first glance that the metaphors in (3) and (4) would cause problems, but it would not necessarily be difficult to find a stylistically marked form in a TL. What is not so clear is how the more subtle differences conveyed in sentences (1) and (2) can be translated. In some languages, in French, for example, the options in (1) and (2) do not exist. The translation would have to be something like, 'J'aimerais vous présenter mon fils', the equivalent of sentence (1) in English.

The point of this example is the meaning of a concept like equivalence in translation when in English the choice of 'introduce' in sentence (1) over 'meet' in sentence (2) pays more attention to one person's role in the process than another's. In other words, the use of a term like equivalence of meaning masks the underlying differences that arise as a result of the nature of the process of translation.[2]

The question of equivalence of meaning across languages within given structures is not necessarily resolved when languages share grammatical structures. Different languages assign different weight to specific grammatical and rhetorical functions, so that the weaving of semantic relations with which a text is constructed is determined by an interpretation of initial relations, and the fact that these initial relations appear identical on the level of individual sentences masks the potential for development of a text along particular topics (Li and Thompson, 1976; van Oosten, 1986; Lambrecht, 1994).

The reading of meaning is also directed by ideological assumptions. These assumptions are inscribed in the vocabulary and structures[3] and in the general act of selection itself. Take, for example, the sentence, 'Clothing is generally laundered in tubs, then hung out to dry.' It is attributed to a *Time* magazine reporter in a book about the economic and political changeover in Eastern Europe, *How We Survived Communism and Even Laughed*, by Slavenka Drakulic. What the author, born in the former Yugoslavia and a reporter herself, understands from this sentence is that the society for whom the article was written not only finds it unusual but 'outrageous' that laundry is done by hand, that the society is unaware that three-quarters of the world's population does their laundry by hand. What the reporter finds interesting in terms of its information value or the addition of local colour becomes a proof of Western naïvety and materialism when viewed from the perspective of those doing the laundering. In addition to the word 'generally', which implies an enunciator familiar enough with the culture to categorise its behaviour, the selection of particular information carries with it the meaning associated with its selection as opposed to what might have been said. Put another way, and here comes the link to translation, the question is not merely one of transfer of meaning between cultures, but the intrinsic potential for readerships to participate in the construction of meaning.

When I mentioned earlier the pragmatic consequences of uttering the sentence, 'I smell smoke', I brought up the issues of time and place. Yet even within one culture the power relationships underlying the ideological differences that lead to cross-cultural differences in interpretation influence the ways in which the meaning of a sentence can be construed in a given context. Back when Pierre Trudeau was prime minister of Canada, it was reported that he uttered this sentence on entering a hotel ballroom. Aides rushed off, with no further encouragement, to pull cigarettes out of people's mouths.

To return, then, to my high school teacher's helpful hints on punctuating sentences. Sorry, but sentences do not *contain* meaning, any more than any other unit of language, for that matter; they *vehicle* meaning. As completeness of meaning does not coincide with typographical sentences, the definition of a sentence as a complete thought is simply inaccurate.

'Well so what,' my teacher might argue, 'my job was to get you to learn to punctuate, and it looks as though I succeeded.' My problem with that argument is that I was never capable of recognising a complete thought, and I don't think the problem is just mine. Given what we know about the pragmatics of

communication, about inference and implication and reading and understanding, it is not clear how anyone could identify exemplars of abstract
attributes like 'complete' and abstract concepts like 'thought'. In other words,
the explanation was perhaps comforting, but not helpful.

What, then, of the explanations about sentences we find in the field of
translation? Are they accurate? Helpful? Comforting? Teaching translation is not
exactly like teaching punctuation. It is similar in that some of what we do in
translation classrooms is to effect a conformity to norms. More than that, of
course, we help develop skills, and in the context of theory courses, transmit
knowledge about the discipline. To further this last goal, an explanation of the
relationship between sentences and translation would have to be accurate in
terms of the current state of knowledge about communication processes. To
further the first and second goals, a definition would have to be helpful in
developing skills or habits.

Translation and the Sentence

Let's start by returning to the relationship between meaning and the sentence
but this time from the perspective of translation. The way the sentence has been
defined in translation has been tied to its status as an operational unit. Peter
Newmark (1991: 66) has put it this way:

> . . . From a translator's point of view, I think the main descriptive units (an
> extension of Halliday) are a hierarchy: text, paragraph, sentence, clause,
> group, word, morpheme. In abstract terms, none of these are more
> important than another (as Halliday states) though in practice, the text is
> the ultimate court of appeal, the sentence is the basic unit of *translating* (not
> of translation), and most of the cruxes are centred in the lexical units, if not
> the words.

This definition of a sentence as a 'unit of *translating*' as opposed to a 'unit of
translation', is expressed in a slightly different way in another of Newmark's
publications where he refers to his own tentative translating process (Newmark,
1988: 21):

> There are two approaches to translating (and many compromises between
> them): (1) you start translating sentence by sentence, for say the first
> paragraph or chapter, to get the feel and the feeling tone of the text, and then
> you deliberately sit back, review the position, and read the rest of the SL
> text; (2) you read the whole text two or three times, and find the intention,
> register, tone, mark the difficult words and passages and start translating
> only when you have taken your bearings.

> Which of the two methods you choose may depend on your temperament,
> or on whether you trust your intuition (for the first method) or your powers
> of analysis (for the second). Alternatively, you may think the first method
> more suitable for a literary and the second for a technical or an institutional
> text. The danger of the first method is that it may leave you with too much
> revision to do on the early part, and is therefore time-wasting. The second
> method (usually preferable) can be mechanical; a translational text analysis

is useful as a point of reference, but it should not inhibit the free play of your intuition. Alternatively, you may prefer the first approach for a relatively easy text, the second for a harder one.

Compare this to a definition of translation units that speaks to the need for concepts in the theoretical discourse on translation (Newmark,1988: 54):

> There is at present a confusing tendency for translation theorists to regard the whole text, the basis of discourse analysis, as the unit of translation (UT), which is the opposite of Vinay's and Darbelnet's original concept. Vinay and Darbelnet define the unit of translation as 'the smallest segment of an utterance whose cohesion of signs is such that they must not be separately translated' — in other words, the minimal stretch of language that has to be translated together, as one unit. The argument about the length of the UT, which has been put succintly by W. Haas, 'as short as is possible, as long as is necessary', is a concrete reflection of the age-old conflict between free and literal translation — the freer the translation, the longer the UT; the more literal the translation, the shorter the UT, the closer to the word, or, in poetry, even to the morpheme. Free translation has always favoured the sentence; literal translation the word. Now, since the rise of text linguistics, free translation has moved from the sentence to the whole text.

Or compare it to the need for definitions of translating and translation units, to use Newmark's distinction, that refer to cognitive units:

> Since the sentence is the basic unit of thought, presenting an object and what it does, is, or is affected by, so the sentence is, in the first instance, your unit of translation, even though you may later find many SL and TL correspondences within that sentence. [Newmark, 1988: 31]

And:

> Nous considérons comme équivalents les termes: unité de pensée, unité lexicologique et unité de traduction. Pour nous ces termes expriment la même réalité considérée d'un point de vue différent. [Vinay and Darbelnet, 1977: 36]

If we summarise the points these different references to sentences in translation seem to be making, it is perhaps easier to see the assumptions they entail and their orientation to either the transmission of knowledge or the transfer and development of norms and skills.

The first of Newmark's definitions of the sentence, the one that refers to a descriptive unit on an abstract level and a basic operational unit in practice, belongs to the descriptive branch of Translation Studies. It is based on an implied probability. The probability is that the translator will carry out activities on the level of the sentence; the precise nature of the activities is not clear. This definition speaks to the individual act of translating, the process.

The second reference is not talking about the individual act of translating, although it is about starting a translation, as much as collective behaviour and the institutional view represented as Newmark, translator, and Newmark, authority on translation. The perspective is the psychological — the temperament, attitude, and competence of the translator — and the normative. The branch of translation to which it belongs in the schema developed by Holmes as cited in Toury (1995: 10) is no longer descriptive, but applied.

The third way Newmark defines translation refers to sentences as a basic unit of thought, not as a hypothesis about the relationship between sentences and meaning, but in the context of a justification of the sentence as a translation unit. A 'basic unit of thought' is not the same as a complete thought, so the objections to the punctuation guideline do not hold here, but still there are questions about what 'basic' means. Does 'sentence' here refer to propositions, i.e. a basic unit in a formal sense, or to typographical sentences, which could include a number of co-ordinate or subordinate clauses?

So the first problem with identifying the sentence as a theoretical construct is to define it. A second problem in associating thought with a given language unit is the implication that all thoughts find expression in language. Sociocultural constraints may determine that some concepts are not expressed verbally, so that a distinction has to be drawn between the existence of thoughts and the vehicles or absence of vehicles for their expression (Wierzbicka,1994: 461).

The reason the relationship between meaning and the sentence has been unclear in translation is that the focus has not been on the nature of the unit but on the unity of the translation operation. Experts say that they translate sentence by sentence, or that in most cases this is what competent translators do. Statements about translation and the sentence as the preferred unit take the form that (a) it has been a general practice over time; (b) certain types of translation are likely to be carried out on the level of sentences; and (c) certain types of people prefer to translate on this level.

There is a sense, then, that there is a probability of occurrence, and it is this probability that leads to what Gideon Toury (1995: 260–3) has referred to as recommended types of behaviour. Using the translation of metaphor as an example, Toury refers to Newmark as saying that metaphors are *normally* transferred in translation. As a parallel to the features of a text determining the relevance of the sentence as a unit, Mary Snell-Hornby, cited in the same passage in Toury, relates the translating of a metaphor to its structure or function in a text. In contrast, a *theoretical* approach to the translation of metaphor, Toury says, would be a description of a closed set of options with a logic for the choice of particular options.

Obviously we are far from the possibility of this kind of description. But what we can ask, in terms of the scientific foundation of statements about the sentence and translation, is whether the sentence is a translation unit from an *operational* point of view, and, if so, under what conditions? In other words, is there empirical proof that supports the anecdotal evidence? Second, is there a better explanation for recommending to budding translators that they translate at this level than an appeal to convention?

Translating and the Sentence

Let's take the idea of translation units, units that exist apart from the individual act of translating, first. The only argument has been the appeal to cognitive units, and given what we know about meaning, translation units would have to be penetrable, i.e. their meaning would have to be open to modification from co-textual and contextual sources. Further, a theory that suggested units of meaning without reference to a person — a writer or speaker of the source text (ST) or the translator or a reader or hearer of the target text — would be assuming that meaning is *transmitted*, whereas we know from reading theory in both linguistic and literary fields that meaning is *constructed*.

In terms of *translating* units, however, there is some indication that the sentence *does* have a special status in translation. My own empirical research has been with professional translators, meaning those who spend whole days translating pragmatic texts (Séguinot, 1988, 1989, 1996a, 1996b). The evidence from videotapes of these translators is that they read and comprehend a typographical sentence before they start, and that they continue translating either until they encounter a problem or their memory fails. The sentence also seems to be a factor in determining where a translator will go back to make changes: there is some evidence that these translators working on pragmatic texts may wait until a sentence is complete to make substantive revisions. Further, there does not seem to be evidence that translators operate consistently on units other than the word and the sentence. The fact that there do not seem to be significant numbers of pauses in the introspective flow at the end of clauses within complex sentences shows that the translators, at least the ones that have been studied in this way, are not working within the boundaries of individual propositions.

Note, though, the difference between expediency and necessity. It may be more productive for translators with word counts to meet to force themselves to produce a preliminary version and then revise it to make sure that it is an adequate translation rather than structure their time to encourage creativity. On the other hand, interpreters clearly do not, and cannot, wait until they have heard an entire sentence to begin. Interpretation and translation must draw on some of the same resources, yet the managing of resources cannot be the same in the transfer from a written text and in simultaneous interpretation.[4]

Saying that the sentence is important as a domain in the processing of information in translation does not mean that meaning is restricted to this level. Outputs are informed and constrained both by text beyond the sentence and by the production of the translation itself. This means that a theoretical model that explains the structures and processes underlying translation has to take into account instances where processes are non-linear, has to provide input for world knowledge and text knowledge, and has to explain the phenomena of self-generated meaning and the development of expectations (or in Lörscher's terms (Lörscher, 1991), the prospective aspect of translation) as a text progresses.

The example that follows shows how text and world knowledge lead to self-generated meaning. It comes from a dialogic translating session (Séguinot, 1996a). The two translators, T1 and T2, were working on a part of a sentence in the ST that read, '. . . as his sons James and Thomas both married daughters . . .'. The transcript of the think-aloud recording with glosses of the French follows. Words that are underlined are the translation as it appears on the computer screen:

T2 _Ah ben écoute écoute puisque son fils . . . ses fils James et Thomas_
Hey listen, listen as his son . . . his sons James and Thomas

T1 _both married daughters of the_

T1 _Ah oui d'ailleurs_
Yes and

T1 _il reste le problème de speaker là on l'a jamais vu_
there's still the problem of speaker — we never had it before

T2 _Oui_
Right
[T1 types out _'puique de'_ then deletes the _'e'_ > _'puique d'_]

T2 _puisque deux de ses fils_ (2.18 sec. pause) [T1 deletes _'ique'_] _parce que je pense qu'il en avait plus que deux_
as two of his sons (2.18 sec. pause) because I think he had more than two

T1 _Remarque il en avait peut-être que deux_
Listen he may only have had two

T2 _Non on dirait his two sons_
No they would have said his two sons

So when the word _deux_ finds its way into the translation, it is not because there was a 'two' or its equivalent in the English text, but because, perhaps under the influence of the 'both', the translator has been working from what she thinks is her knowledge of the family about which she is writing.

In terms of modelling the translation process, then, a linear model that suggests a transfer of the kind:

$$\text{Source sentence} \rightarrow \text{Target sentence}$$

is an oversimplification because it implies linearity in the production phase, which may not be the case (Jääskeläinen, 1990: 55), and does not include access to world knowledge, text knowledge, constraints that translating puts on the translation that follows, the nature of the assignment, the audience . . . in other words, all those sources of meaning and influences other than the immediate text.

But what of the other argument, the one that says that an explanation that may not be accurate scientifically can still be useful in the classroom? In this case, it just might work. Teachers of translation know that beginning translation students tend to pay undue attention to lexical information, which leads to unhelpful strategies (Séguinot, 1991: 84–5). To some extent, the highlighting of information through the syntactic and accentual system causes students to focus on these items. The disengaging of information from the form of its expression is one of the differences between successful and unsuccessful strategies (Jääskeläinen, 1990: 220). In the case of expert translators, there is an ability to learn from experience and actually recognise that the sentence might not be the appropriate level to work with as a unit. The transcript that follows comes from a study of two professional translators working on the same annual report (Séguinot, 1991). The more junior translator had four years' experience in translation but less than a year in the area of finance. Here is part of her think-aloud protocol:

> Yeah . . . okay . . . it's ah very technical terms in the . . . it's terms that appear in the Fren . . . in the report and uh they have to be exactly the same as uh what we have here in the financial statements so I have to make sure that I use those . . .

In contrast, the other translator had worked for over ten years in this field and had done this company's report before. Her interpretation was that the problems in the text were not in the terms, but in the syntax, and she chose to separate the propositions in the sentences of the ST.

> There's always so many pieces in these sentences of Cambridge, you don't know how to fit them in . . . it's terrible . . . okay . . . It's very typical of this particular annual report. It's very dense, so that they'll say something like the 52,437,000 square ft., wholly owned shopping centre and then it carries on, so you just, you know, you get lost. Hmmm And we generally revise it quite significantly. I think the most important thing at the beginning is to make sure that all the elements are there, and then you have to play around with them a little bit . . . And sometimes you have to break down the sentences differently.

Conclusion

To return now to our starting point: as with punctuation, a sentence in isolation is a different kind of animal from a sentence embedded in a text. From a theoretical perspective, the sentence may have a relationship to thought, but it is difficult to prove that the expression of meaning in translation is captured by a transfer or transmission of individual sentences. On the other hand, a process view of translation shows that sentences are very real operational units in routine types of translation performed by people with some degree of expertise.

Notes

1. See Schäffner (1991) for discussions of extra-textual knowledge and translation.
2. For a fuller discussion of this issue see Barbara Folkart's book, _Le conflit des énonciations. Traduction et discours rapporté._
3. See the work of Teun A. Van Dijk, for example.
4. For theories about the processes underlying interpretation, see De Groot (1996), Gile (1996), and Moser-Mercer (1996).

References

Danks, J.H., Shreve, G.M., Fountain, S.B. and McBeath, M.K. (eds) (1996) _Cognitive Processes in Translation and Interpreting._ Thousand Oaks, London & New Delhi: Sage Publications.

De Groot, A.M.B. (1996) The cognitive study of translation and interpretation: Three approaches. In J.H. Danks, G.M. Shreve, S.B. Fountain and M.K. McBeath (eds) (pp. 25–56).

Folkart, B. (1991) _Le conflit des énonciations. Traduction et discours rapporté._ Candiac, Québec: Collection L'Univers des discours, Les Éditions Balzac.

Gile, D. (1996) Conference interpreting as a cognitive management problem. In J.H. Danks, G.M. Shreve, S.B. Fountain, and M.K. McBeath (eds) (pp. 196–214).

Jääskeläinen, R. (1990) *Features of Successful Translation Processes: A Think-Aloud Protocol Study*. Unpublished Licentiate Thesis, Savonlinna School of Translation Studies, University of Joensuu.

Lambrecht, K. (1994) *Information Structure and Sentence Form*. Cambridge: Cambridge University Press.

Li, C. and Thompson, S. (1976) Subject and topic: A new typology of language. In C. Li (ed.) *Subject and Topic* (pp. 457–90). New York: Academic Press.

Lörscher, W. (1991) *Translation Performance, Translation Process, and Translation Strategies*. Tübingen: Narr.

Moser-Mercer, B. (1996) Beyond curiosity: Can interpreting research meet the challenge? In J.H. Danks, G.M. Shreve, S.B. Fountain and M.K. McBeath (eds) (pp. 176–95).

Newmark, P.P. (1988) *A Textbook of Translation*. New York & London: Prentice Hall.

Newmark, P.P. (1991) *About Translation*. Clevedon: Multilingual Matters.

Schäffner, C. (1991) Semantic relations in the lexicon and in the text: Reflections on adequate translation. In S. Tirkkonen-Condit (ed.) (pp.111–20).

Séguinot, C. (1988) Pragmatics and the explicitation hypothesis. *TTR* 1(2), 103–13.

Séguinot, C. (1989) The translation process: An experimental study. In C. Séguinot (ed.) *The Translation Process* (pp. 21–53). Toronto: H.G. Publications, School of Translation, York University.

Séguinot, C. (1991) A study of student translation strategies. In S. Tirkkonen-Condit (ed.) (pp. 79–88).

Séguinot, C. (1996a) Some thoughts about think-aloud protocols. *Target* 8(3), 75–95.

Séguinot, C. (1996b) Accounting for variability in translation. In J.H. Danks, G.M. Shreve, S.B. Fountain, and M.K. McBeath (eds) (pp. 25–56).

Tirkkonen-Condit, S. (ed.) (1991) *Empirical Research in Translation and Intercultural Studies*. Tübingen: Gunter Narr.

Toury, G. (1995) *Descriptive Translation Studies and beyond*. Amsterdam & Philadelphia: Benjamins.

Van Dijk, T.A (1989) Structures of discourse and structures of power. In J.A. Anderson (ed.) *Communication Yearbook 12* (pp. 18–59). Newbury Park, Ca.: Sage.

Van Dijk, T.A. and Kintsch, W. (1983) *Strategies of Discourse Comprehension*. London: Academic Press.

Van Oosten, J. (1986) *The Nature of Subjects, Topics and Agents: A Cognitive Explanation*. Monograph reproduced by the Indiana University Linguistics Club.

Vinay, J.P. and Darbelnet, J. (1977) *Stylistique comparée du français et de l'anglais: méthode de traduction*. Paris: Didier.

Wierzbicka, A. (1994) Semantic primitives across languages. In C. Goddard and A. Wierzbicka (eds) *Semantic and Lexical Universals* (pp. 445–500). Amsterdam & Philadelphia: Benjamins.

Chapter 10

The 'Ultimate Confort': Word, Text and the Translation of Tourist Brochures

Mary Snell-Hornby

> *Communicative translation attempts to produce on its readers an effect as close as possible to that obtained on the readers of the original.*
>
> (Peter Newmark, 1981: 39)

The following extract, taken from a tourist brochure, will sound familiar to many travellers:

> Equiped with the latest facilities to give ultimate confort, it has 232 rooms all with bath and toilette, telephone direct line, music, private TV facilitie, air conditioning and balcony with sea view.

This is an exact quotation from a glossy, richly illustrated brochure in four languages singing the praises of a brand new hotel in a smart seaside resort in Southern Spain. To the seasoned translation teacher and researcher, the language comes as no surprise: elementary errors are unfortunately still a common feature of multilingual tourist brochures, making it painfully obvious that translation is still not given the professional attention now taken for granted in most other aspects of the tourist trade. It is not our aim here to analyse what went wrong with the English in the above quotation: to explain when consonants are doubled, how plurals are formed and how interferences can be avoided lies in the domain of language teaching and not of Translation Studies. This chapter rather seeks to approach the problem of translation for the tourist industry from the other end of the spectrum: we shall first investigate the tourist brochure as a text type within the context of Translation Studies today, then look at the advertising conventions found in tourist brochures from different linguistic and cultural backgrounds, and finally create texts which harmonise with those conventions and fulfil their function as instruments of persuasion.

The Tourist Brochure as Text Type

In the classic typology of Katharina Reiss (1971, 1976) the tourist brochure is an operative text. Its dominant function is to present material in such a way that it attracts attention and invites patronage. The main focus is on the appeal to the addressee, and — even in an age of increasing globalisation — tourist brochures and other advertising texts are culture bound; their impact varies with the reader, his or her age, background, origin and mentality. Stories abound of disastrous publicity campaigns which failed because their managers were unaware of simple but vital cultural differences, for example, that in some cultures white is the colour of mourning, and in others Venus de Milo would not symbolise beauty but would be taken for a thief. However, despite their dominant operative function, tourist brochures usually convey essential information (and are hence also content-oriented) and they often rely on distinctly expressive elements (metaphor, pun, alliteration, allusion) for their effect. In other words, their message depends on an interplay of all three textual functions: informative, expressive and operative.

Apart from this, however, the tourist brochure rarely consists only of a verbal text. On the contrary, illustrations and other visual elements — in particular photographs, but also maps, diagrams, street plans, logos — are often given more prominence than language. Layout is an important issue (cf. Schopp, 1996), and here again the overall impact depends, not on individual characteristics, but on the interplay of all the features involved.

Marketing, publicity, advertising, mass tourism are by-products of our modern consumer society with its emphasis on individual freedom and self-fulfilment. Once associated with 'Western' society, advertising has in recent years become a global feature. The lack of advertisements — whether television commercials or billboards on the streets — was a conspicuous feature of communist countries, but the years since 1989 have brought changes, and we can now witness the development of a completely new genre of text, alongside new markets for translation, in the countries of former Eastern Europe. The former vacuum has been filled, not only by linguistic innovations but by the influence of Western values and models:

> The present decade — a period of incredible expansion of the advertising industry in the East European markets — is a scene of obvious foreign (i.e. West European and American) impact. As a genre representing very strong correlation between the text and culture, as consumer-oriented and overtly persuasive texts recommending not only goods for sale but also attitudes, advertisements produce and are themselves the result of cultural stereotyping. Translated advertisements import social values and often unrecognised beliefs, as well as linguistic patterns. New text type conventions are being created through the adoption of foreign textual features, partly mediated by literal translations, which sometimes cause a clash of linguistic and cultural norms. [Jettmarova, Piotrowska and Zauberga, 1997: 186]

Even in the long-standing consumer societies of the West, however, cultural stereotyping is a noticeable feature of advertising material, including tourist brochures, and the varying cultural and linguistic conventions pose considerable problems in translation.

Translation Studies and the Language of Advertising

For a long time Translation Studies paid only scant attention to the phenomenon of advertising and tourism, and in translator training it is still often completely ignored — despite the large amount of translation work done for the tourist industry. In recent years, however, studies have appeared, highlighting its potential both for Translation Studies and for the development of new job profiles. Séguinot (1994) points out the multiple issues involved in the translation of advertisements and the varied fields of competence demanded of the translator:

> In translating advertising, translators are expected to take responsibility for the final form of an advertisement. Globalisation of the translation business sometimes means providing full marketing services in addition to translation and interpreting. Therefore, in the marketing of goods and services across cultural boundaries, an understanding of culture and semiotics that goes well beyond both language and design is involved. Translators need to understand the basics of marketing; they need to know the legal jurisdictions of their market; they must know how cultural differences affect marketing; they must be aware of constraints placed by the form and functions of the source text, and they must be able to interpret the visual elements which are of key importance in advertising. Going global successfully means taking control of the final product, researching the cultural and marketing aspects, and making sure the translation conforms to legal constraints. All this shows that the range of knowledge and skills needed by the profession of the translator is changing. [Séguinot, 1994: 249]

Smith and Klein-Braley (1997) emphasise the range of theoretical and practical issues involved in translating advertising texts, which provides material both for research and translator training:

> For translation studies, the translation of advertisements provides us with a microcosm of almost all the prosodic, pragmatic, syntactic, textual, semiotic and even ludic difficulties to be encountered in translating. By analysing such short but complex and structurally complete texts we can derive valuable insights into possible strategies and methods for dealing with these phenomena in other longer texts, whether literary or non-literary. [Smith and Klein-Braley, 1997: 173]

Despite the complexities involved, and despite the obvious convenience of the advertising text as a tool in teaching, the language of advertising is still inadequately researched. In a recent study (cf. Snell-Hornby, 1996: 101–3) I analysed a corpus of over 100 written advertisement texts in German and English to identify linguistic and cultural differences. It appeared, not surprisingly, that in both languages clear, terse, rhythmical prose was predominant, with simple syntax, whether in the form of complete sentences or what Quirk and Greenbaum call 'block language' (1973: 205). Secondly, the actual devices used to achieve this end differ: in German block language, for example, nominal forms dominate more than in English, which favours verb phrases. Both, however, favour unmarked forms of the verb, in English the imperative ('Save time and money'), in German the infinitive ('Jetzt unverbindlich anfordern . . .'). This means that in English advertisements the reader is more often implicitly addressed than in German. Thirdly, in both languages common use is made of devices such as wordplay, metaphor and fixed idioms, while in their concrete realisation such devices are of course language-specific, usually making a literal translation impossible. Fourthly, in both languages local and cultural associations are frequent, and as these are culture-specific in their concrete realisation, they too provide a problem for the translator.

The Hotel Brochure: The Spanish Example

Let us now compare these findings with the text provided in our hotel brochure from the seaside resort in Southern Spain. The brochure consists mainly of a selection of exactly twenty brightly coloured photographs showing the seaside panorama, views of the hotel foyer, dining room, bedrooms, swimming pool and balconies, and beside them the nineteen lines of verbal text seem paltry and inadequate. It is presented in four versions, clearly recognisable as a Spanish source text (ST) with translations into German, English and French. The Spanish version of our opening quotation runs as follows:

> Dotado del más moderno confort, con 232 habitaciones, con baño completo, teléfono directo al exterior, música ambiental, posibilidad de TV privada, aire acondicionado y terraza con vistas al mar.

All three translations can be described as literal transcodings containing elementary language errors in grammar, lexis and syntax. They all lack coherence and textual cohesion and for that reason alone fail to function as texts. Apart from individual language errors that could be corrected (*equipped, comfort, toilet, facilities*), the attempt to reproduce the Spanish syntax as exactly as possible has in all three translated versions resulted in an anomaly: in the English version the referent of *it* (the hotel) can only be inferred from the photographs above the text. Even more disastrous in translation is the last of the three paragraphs of text, here in Spanish, German and English:

> Situado en primera linea de la playa de San Cristóbal, en el paseo de mayor atractivo de Almuñécar, ciudad ubicada en la Costa Tropical de Granada, donde durante todo el año se disfruta de un privilegiado microclima con temperaturas medias de 18° en invierno y 25° en verano, siendo la única área de España donde se desarrollan los cultivos tropicales (chirimoyas, aguacates, . . .).

> Gelegen am Strand von San Cristobal, der schönsten Promenade Almuñecars, einer Stadt der Costa Tropical in der südspanischen Provinz Granada, an der man das ganze Jahr über ein aussergewöhnlich mildes Klima mit temperaturen zwischen 18° Celsius im Winter und 25° Celsius im sommer geniessen kann, in dem Teil Spaniens wo tropische Früchte cultiviert werden. (Advokatenbirne, Zuckerapfel, . . .)

> It has the best view to the beach of San Cristobal. Situated on the most attractive promenade of Almuñecar. This city is located on the Costa Tropical of Granada with its very special microclimate; an average temperature in the winter of 18°C and 25°C in the summer, makes possible to be the only place in Spain where tropical fruit can be grown (avocado, cherimoya . . .).

The translators' problem seems to have been that the Spanish sentence, as in our first example, operates without a main verb. The German translation tries to imitate this, and the reader wades through four lines in vain, naturally expecting the series of dependent clauses and appositional phrases to lead into a main clause. The English translation goes to the other extreme and chops up the one sentence into a series of barely connected and syntactically incomplete statements. Here again, both versions fail to function linguistically as texts, quite apart from their operative function as publicity material. One can only assume, as one hotel receptionist said by way of explanation for the abysmal quality of these and other translations of tourist brochures, that they were never seriously intended to be read.

The Advertising Text as Creative Writing

The most glaring reason for the failure of the Spanish translations was the lack of even modest linguistic competence on the part of the translator(s). Highly questionable, however, is also the strategy of literal transcoding: if they are intended to function as advertising texts in their specific target culture, these are, in Newmark's terms (1981), not semantic but communicative translations. Moreover, as was observed above, devices are used in advertising language which defy transcoding or literal translation. This is confirmed by a look at any authentic English parallel text: let us take for example the brochure (a ten-page booklet) published by the Regent Palace Hotel in London. On the front cover is the name and logo of the hotel with its immediate location (Piccadilly Circus) and a slogan: *You can't get closer to London.* The back cover is purely informative: we find address, fax and phone numbers, and, in large print, numbers for making reservations at any hotel in the same chain. The inside back cover shows a simplified street plan, indicating the exact position of the hotel, along with the slogan *The capital's liveliest location.* The rest of the brochure has mainly operative function, with a number of brief passages of text, copiously illustrated by photographs or drawings, and with ample use of creative and expressive devices. Here are two examples:

Feel the pulse of Piccadilly

Just step out of the hotel's door and you're right in the liveliest part of London: Piccadilly Circus. The most famous theatres, restaurants and shops are all within a few minutes walk of the hotel.

The choice of entertainment within a few hundred yards is absolutely unbeatable — you'll feel the pulse of Piccadilly from the Regent Palace: it's right at the heart of London.

Perfect accommodation for Families

Unique in the West End, the Regent Palace has an area wholly dedicated to family accommodation. There is a choice of over twenty rooms with a variety of bed combinations and inter-connecting room options to accommodate family members of all ages.

If you're coming to London with children, then there is no better place to stay than the *Piggadilly* rooms at the Regent Palace!

The second text is illustrated by a drawing of a comic, brightly-dressed 'Piggy' figure, with a 'hand' raised in welcome.

The two texts show elements we have already described as characteristic of advertising: clear, rhythmical prose, with simple syntax and explicit involvement of the reader (*just step out, you'll feel*, etc.). Creative devices used are wordplay (*Piggadilly*), metaphor — cliché and stock metaphors in Newmark's terminology (1981) — *the heart of London* and *the pulse of Piccadilly*, the latter with the additional device of alliteration. These are all supported by superlative adjectives and turns of phrase with clear positive connotations: *liveliest, most famous, absolutely unbeatable, unique*. It is the task of the translator not to find an individual equivalent for each of the devices, but to create a text, based on the given information, which would rouse the burning desire in the target reader's mind to go to London and stay at the Regent Palace.

The Brazilian Example: A Holistic Approach

The tourist brochure can be either a booklet or a leaflet that presents a more or less balanced blend of information and persuasive elements. In the case of hotel brochures, the basic information, as was the case with the Regent Palace, includes the name and logo, address, telephone and fax numbers along with the location (possibly marked on a simplified street plan) — these are featured prominently, usually on the front page or panel. Information concerning rooms and facilities is generally incorporated in a verbal text inside the brochure, and is presented in as positive a light as possible. Other features, whether verbal, such as slogans, or visual, such as photographs, are used as further persuasive elements to heighten the effect.

The blend of information and persuasion through word and image is a crucial issue, and clumsy presentation of either can be counter-productive. A hotel in Fortaleza, Brazil, for example, has a publicity leaflet with an address that is barely visible. Two outer panels show, in prominent position, the logo of the hotel chain, with the name of the hotel itself only at the bottom of the page, and irrelevant photographs in central position. Two other panels show, in oversize letters, the names of the town and province with a rough map of Brazil and an aerial view of the town's skyscrapers and coastline; above this in small print, a list of information items is presented in Portuguese and English:

FORTALEZA	FORTALEZA
Área: 336 km^2	Area: 336 km^2
Altitude: 26 m	Altitude: 1014 inches
Clima: quente e úmido,	Climate: hot and wet,
temperatura média	temperature anual
anual de 26,5°C.	average 79°F.

A diagram the size of a postage stamp turns out to be, upon closest scrutiny, a miniature street plan with the name of the hotel, Colonial Praia, in minute letters.

The material on hotel facilities is presented in the same way: at the top of the page, placed above four poor quality photographs (recognisable as part of the garden, one of the bedrooms, the dining room with buffet and an aerial view of the hotel) we perceive, in very small letters, the following list of items in Portuguese and English:

106 apartamentos e suites	106 rooms and suites
2.400 m² de jardins	2.400 square meters of garden
A 8 km do aeroporto	8 km from airport
Localização privilegiada para compras	located nearby shopping area
Piscina para adultos e infantil	2 swimming pool
Restaurante	Restaurant
Room service 24 horas	24 h room service
Salão de beleza	Beauty parlour
Salão para convenções	Banquet and meeting rooms
Agência de viagem	Travel agency
Estacionamento	Parking
Apartamento com ar condicionado, banheiro privativo, tv a cores, minibar e água quente central	All rooms with air conditioning, bath and shower, TV, direct dial phone, minibar

The result of this strategy is a complete imbalance of informative and persuasive elements, and as publicity material the leaflet is ineffective. The above list of items creates no coherent impression of the hotel, its style or ambience, for which a more imaginative verbal text, well supported by illustrative material, would be more suitable. In fact the entire brochure presents a fragmentary confusion of conflicting elements, distorted in their relevance for an operative text. What is needed in prominent position is not the name and logo of the hotel chain, but the name of the hotel itself with address, telephone and fax numbers, and the location clearly indicated on a legible street plan. Singularly unfortunate, especially for the European tourists (a large target group for this Brazilian 'Costa do Sol' with its 573 kilometres of beaches) is the photograph with the view of the town's skyscrapers, which are more reminiscent of concrete and stress than of holidays and comfort. The information on Fortaleza is partly irrelevant and partly misleading: irrelevant are the statistics on the area of the town in square kilometres and the altitude in inches; misleading is the description of the climate as *hot and wet*, giving the impression of frequent rain — what is meant is a *hot and humid* equatorial climate. Much more interesting for the sun-seeking European tourist would be a mention of the many sandy beaches and Fortaleza's position just 3° south of the equator (it has in fact an enviable record of 2,800 hours of sunshine per year). For this a brief text would be sufficient with both informative and operative function: *Fortaleza, the seaside city 3° south of the equator (average temperature 80°F), situated on the Brazilian 'Costa do Sol' with its stupendous 360 miles of beaches.*

Similarly, the gracious and charming hotel deserves more than the meagre list of facilities offered above. The information they provide plus the experience of staying there led me to write the following description:

> Just round the corner from the Iracema Beach and only 2 miles from Fortaleza's bustling Old Town, you will find a haven of peace and comfort: the **Colonial Praia Hotel.** Built in rambling colonial style round court-yards of lush tropical gardens, it has 98 bedrooms and 7 suites — all with air-conditioning, minibar, TV, direct dial telephone and bathroom — as well as a souvenir shop, hairdresser's and facilities for banquets and conferences.
>
> Staying at the **Colonial** makes business a pleasure and turns a holiday into sheer delight. Whether tasting our sumptuous buffets in the dining room, enjoying a cool breeze on the verandah or relaxing by the pool beside hibiscus, coconut palms and banana trees, at the **Colonial Praia** you will discover the essence of gracious living.

Like the texts describing the Regent Palace Hotel, this passage has many features typical of advertising in English, including simple syntax with paratactic sequencing and strong end-focus, and the explicit involvement of the reader (*you will find, you will discover*). The persuasive elements lie mainly in the lexical items: apart from adjectives and phrases with strong positive connotations (*lush, sumptuous, enjoying a cool breeze, relaxing by the pool, essence of gracious living*), there is the positively marked metaphorical phrase *haven of peace and comfort* (recognisable as a cliché metaphor in Newmark's terminology), and in particular the use of such expressive devices as lexical opposition and intensification (*makes business a pleasure and turns a holiday into sheer delight*). And of course there are the stock images which the European associates with a tropical paradise: *hibiscus, coconut palms and banana trees.*

Even the most expressive or persuasive verbal elements are not complete as publicity material, however, without suitable and high-quality photographs for illustration and an optimal layout, including factors such as position, size, colour and type of lettering. In the age of desktop publishing, the awareness is growing that this too is a vital concern of the translator and of translator training (cf. Schopp, 1996), and it is a major question to be considered if, as Candace Séguinot put it, the translator is to take the responsibility for the final form of his or her product.

In the globalised society of the outgoing twentieth century, marketing is one of the driving forces, and in it advertising has a key role. For countries that rely on the tourist trade, and those now include Spain and Brazil, effective publicity is essential, and multilingual text material will need to be taken much more seriously than has hitherto been the case. At the interface between a globalised consumer society on the one hand and the varying conventions, constraints and culture-bound stereotypes of the different target groups on the other, advertising is fruitful ground for the translator. Though it goes far beyond language, it would be a first step if linguistic competence could at last be a condition *sine qua non* for anyone working with multilingual material, including tourist brochures, and it is also high time for translatorial competence and subject expertise to be likewise taken for granted, so that the translated material can attain the same degree of excellence that the advertisers seek to praise in their products. We need in fact to translate such bungled linguistic products as the 'ultimate confort' into what is understood by the target reader as the last word in luxury.

References

Jettmarova, Z., Piotrowska, M. and Zauberga, I. (1997) New advertising markets as target areas for translation. In M. Snell-Hornby, Z. Jettmarova and K. Kaindl (eds) *Translation as Intercultural Communication. Selected Papers from the EST Congress — Prague 1995* (pp. 185–94). Amsterdam: John Benjamins.

Newmark, P.P. (1981) *Approaches to Translation.* Oxford: Pergamon Press.

Quirk, R. and Greenbaum, S. (1973) *A University Grammar of English.* London: Longman.

Reiss, K. (1971) *Möglichkeiten und Grenzen der Übersetzungskritik. Kategorien und Kriterien für eine sachgerechte Beurteilung von Übersetzungen.* Munich: Max Hueber.

Reiss, K. (1976) *Texttyp und Übersetzungsmethode: Der operative Text.* Heidelberg: Julius Groos.

Schopp, J. (1996) The typographic competence of the translator — Visual text design and desktop publishing. In *XIV World Congress of the Fédération Internationale des Traducteurs (FIT) February 1996, Melbourne, Australia, Proceedings, Volume 1* (pp.189–95).

Séguinot, C. (1994) Translating and advertising: Going global. *Current Issues in Language and Society* 1/3, 247–65.

Smith, V. and Klein-Braley, C. (1997) Advertising — A five-stage strategy for translation. In M. Snell-Hornby, Z. Jettmarova and K. Kaindl (eds) *Translation as Intercultural Communication. Selected Papers from the EST Congress — Prague 1995* (pp.173–84). Amsterdam: John Benjamins.

Snell-Hornby, M. (1996) *Translation und Text. Ausgewählte Vorträge.* Vienna: Vienna University Press.

Chapter 11

Translating Terms in Text: Holding on to Some Slippery Customers[1]

Margaret Rogers

> *... some words are more context-dependent or bound than others ...*
> (Peter Newmark, 1991: 87)

Words, Terms and Context

The translation of words in text — 'slippery customers' according to Labov (1973: 341) — is the everyday task of the translator. To perform this task, the translator is said to need an understanding of the 'context' in which the words operate. Peter Newmark (1988: 193, cf. also Newmark, 1991) has identified four types of context: the linguistic (for example, collocations); the referential (the topic); the cultural; and the individual (the ideolect of the writer). Implicit in this view is the belief that words cannot be isolated from their context without their meaning becoming more elusive. A functionalist view of translation might add the purpose of the translation commission as a further contextual aspect which shapes the translator's decisions (cf., for example, Hönig, 1997). Yet claims about the importance of context are often relativised where LSP (language for special purposes) translation is concerned: the translation of technical words — or 'terms' — is often said to be context-free (cf., for example, Coseriu, 1975: 28). As Newmark neatly puts it: 'Such words bring their contexts with them' (1988: 194, cf. also Newmark, 1996: 56).

The view that the meaning of terms is context-independent, i.e. that terms are not slippery customers, is also found in the discipline known as terminology science or the general theory of terminology (*die AllgemeineTerminologielehre*, cf. Wüster, 1974) which is concerned with the study of terms and concepts and the relations between them. Felber (1984: 108) has stated, for instance, that a term 'retains the particular meaning [. . .] within any context', by which I understand him to mean that the meaning of a term does not vary within a particular subject field, at least once any polysemy has been identified and eliminated through standardisation. The motivation for this view lies in the onomasiological approach adopted in terminology science to the study of the specialist lexicon and the compilation of specialist lexica — or 'terminologies'.

In contrast to the word-oriented methods of lexicography, where the various linguistic contexts of words are used to infer the range of senses which that word form denotes, in terminology, analysis begins with the 'meanings' — or concepts — of a particular subject field. This meaning-driven approach, attempted in language for general purposes in thesauri such as Roget in English (Kirkpatrick, 1987/Roget, 1852) and Hallig and Wartburg (1952) and Dornseiff (1954) in German, is arguably better motivated for LSPs and their related domains, since a consensual view may be more easily reached on the conceptual organisation of specialised fields than on the world in general. Once a system of concepts is established, terms may be assigned to each concept in order to identify cases of synonymy (two or more terms designate a single concept) and polysemy (one term designates two or more concepts). Where appropriate, standardisation may follow this descriptive phase with the object of establishing a preferred use of terms based on a one-to-one term-concept/concept-term relation within the subject field concerned (*Eineindeutigkeit*, cf. Arntz and Picht, 1995: 117). Accordingly, the meaning of a term is said to be the concept which it designates; that concept, in turn, belongs to a system of concepts which maps out the structure of the subject field. Since this can be viewed as relatively stable at any given time — and indeed must be for standardisation purposes — the meaning of the term is said to be constant, regardless of its context.

Context-dependency and Translation

The implication of a context-independent interpretation of the meaning of terms is that translation consists — for those words — of a simple cross-linguistic substitution exercise. What we might call text-based work in terminology has, however, cast some doubt on this view.

In a well-known study of technical terms in special-language texts, Schmitt (1986: 254) demonstrates that the translation of a term such as *alloy steel* by 'legierter Stahl' (in accordance with authoritative specialised dictionaries such as Ernst) may be correct in some textual contexts but not in others, since the alloy level differs in German and British standards. In cases where the composition of the alloy steel is made explicit, a translation of 'hochlegierter Stahl' would, Schmitt argues, be more appropriate, since the German DIN standard specifies a lower alloy composition for 'legierter Stahl' than is the case for *alloy steel*.

On the one hand, Schmitt's observations provide support for the terminological view that terms and concepts are embedded in a system from which they derive their meaning. On the other hand, his translation-oriented perspective points to cultural differences in such systems, even in technical areas. He describes (1986: 257–8) in some detail the complexities of trying to match the meanings of two terms whose form suggests equivalence, from two different but partially overlapping systems. While dictionaries give 'Kohlenstoffstahl' as the translation of *carbon steel*, Schmitt points out that since the subject field of steels is classified differently in German (for example, *Baustähle* and *Werkzeugstähle* at the top level) and English (*carbon steels* and *alloy steels*), this suggested equivalent turns out to be incorrect, since each term/concept assumes a quite different position in its respective system.

Another perspective on the claimed *Eindeutigkeit* (the assignment of only one concept to a term, i.e. the exclusion of polysemy, cf. Arntz and Picht, 1995: 117) of terms is provided by recent work on the terminology of economics by Gerzymisch-Arbogast (1996). While one might expect terms from the social sciences to be subject to greater variation than technical terms — since they designate concepts which represent immaterial rather then material objects — Gerzymisch-Arbogast's work suggests a more fundamental objection to *Eindeutigkeit*. Her argument goes to the heart of the difference between the use of terms in texts and their representation in dictionaries, giving the lie to the common perception that the translation of terms is a straightforward matter of the substitution of an easily identifiable target language (TL) term for a source language (SL) term with little or no discretion left to the translator. By analysing the use of terms such as *money, money supply* and *money stock*, she clearly shows that translational competence is essential alongside linguistic competence in the translation of terms within special-language texts. Furthermore, the role of context — the place and function of the term in the text — is shown to be a reality of which terminology science needs to take serious account, not only in relation to its various applications including translation but also with regard to its own future development as a discipline. To view language use primarily as a bit of a mess which needs to be fixed through standardisation (I overstate the case) is, Gerzymisch-Arbogast's work implies, not only a simplification of the true situation, but also theoretically insupportable, since terms within text also have their own system. In the 'ideal' case, this would match the system of terms represented in, for instance, specialist dictionaries or term bases, as is implicit in Wüster's model. An example would be the faithful use of a terminological standard in the creation of a text. However, as translators' daily experience tells them, the ideal case is often an elusive shadow.

A Case Study: Concept Systems and Terms in Text

One referential context in which we might, however, expect to find something close to the ideal case is that of a well-established technology within one company for which bilingual documentation is required. It would seem reasonable, for instance, to assume that the terms in a well-established field would have achieved a certain stability, particularly if inter-company variation were not a consideration. Since large companies operate in a global market, it also seems reasonable to assume that the relevant terms in other widely-used languages would also have achieved a certain stability within these languages. Consequently, establishing equivalence at term level seems not to pose any particular problems, particularly if the objects discussed in the texts are material rather than immaterial, and the products described in each language are the same.

Precisely such a context is offered by the automotive handbooks produced by the German company Bosch, which markets its electrical products globally. In what follows, I have chosen to analyse extracts from the German and English versions of the handbook dealing with the braking systems in vehicle combinations (Newmark's referential context), by which I understand articulated vehicles. No illustration is provided.

The texts are functionally informative and therefore not author-focused (expressive), potentially neutralising Newmark's individual context. There is no indication in the texts that the objects described in each language vary in any material respect, thereby indicating that no cultural differences such as varying

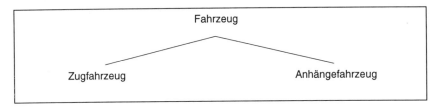

Figure 11.1 A genus-species representation of the three main concepts in German

standards are concerned. Furthermore, since the function of the translated text is the same as that of the source text (ST), and given the close contextual relations of the ST and the target text (TT), it would be reasonable to expect that the translator has simply substituted a set of SL terms (German) by a set of TL terms (English) which designate a common conceptual structure. (The texts in question are given in an appendix.)

The purpose of the following analysis is therefore to examine the claim that context has little, if any, influence on the translation of technical terms where contextual variation seems to be largely neutralised. After establishing a conceptual system for the principal concepts (here representing material objects), the linguistic expression of these concepts in the chosen text extracts will be compared.

It seems that we are dealing with three main concepts. These can be described as the vehicle which tows, the towed vehicle, and the vehicle which is the combination of these two. Figure 11.1 shows one possibility for organising these three concepts into a genus-species hierarchy.

We can interpret this diagram to mean that a *Zugfahrzeug* is a kind of *Fahrzeug* and that an *Anhängefahrzeug* is also a kind of *Fahrzeug*. Each of the two types of *Fahrzeug* are distinguished from each other as co-ordinate concepts by characteristics regarding, for instance, their function. However, if we return to the text, it becomes clear that the terms used to refer to the whole vehicle are *Fahrzeugkombination* and *Zug*, not *Fahrzeug*. Since it is not possible to maintain that an *Anhängefahrzeug* is a kind of *Fahrzeugkombination* or that a *Zugfahrzeug* is a kind of *Zug*, a part-whole representation seems preferable to a genus-species organisation for the concepts in this narrowly-defined domain: an *Anhänge-fahrzeug* is a part of a *Fahrzeugkombination*; a *Zugfahrzeug* is a part of a *Fahrzeugkombination* , as shown in Figure 11.2.

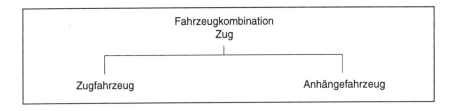

Figure 11.2 A part-whole representation of the three main concepts in German

It turns out, however, that *Fahrzeugkombination* and the lexically less explicit *Zug* cannot be considered synonyms, since they cannot easily be interchanged in the text. The term *Zug* actually only appears in the text as a genitive attribute of *Fahrzeug*, as in *Kombination von Bremsanlagen der Fahrzeuge eines Zuges*. So what is a suitable candidate for the designation of the superordinate concept (i.e. the whole vehicle)? One possibility might be the phrase *Fahrzeuge eines Zuges* rather than just *Zug*. However, we must also take into account the fact that the the plural form *Fahrzeuge* also occurs without the accompanying genitive attribute *des Zuges*. It does so as a generic term when neither the towing vehicle nor the towed vehicle is specifically meant but only one part of the whole vehicle is being referred to, for example *die Bremsanlagen der einzelnen Fahrzeuge*. In this interpretation, the form *Fahrzeuge* is always modified by *einzeln*. In fact, the word form *Fahrzeuge* cannot appear in our chosen text without pre-nominal modification by the adjective *einzeln* and/or post-nominal modification through the genitive attribute *des Zuges*. The actual phrases which occur are: *der Fahrzeuge eines Zuges; der einzelnen Fahrzeuge; der einzelnen Fahrzeuge eines Zuges*. Without the adjective *einzeln*, the collective perspective of the articulated vehicle is emphasised; with the adjective, the respective roles of each of the parts of the articulated vehicle are in the foreground but without their particular function being made explicit.

Figure 11.3 gives a revised picture of the designations which could be assigned to each of the conceptual positions, showing a typical pattern of the hyperonymic (or generic) part of a compound serving as a synonym for the whole compound.

However, this rather clean and neat picture does not adequately represent the rather complex textual situation in which word forms enter into particular combinations, reflecting different views of the same objects (cf. Bowker, 1997; Kageura, 1997). When trying to assign linguistic designations to particular conceptual positions in a structure — the traditional onomasiological approach to the compilation of a terminology — the designations in question are in the abstract form of lexemes not of particular word forms. Hence, in cases such as that described here, problems arise when trying to match language use (as exemplified by word forms in the text) with a systematic representation in which concepts are labelled by lexemes. It is a little like trying to compare two views of reality: the view that one might get from a moving camera and that which might be gleaned from a two-dimensional photograph. It does not matter how many times you change the angle from which you view the photograph, the

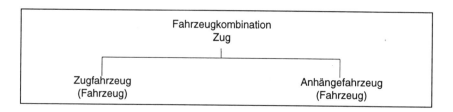

Figure 11.3 A part-whole representation of the three main concepts in German showing possible synonyms

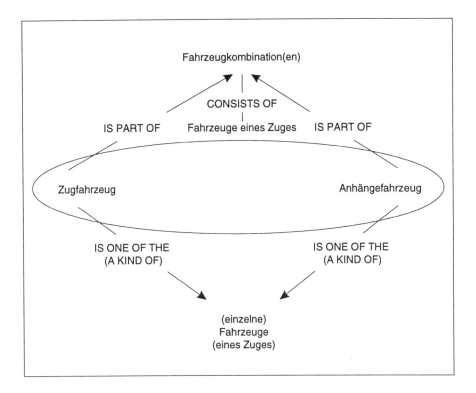

Figure 11.4 A textual view of the terms designating the three main concepts and the relations between these terms

perspective does not change. In a text, the view of an object may be dynamically built up from many different perspectives; the labelling of a system of concepts is, however, static. Figure 11.4 is an attempt to represent the textual view of our chosen subject, showing the interaction of various relations between word forms and expressions.

A Translation Perspective

The terms in an LSP text may be characterised as the main carriers of specialist information (Arntz and Picht, 1995: 35): their accurate translation is therefore crucial to the success of the communication in the TL. But how should this task be understood? A comparison of Figures 11.3 and 11.4 suggests that, even monolingually, the relations between terms on the system level of lexemes and the text level of word forms are rather different. So what implications does this have for definitions of equivalence? And for the translator's task?

Continuing with our descriptive approach, there follows a comparison of the phrases in the German ST and the English TT in which the key terms and expressions appear. The parallel phrases are presented in the order in which they appear in the texts:

(1a)   (Bremsanlagen von) Fahrzeugkombinationen
(1b)   Vehicle Combinations

(2a)   die Bremsanlagen der einzelnen Fahrzeuge
(2b)   the braking systems of the individual vehicles

(3a)   zur Betätigung der Bremsanlage des Anhängefahrzeug (*sic*)
(3b)   for the control of, the braking system of the towed vehicle

(4a)   die Bremsanlagen der einzelnen Fahrzeuge
(4b)   the braking systems of the individual vehicles

(5a)   die Betätigung der Bremsanlage des Anhängefahrzeugs
(5b)   for the control of, the braking system of the towed vehicle

(6a)   Kombination von Bremsanlagen der Fahrzeuge eines Zuges
(6b)   Combination of braking systems for vehicles forming a vehicle combination

(7a)   eine Betätigungseinrichtung im Zugfahrzeug direkt (betätigen)
(7b)   a directly operated control device on the towing vehicle

(8a)   eine Betätigungseinrichtung im Anhängefahrzeug indirekt (betätigen)
(8b)   an indirectly operated control device on the towed vehicle

(9a)   die zur Bremsung der einzelnen Fahrzeuge eines Zuges benötigte Energie
(9b)   the energy used for the braking of each of the vehicles forming the combination

(10a)   gleichzeitige oder geeignet zeitlich verschobene Bremsung der einzelnen Fahrzeuge eines Zuges
(10b)   simultaneous or suitably phased braking of each of the vehicles forming the combination

(11a)   Kombination von Bremsanlagen der Fahrzeuge eines Zuges
(11b)   Combination of braking systems for vehicles forming a vehicle combination

(12a)   eine Betätigungseinrichtung im Zugfahrzeug direkt (betätigen)
(12b)   a directly operated control device on the towing vehicle

(13a)   eine Betätigungseinrichtung im Anhängefahrzeug indirekt (betätigen)
(13b)   an indirectly operated control device on the towed vehicle

(14a)   die zur Bremsung der einzelnen Fahrzeuge eines Zuges benötigte Energie
(14b)   the energy used for the braking of each of the vehicles forming the combination

(15a)   gleichzeitige oder geeignet zeitlich verschobene Bremsung der einzelnen Fahrzeuge eines Zuges
(15b)   simultaneous or suitably phased braking of each of the vehicles forming the combination

(16a)   Kombination von Bremsanlagen der Fahrzeuge eines Zuges
(16b)   Combination of the braking systems of the vehicles forming a combination

These phrases can be regrouped in order to allow patterns of equivalence to emerge. The same numbering is retained so that the connection with their relative position in the text is not lost.

Fahrzeugkombinationen

(1a)   (Bremsanlagen von) Fahrzeugkombinationen
(1b)   Vehicle Combinations

. . . der einzelnen Fahrzeuge
(2a)   die Bremsanlagen der einzelnen Fahrzeuge
(2b)   the braking systems of the individual vehicles

(4a)   die Bremsanlagen der einzelnen Fahrzeuge
(4b)   the braking systems of the individual vehicles

. . . . der Fahrzeuge eines Zuges
(6a)   Kombination von Bremsanlagen der Fahrzeuge eines Zuges
(6b)   Combination of braking systems for vehicles forming a vehicle combination

(11a)   Kombination von Bremsanlagen der Fahrzeuge eines Zuges
(11b)   Combination of braking systems for vehicles forming a vehicle combination

(16a)   Kombination von Bremsanlagen der Fahrzeuge eines Zuges
(16b)   Combination of the braking systems of the vehicles forming a combination

. . . der einzelnen Fahrzeuge eines Zuges
(9a)   die zur Bremsung der einzelnen Fahrzeuge eines Zuges benötigte Energie
(9b)   the energy used for the braking of each of the vehicles forming the combination

(10a)   gleichzeitige oder geeignet zeitlich verschobene Bremsung der einzelnen Fahrzeuge eines Zuges
(10b)   simultaneous or suitably phased braking of each of the vehicles forming the combination

(14a)   die zur Bremsung der einzelnen Fahrzeuge eines Zuges benötigte Energie
(14b)   the energy used for the braking of each of the vehicles forming the combination

(15a)   gleichzeitige oder geeignet zeitlich verschobene Bremsung der einzelnen Fahrzeuge eines Zuges
(15b)   simultaneous or suitably phased braking of each of the vehicles forming the combination

. . . des Anhängefahrzeugs
(3a)   zur Betätigung der Bremsanlage des Anhängefahrzeug (*sic*)
(3b)   for the control of, the braking system of the towed vehicle

(5a)   die Betätigung der Bremsanlage des Anhängefahrzeugs
(5b)   for the control of, the braking system of the towed vehicle

. . . im Anhängefahrzeug
(8a)   eine Betätigungseinrichtung im Anhängefahrzeug indirekt (betätigen)
(8b)   an indirectly operated control device on the towed vehicle

(13a)   eine Betätigungseinrichtung im Anhängefahrzeug indirekt (betätigen)
(13b)   an indirectly operated control device on the towed vehicle

. . . im Zugfahrzeug
(7a)   eine Betätigungseinrichtung im Zugfahrzeug direkt (betätigen)
(7b)   a directly operated control device on the towing vehicle

(12a)   eine Betätigungseinrichtung im Zugfahrzeug direkt (betätigen)
(12b)a directly operated control device on the towing vehicle

The clearest equivalents emerge when each specific part of the vehicle is referred to, i.e. *towed vehicle* and *towing vehicle* for *Anhängefahrzeug* und *Zugfahrzeug* respectively (cf. examples 3, 5, 8, 13, 7 and 12). The superordinate term *Fahrzeugkombination* also seems to be clearly matched by *vehicle combination* in the headings. Hence, our first picture of a bilingual conceptual plan can be represented as in Figure 11.5.

Figure 11.5 suggests that no other linguistic designations may be used to express the concepts concerned. However, if we look at the remaining examples taken from the text extracts, it quickly becomes apparent that such a representation permits only one perspective, namely a view of each functionally-specific part of the vehicle combination or of the combination itself as a whole. But the text extracts clearly show that it is possible to mention the parts of the combination without referring to them specifically. As we have seen, this is achieved in the German ST by using the generic term *Fahrzeug* to designate the subordinate concepts, and in the English TT by the generic *vehicle*. In fact, there

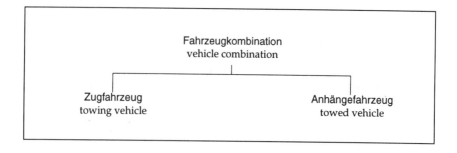

Figure 11.5 A bilingual conceptual plan of the chosen domain

actually seem to be two conceptual organisations manifest in the texts: an ontological part-whole system (cf. Figure 11.2) and a logical genus-species system (cf. Figure 11.1). This is reflected at the textual level where different expressions are used to represent each case in both the German and the English texts: on the one hand, to refer to the specific parts of the whole vehicle according to its function (*Zugfahrzeug; Anhängefahrzeug* and *towing vehicle; towed vehicle*); on the other hand, to refer to the same parts but non-specifically using a range of expressions. A certain regularity can be noted in the translations of these expressions:[2]

(17a)   . . . der einzelnen Fahrzeuge
(17b)   . . . of the individual vehicles

(18a)   . . . der Fahrzeuge eines Zuges
(18b)   . . . (for) vehicles forming a vehicle combination

(19a)   . . . der einzelnen Fahrzeuge eines Zuges
(19b). . . of each of the vehicles forming the combination

If we are compiling a terminology which is to be useful for translation purposes, such correspondences are clearly of some interest. Turning our attention to the term *Zug,* which was originally proposed as a potential synonym for *Fahrzeugkombination,* we can see that it has been translated in two ways, namely, *vehicle combination* and *combination.* However, as we have seen, in the present ST, *Zug* only appears as a post-nominal attribute of the generic term *Fahrzeug* and not independently as does its apparent synonym *Fahrzeugkombination.* The German ST expression also varies according to whether *Fahrzeug* is modified pre-nominally (*der einzelnen Fahrzeuge*) or not (*der Fahrzeuge*), reflected in the English translation as 'individual vehicles' or 'vehicles' respectively. What is the reason for these variations and what implications does it have for establishing equivalence relations?

If we extend our consideration of terms beyond their linguistic, or phraseological, context to the textual level, we begin to see a relation between the expressions used and their positions relative to each other within the text, or more precisely, their positions relative to each other within a section. The examples below show the progression of phrases within the section *Durchgehende Bremsanlage*:

(6a)   Kombination von Bremsanlagen *der Fahrzeuge eines Zuges*

(9a)   die zur Bremsung *der einzelnen Fahrzeuge eines Zuges* benötigte Energie

(10a)   gleichzeitige oder geeignet zeitlich verschobene Bremsung *der einzelnen Fahrzeuge eines Zuges*

The English versions in the same section (*Continuous braking system*) show the following progression:

(6b)   Combination of braking systems for *vehicles forming a vehicle combination*

(9b)   the energy used for the braking *of each of the vehicles forming the combination*

(10b)   simultaneous or suitably phased braking *of each of the vehicles forming the combination*

A number of comments can be made concerning the English translations. Firstly, the change from *vehicle combination* to *combination* seems to be motivated not only by the tendency of compounds to be clipped on subsequent mentions in a text for the sake of economy, but also by the occurrence of the polyseme *combination* initially, referring to the combination of the braking systems, not to the overall vehicle. The use of the compound *vehicle combination* therefore serves to disambiguate the polysemous *combination*. Secondly, we can note a concomitant change in the use of the article as the compound is clipped. So, while an indefinite article is used in (6b) with the full compound (*vehicles forming* a *vehicle combination*), in examples (9b) and (10b) *combination* occurs with a definite article (*each of the vehicles forming* the *combination*). This can be contrasted with the original German in which the unmodified *Zug* always occurs in an indefinite phrase (*der Fahrzeuge eines Zuges; der einzelnen Fahrzeuge eines Zuges*). The indefinite-definite shift in the English is consistent with a move from new to given information, a move which is explicitly indicated by the clipping of the compound. Thirdly, the focus of attention shifts, in both the German and the English, from the vehicle functioning as a whole (*der Fahrzeuge eines Zuges; vehicles forming a vehicle combination*) to the vehicle functioning as two parts (*der einzelnen Fahrzeuge eines Zuges ; each of the vehicles forming the combination*). What changes here is not the objects themselves in the real world, but the way in which they are presented by the author of the ST and consequently by the translator of the TT. It is not straightforward to view such shifts within a framework which presupposes a stable relation not only between terms cross-linguistically but also between terms and the concepts which they designate.

Conclusion

I have tried to show that the interlinguistic view of technical terms as static pairs which can be slotted in and out of texts in each language can be a misleading one. Yet one of the objectives of terminology work is to establish precisely such pairs in order to ensure consistency and hence clarity of communication. While the examples discussed here show that this is possible in some cases, for example *Anhängefahrzeug — towed vehicle* and *Zugfahrzeug — towing vehicle*, other cases present more difficulties, for example *Fahrzeug* and *Zug*. A number of reasons suggest themselves which are often non-discrete and include relations with other terms intralingually, for example *combination — (vehicle)combination*, the ordering of terms within a text, for example *vehicle combination — combination*, and the marking of given new relations, for example *vehicles forming a vehicle combination* and *each of the vehicles forming the combination*. It is precisely such relations and shifts which pose problems for the kind of conceptual representation which is usual in terminology science, but which can be expressed in texts, reflecting the many perspectives of the text producer/recipient with which the translator must deal.

Appendix

Begriffe, die sich auf Bremsanlagen von Fahrzeugkombinationen beziehen:

Definitions Relating to Vehicle Combinations

Einleitungs-Bremsanlage
Anordnung, bei der die Bremsanlagen der einzelnen Fahrzeuge so miteindander verbunden sind, daß eine einzige Leitung abwechselnd zur Energieversorgung oder zur Betätigung der Bremsanlage des Anhängerfahrzeug benutzt wird.

Single-line braking system
Assembly in which the braking systems of the individual vehicles act in such a way that a single line is used both for the energy supply to, and for the control of, the braking system of the towed vehicle.

Zwei- oder Mehrleitungsbremsanlagen
Anordnung, bei der die Bremsanlagen der einzelnen Fahrzeuge so miteinander verbunden sind, daß die Energieversorgung und die Betätigung der Bremsanlage des Anhängerfahrzeugs getrennt über mehrere Leitungen gleichzeitig erfolgt.

Two- or multi-line braking systems
Assembly in which the braking systems of the individual vehicles act in such a way that several lines are used separately and simultaneously for the energy supply to, and for the control of, the braking system of the towed vehicle.

Durchgehende Bremsanlage
Kombination von Bremsanlagen der Fahrzeuge eines Zuges mit folgenden Eigenschaften:
— Der Fahrzeugführer kann vom Führersitz aus mit einem einzigen Vorgang eine Betätigungseinrichtung im Zugfahrzeug direkt und eine Betätigungseinrichtung im Anhängerfahrzeug indirekt abgestuft betätigen;
— die zur Bremsung der einzelnen Fahrzeuge eines Zuges benötigte Energie wird durch die gleiche Energiequelle (die die Muskelkraft des Fahrzeugführers sein kann) geliefert;
— gleichzeitige oder geeignet zeitlich verschobene Bremsung der einzelnen Fahrzeuge eines Zuges.

Continuous braking system
Combination of braking systems for vehicles forming a vehicle combination offering the following characteristics:
— the driver, from his driving seat, can operate gradually by a single operation a directly operated control device on the towing vehicle and an indirectly operated control device on the towed vehicle;
— the energy used for the braking of each of the vehicles forming the combination is supplied by the same energy source (which can be the effort of the driver);
— simultaneous or suitably phased braking of each of the vehicles forming the combination.

Teilweise durchgehende Bremsanlage
Kombination von Bremsanlagen der Fahrzeuge eines Zuges mit folgenden Eigenschaften:
— Der Fahrzeugführer kann vom Führersitz aus mit einem einzigen Vorgang eine Betätigungseinrichtung im Zugfahrzeug direkt und eine Betätigungseinrichtung im Anhängerfahrzeug indirekt abstufbar betätigen;
— die zur Bremsung der einzelnen Fahrzeuge eines Zuges benötigte Energie wird von meistens zwei Energiequellen geliefert (die eine davon kann die Muskelkraft des Fahrzeugführers sein);
— gleichzeitige oder geeignet zeitlich verschobene Bremsung der einzelnen Fahrzeuge eines Zuges.

Semi-continuous braking system
Combination of braking systems for vehicles forming a vehicle combination offering the following characteristics:
— the driver, from his driving seat, can operate gradually by a single operation a directly operated control device on the towing vehicle and an indirectly operated control device on the towed vehicle;
— the energy used for the braking of each of the vehicles forming the combination is supplied by at least two different energy sources (one of which can be the muscular effort of the driver);
— simultaneous or suitably phased braking of each of the vehicles forming the combination.

Nicht durchgehende Bremsanlage
Kombination von Bremsanlagen der Fahrzeuge eines Zuges, die weder durchgehend noch teilweise durchgehend sind.

Non-continuous braking system
Combination of the braking systems of the vehicles forming a combination which is neither continuous nor semi-continuous.

Source:
Bosch, 1984: Kraftfahrzeugtechnisches Taschenbuch, *19. Auflage, 502–3.*

Source:
Bosch, 1986: Automotive Handbook, *2nd edition, 504–5.*

Notes

1. I have chosen this topic because it was the subject of a talk which I gave for the Translating Division of the Institute of Linguists in March 1995 at which Peter Newmark was present. I would like to thank Dr John Mitchell for inviting me on that occasion. I am also very grateful to Dr Ingrid Meyer of the School of Translation and Interpretation, University of Ottawa and Dr Lynne Bowker of the School of Applied Language and Intercultural Studies, Dublin City University, for their helpful and constructive comments on an earlier version of this chapter.
2. Example 17 is the expression used in examples 2 and 4; example 18 is taken from examples 6, 11 and 16; example 19 has been extracted from examples 9, 10, 14 and 15.

References

Arntz, R. and Picht, H. (1995) *Einführung in die Terminologiearbeit*. Hildesheim: Olms. 3te Auflage.

Bowker, L. (1997) Multidimensional classification of concepts and terms. In Wright and Budin (pp. 133–43).

Coseriu, E. (1975) *Die Geschichte der Sprachphilosophie von der Antike bis zur Gegenwart*. Bd.1. Tübingen: Gunter Narr. 2te Ausgabe.

Dornseiff, F. (1954) *Der deutsche Wortschatz nach Sachgruppen*. Berlin. (1st edition 1934.)

Ernst, R. (1980) *Wörterbuch der industriellen Technik*. Wiesbaden: Brandstetter Verlag. 4te Auflage.

Felber, H. (1984) *Terminology Manual*. Paris: General Information Programme & UNISIST, UNESCO, Infoterm.

Gerzymisch-Arbogast, H. (1996) *Termini im Kontext. Verfahren zur Erschließung und Übersetzung der textspezifischen Bedeutung von fachlichen Ausdrücken*. Forum für Fachsprachenforschung. Band 31. Tübingen: Gunter Narr Verlag.

Hallig, R. and Wartburg, W. von (1952) *Begriffssystem als Grundlage für die Lexikographie. Versuch eines Ordnungsschemas*. Berlin: Akademie-Verlag.

Hönig, H.G. (1997) Positions, power and practice: Functionalist approaches and translation quality assessment. *Current Issues in Language and Society*, 4 (1), 6–34.

Kageura, K. (1997) Multifaceted/multidimensional concept systems. In Wright and Budin (pp.119–32).

Kirkpatrick, E. (1987) *Roget's Thesaurus*. London: Longman. New Edition. (Roget's 1st edition 1852.)

Labov, W. (1973) The boundaries of words and their meanings. In C-J. Bailey & R. Shuy (eds) *New Ways of Analyzing English* (pp. 340–73). Georgetown University School of Language and Linguistics.

Newmark, P.P. (1988) *A Textbook of Translation*. Hemel Hempstead: Prentice Hall International.

Newmark, P.P. (1991) Word and text: Words and their degree of context in translation. In P.P. Newmark *About Translation* (pp. 87–100). Clevedon: Multilingual Matters.

Newmark, P.P. (1996) Looking at English words in translation. In G.M. Anderman & M.A. Rogers (eds) *Words, Words, Words* (pp. 56–62). Clevedon: Multilingual Matters.

Schmitt, P. A. (1986) Die 'Eindeutigkeit' von Fachtexten: Bemerkungen zu einer Fiktion. In M. Snell-Hornby (ed) *Übersetzungswissenschaft — eine Neuorientierung* (pp. 252–82). Tübingen: Francke.

Wright, S.E. and Budin, G. (eds) (1997) *Handbook of Terminology Management*. Amsterdam/Philadelphia: John Benjamins.

Wüster, E. (1974) Die allgemeine Terminologielehre — Ein Grenzgebiet zwischen Sprachwissenschaft, Logik, Ontologie, Informatik und den Sachwissenschaften. *Linguistics* 119, 61–106.

Part 3 Text

Chapter 12

Words and Texts — Which Are Translated? A study in Dialectics

Albrecht Neubert

> *On the basis of these criteria the theorist decides whether to*
> *translate 'communicatively' or 'semantically'*
>
> (Peter Newmark, 1981: 22)

Introduction

Doing translations, literary or technical, is inextricably bound up with words, words of the source language (SL) as well as words of the target language (TL), words translators know well, sometimes too well, or words they do not know and have to look up and often enough they cannot find, at least not in time to meet a deadline. Of course, grammar and style are intriguing too but their niceties invariably end up in words. It is through words that grammatical framing and stylistic patterning challenge the translator. Words and sequences of words are like the eye of the needle through which translators have to thread their message, literally or sense-wise. It looks as if the dimension of the word level cannot be overestimated. Words appear to be the most tangible element in the translation process. In the public mind translation is about words. And translation students too tend to be discouraged if a text abounds in many 'difficult words'.

Words and their 'Matter': Context in the Background

This almost trivial argument about words is borne out by the translators' tools. Over the ages dictionaries have not only been widely used but are regarded as the most important helpers available for translators. There are no special grammars or style manuals for translators that can compete with the innumerable dictionaries of the most diverse kind. The so-called contrastive grammars which appeared in recent years (cf., for example, Lohnes and Hopkins, 1982) or *stylistiques comparées* (cf., in particular, Vinay and Darbelnet, 1972), though highly illuminating as reference works for the translation student, have never had a serious impact on the practising translator. They have been only indirectly associated with the translator's task but are rarely consulted in a concrete translation assignment.

Thus it appears as if the right or adequate choice of words determines the success of a translation. Addressing the translator, let us rephrase Polonius's famous question to Hamlet 'What do you read, my lord ?' by 'What do you translate?'. Like Hamlet, translators might answer 'Words, words, words'. But this in only half the truth. What is often forgotten about this famous quotation is that Polonius does not give up, insisting ' I mean, the matter that you read, my lord'. We should then keep asking translators, analogously, about 'the matter of the words' which they translate'. This puts them seriously in a bind. What is their 'matter'? What is the 'matter' behind the words, what do they stand for ? How can the matter of the words in the SL be placed behind the matter of the TL words so that words can really get across?

Let us try to approach this most crucial of the translators' plights by an aside. It concerns a telling remark made by the reviewer of an English translation of Miroslav Holub's collection of 'anti-romantic' poems *Supposed to fly*. In the *Times Literary Supplement* John Redmond of St Hugh's College Oxford makes the interesting point that:

> One of the reasons why Holub's 'non-sounds' translate so well is that, like Wilde, he makes extensive use of aphorism . . . and other rhetorical features that are *closer to the deep structures of thought*: paradox; inversion; omission. Consequently, one is most struck *not by the surface patterns of sound — but by the ideas moving behind the* patterns [emphasis added].[1]

Evidently, words are unique vehicles of meaning. Often they leave indelible marks that resist easy rendering into the words of another language. Sometimes, however, they serve just as vessels of thought that can shed their meaning neatly into new containers which the translator has located in the TL. Of the latter kind are obviously the words which were made out as 'easily translatable' in Holub's poetry. This is quite remarkable because in poems words, as 'surface patterns of sounds', can rarely be separated from their conventional meanings but form a symbiosis that is uniquely language-specific and hence impossible to translate into another language where identical form-and-meaning wholes rarely exist. In Holub's case, however, meanings lie deeper than on the lexical surface of a particular language and can be actually ascertained 'behind the sounds'. If we can believe the reviewer, the Czech original translates, for example, into a sentence like 'Noise is the school of silence and death is the basic practice text of what we call life' (Redmond, 1997), which sheds its total meaning into English, divested of the 'surface sound' of the Czech source.

Other examples are legion, if we think of the extensive literature of aphorisms in translation, which can be traced from antiquity down to more recent times. Take the translation of the *reflections* or *maximes* of French moralists such as La Rochefoucauld, Vauvenargues, Montesquieu, Chamfort, or, in particular, of the *Pensées* of Pascal. Their high degree of translatability exhibited time and again with regard to many TLs is a case in point. It is evidently the pervasive clarity and, hence, the often clear-cut meaning profile of aphoristic diction that facilitates translation and catches on in the TL version. Translators can pick up the thread of thought, so to say, directly from individual words, that is, from those words that carry the key meanings. The reason could be that the purported general validity of the sentences renounces any idiosyncrasy that might hide in the words of a particular language. As a result, the meanings of words that figure prominently in such 'general moral verdicts' follow closely their prototypical dictionary denotations.

Another feature of aphorisms is their generality. Their lack of individuality is paralleled by the *minimal contextuality* which is a characteristic feature of short and self-sufficient texts. It affects the words of these apodictic propositions, lending them generic validity.

For instance, La Rochefoucault's dicta 'Nos vertus ne sont le plus souvent que des vices déguisés' or 'L'amour-propre est le mobile de toutes nos actions', translate directly into English: 'Our virtues are often nothing but vices in disguise', and into German: 'Unsere Tugenden sind oft nichts anderes als verkappte Laster'; or 'Self-interest drives all our actions', and 'Eigenliebe treibt all unser Tun'. Or a more modern aphorism from Valéry's *Mauvaises pensées et autres* like 'Ce qui ne resemble pas à rien n'existe pas' could be translated as 'He who doesn't resemble anyone does not exist' or 'Wer niemand ähnlich ist, den (oder die) gibt es nicht'.

The overall wording of the individual renderings (by different translators) might, of course, vary. What matters in these translations is, however, that the individual words of the original do not normally pose any serious obstacle for the translator. Another question is the 'arrangement of the words' such as style or 'dynamic sentence perspective'. Thus Valéry's dictum might also be rendered: 'Nobody exists who does not resemble someone else' ('Es gibt niemanden, der (oder die) keinem (oder keinem) anderen ähnlich ist', or 'Es gibt keinen Menschen, der nicht einem anderen ähnlich ist') where the theme/rheme structure is reversed. Similarly, the above examples might easily be rendered differently, since not a single translation is entirely predictable. For example, La Rochefoucault would also translate as 'Our virtues are but disguised vices' and 'Self-interest is behind all our actions' or 'motivates whatever we do'. The same holds true for variants in German. In fact, the French moralists have been translated many times, with words fitting the spirit of the period and, of course, also the tastes of individual translators. But the key words have not been significantly altered by consecutive translators to the present day.

The vocabularies of French, English, German, and other languages belonging to the so-called 'Standard Average European (SAE) language-culture complex' (Whorf, 1954: 248), share many semantic features due to parallel developments in the cultural history of the 'Christian western world'. Aphorisms appear to represent common 'universal truths' about experiences that are ingrained in people's minds and represent 'habitual thoughts'. And it is certainly the case that abstract words often mirror highly similar concepts across cultures of an overarching cultural whole, although they seem to differ slightly from language to language. It is against this background that words translate 'more easily'. In a way, the translation of aphorisms and similar kinds of (often relatively brief) texts could be said to follow bilingual dictionary entries quite closely.

Of course, this is not to be taken literally. Good dictionaries, provided that they reflect the usage at the time when the original was composed, define the meanings of those key words and relate them to their TL counterparts. Translators can safely assume that the decisive words in these aphoristic texts are almost entirely 'dictionary-derived'. Their meanings are part of what Agar

(1996) and, following him, House (1997) aptly call the *linguaculture* of French, English, and German. And it is precisely in this (restricted) sense that *words are translated*: or, as Peter Newmark would put it, it is a case of *semantic* opposed to *communicative* translation (1981: 22). He has proposed 'only two methods of translation that are appropriate to any text: (a) *communicative* translation, where the translator attempts to produce the same effect on the TL (target language) readers as was produced by the original on the SL (source language) readers, and (b) *semantic* translation, where the translator attempts, within the bare syntactic and semantic constrains of the TL, to reproduce the precise contextual meaning of the author' (Newmark, 1981: 35).

Ironically, what Newmark calls 'precise contextual meaning' is in our examples not primarily that of 'the author' but of the contemporary speech community at the time of writing. This is what we understand by 'dictionary-derived' . The text to be translated seems to be composed of units that allow direct translation into the target text. The *units of translation* (Neubert, 1968: 32) follow in the wake of bilingual dictionary entries, by all means not exclusively those equivalents actually recorded in a bilingual dictionary.[2] But the translator can and in fact often has to search for other options not printed in a particular dictionary at hand. His/her search, however, and this is the point at issue, is essentially determined by the lexical SL item and not primarily or entirely by the textual context. It is rather a case of a lexical TL variant that is the outcome of the translator's *Sprachgefühl* triggered off by the meaning of the TL word, i.e. the specific meaning variant listed among others in the TL lexicon.

Words and their 'Matter': Context in the Foreground

Unfortunately, I think, such an essentially 'lexically-conditioned' but by no means easy translation procedure can hardly be extended to encompass the majority of translation assignments. With many other source texts, both literary and non-literary or pragmatic, the bilingual dictionary does not hold up. Not that dictionaries would not be useful. Their design, which breaks up the vocabulary of a language or *linguaculture* into manageable chunks of meaning or meaning complexes, is modelled on the semantic system of a single language or a language pair. Lexicographers give the appearance of the lexicon of a language as a closed system. Words are defined within the frame of reference of their relationship to other words, again fully explicated within the semantic system of a particular language. The result is *paradigmatic*: words exhibit their semantic potential exclusively by virtue of their systemic 'place value' in the lexical system of the SL, correspondingly, in the TL system, as, for example, the French words of the above maxims, such as *vertu* or *l'amour-propre*, whose meanings as well as those of their English and German translation equivalents are fully recoverable from the semantic systems of the respective languages. They share their 'place values', which result from the dictionary meanings shared by the members of the respective speech communities.

An analogous situation prevails in scientific and technical discourse where words adhere to their established meanings, allotted to them not by the semantic system of the common language but through conventions of the community of experts. They refer reliably to a closed semantic system shared exclusively by the initiated. The translation of scientific texts profits considerably from the relative immutability of the experts' meaning code, which extends beyond linguistic barriers. The translation of words (within larger texts) is possible in most cases, although there are, of course, quite a number of areas where lexical realisation of scientific codes varies between 'technical linguacultures',[3] the striking differences between steel specifications and, consequently, their designation in English and German being an often quoted case in point (Schmitt, 1986: 256–9).

The state of affairs and hence the translation problems, however, get out of hand (beyond the reach of the dictionary) when words in a text are no longer fully supported by the lexical system *per se* or by clearly circumscribed terminological subsystems. This becomes the rule as soon as word meanings — in addition to and often in subtle contrast with the general semantic system — are funnelled through specific textual contexts. Meanings, then, turn out to be *syntagmatic*. They develop their semantic profile as constituents of lexico-grammatical sequences that can comprise long passages, even whole texts. Arguably, this may be a deviation from the prototypical systemic meaning. More often it is an expansion or specification of, a shift or a transfer from, the accepted lexical denotation. In addition, it may be a change in connotation.

Putting meanings across, then, becomes an exercise in dialectics. Words mean what the dictionary says they mean but, at the same time, they mean something else. Words carry over their semantic values while simultaneously giving them up or at least transforming their seemingly immutable systemic properties. In exchange, words get immersed in the text. Their meanings receive a textual charge. They function as *textwords* deriving their meanings from the *actual system* of the text of which they form an integral part. The translator's frame of reference has shifted from word meanings to text meanings. And, as a result, text meanings percolate to 'word-in-text' meanings. Therefore, we should no longer speak of *translating words* but of *translated texts*, or rather *words in texts*. The way a word has to be rendered is a function of its role in the text. In a way, words in texts acquire a similar status to words in the lexical or semantic system of a language. Translating them involves translators taking both the lexical and the textual system requirements into account. Though the latter are elements of an *actual system* in contrast to their membership in the *virtual system* of the vocabulary (Beaugrande and Dressler, 1981: 35), their discourse determination is at least as real.

It is particularly in literary translation but actually also, though less intensely, in translations of almost any other kind of text that individual words acquire such an overarching discourse orientation. Rendering words becomes inextricably bound up with rendering texts. Generally speaking, context has to be taken into account whenever the re-creation of the meaning of the text as a whole is demanded by the translational situation.

Here, we have to include not only the linguistic context, i.e. the immediate syntagmatic environment as well as the textual totality, but also the use and distribution of words in so-called conventionalised settings. Words, then, cannot be translated by selecting any variant, which in its context represents a lexically and grammatically correct 'equivalent', that is, correct with respect to the TL.

Instead only those lexical items may be chosen which are the outcome of a particular *textual style* that has become conventionalised in the speech community of the TL just as this had been the case for the SL speakers. *Words* are then indeed translated but not as individual words: they are translated as *quite rigidly fixed constituents of almost prefabricated patterns,* which are in fact *patterns of the text.*[4]

Furthermore, the situation affecting translation includes the context of culture. Anthony Burgess, who excelled not only through his writing but also through his sensitive remarks on language and languages (cf. Burgess, 1993), neatly expresses this limitation or rather transcendence of words in a translated text: 'Translation is not a matter of words only: it is a matter of making intelligible a whole culture' (Burgess, 1984: 4). Burgess shared this view with several other well-known writers and experienced translators, contributing to a symposium on literary translation organised by the prestigious journal *TRANSLATION,* among them Eco translator William Weaver who put our problem of the translation of words in a nutshell: 'I learned quickly that, in literary translation, dictionaries are of little help. As my Italian improved, I realised that to understand a word, you have to live it.' (Weaver, 1984: 17.) And Weaver is quite explicit about what he means by 'living it', namely, the awareness of the word meanings in living discourse, in the context of daily conversation and reading. In his paper aptly titled 'The Start', referring to the start of his career as a professional translator, he vividly recalls that he could not really begin to translate after he had become acutely aware of the insufficiency of the bilingual dictionary. For translation equivalents to arise in his translator's mind, he had to give up individual word equations to discover the impact of connected words in his Italian SL culture:

> I became an alert, greedy eavesdropper. From the ironic snarl in a bus conductor's voice, I finally grasped the meaning of *magari* (try looking up that many faceted word in a dictionary and see the lexicographer flounder). Listening to the simplest words, I learned how an inflection can change their meaning. Spoken in a certain way, *si* can actually mean *no.* [Weaver, 1984: 17–18].

Time and again translators rediscover the 'rootedness' of words and their meanings in the variable contexts of life. It was J.R. Firth, incidentally, who a couple of years before the academic study of translation entered into its first, linguistic stage (Catford, 1965) set this *contextual* tone. In a paper read to an audience at Birkbeck College in the University of London, June 1956, he applied his contextual theory of meaning to translation by seminal formulations and illuminating examples (Firth, 1968). In contrast to a rationalist conceptualisation of semantics ('to refer structure and systems of language to structure and systems of thought'), which unfortunately was to dominate linguistic thought and, to a large extent, also scholarly thinking about translation for decades, he embraced 'the alternative of regarding language as embedded in the matrix of living experience and the human body as the primary field of human expression and as continuous with the situations of life'. It is not the abstract relationship between words and ideas, the seemingly immediate and systematisable form/content nexus, frozen into the dictionary entry, that may be of use to the translator, it is rather 'that the *situational matrix* is the more manageable one and more easily related to problems of translation' (emphasis added). More importantly even, situations can and, in fact, have to be accessed through 'language texts which are characteristic of them' since the two 'are intimately wedded' (Firth, 1968: 90–1).

Thus texts overrule the meaning of words, or rather give them an additional twist. An only too well-known case is the translation of titles. These must never be translated without taking into cognisance the text which they are meant to represent. This well-known rule-of-thumb procedure can still pose serious problems as we found out in a detailed study dealing with the translation of John Updike's short story 'Slippage' (Neubert, 1992a). In order to render this title convincingly into German we had to conduct a highly complex analysis of the whole story. The 'title problem' was compounded because the single word of the title was fashioned by Updike's word mastery into a highly intricate network of lexical interrelationships recurring like a leitmotif throughout the story. Repetitions of the word 'slippage' as well as derivations alternated with synonyms and hyponyms creating a veritable word system (Aphek and Tobin, 1981).

Reading the story from beginning to end we become progressively aware of an overall, or rather, overarching, textual strategy for which the title 'Slippage' acts as a thematic focus. It stands for the many-faceted *slipping* or *sliding away* of the hero's perceptual, academic, social, sexual, and emotional powers to cope with his world, a world he had been proud to control for years. The story relates how Professor Morison lives through his *last* day of teaching and socialising in an American university community. Actually, *slippage* pervades every detail of his physical and mental experience *turning* all his former abilities and strengths *downward*. Starting with *the sluing of his bed [like] a boat in a wave trough*[5] as a result of a *quite slight earthquake* which woke him up in the morning when he was lying beside his young wife, who had *slipped down* toward the foot of the bed. He receives nothing but *compassionate applause* from his students after his *last* class, has *regrets about his failed career as a scholar* (his big plans of publishing a book: (*he had failed to nail it*). He admits that *gone* is his desire for beautiful women: sex had *slid away*; his daughters of his first marriage *drifted off, . . . he was aging, he would read in their eyes*. Even his teeth — on this particular day it was the left lower bicusped, which he could not stop touching — *felt palpably loose to Morison's tongue.*

One sign after another keeps tugging at his exhausted perceptions, *himself now history, a flake of consciousness lost within time's black shale.* Somehow Morison's experience of life becomes *blunted. It was a kind of deafness, a turning down of the sound on a television set.* The climax of these subtle but to Morison acutely perceptible symptoms of decline happens when, at a colleague's dinner party, he is closely followed by a beautiful woman who is shunned by the other guests, because she clearly has psychological problems. Facing her, a woman who would formerly have aroused him, he can not control his *sagging* features. *And she, seeing what must have been a change, a slippage in his own face, tipped back her face in triumph and attached herself to him with a slim, nervous, hard hand.* Back home with his young wife after his terrifying experience, he gets but her telling comment that he did not look more foolish *than old guys on the make ever look.*

What then do dictionaries[6] tell us about how the title of the story might be translated? Of course, we are now prepared to approach the title after we have read and experienced the whole story. Somehow we try to cope with the title in a backward fashion. *Slippage,* actually now an afterthought, gets reinstated as the focal head of the story, fashioned by a master storyteller.

Unfortunately, or as was to be expected, none of the four sememes or systemic meaning variants listed in the most comprehensive English dictionaries nor the one or two mere 'equivalents' in English-German dictionaries will do. As usual, monolingual paraphrases contain the best information for translators. In the case of *slippage* they form the raw material for Updike's word magic. Our quotations, which are just fragments of the many more *textonymic* (Neubert, 1979: 22) occurrences of *slip* and its lexical and semantic cognates, reflect the complexity of practically all the (four) sememes of *slippage.* The text of the story unfolds those meanings or sememes. Perceptive American readers approach the text with this meaning totality in their minds. Individual occurrences in the story can activate various slightly vacillating shades of the word meanings. And the title represents a highly condensed version of all of them together. Actually, it is only when the reader has finished reading the book that s/he will be able to grasp and remember the textuality of the title word. In this sense the meaning of *slippage* is simply the result of the textual situation. In short, it is a creation of the author, just as any *textword,* for that matter, is a product of a language user's *contextual awareness.* Like *slippage* it is based on the socially accepted norms of the user's knowledge of the lexical and semantic system (of English). But in actual fact it is (in)definitely more than that.

Translating the title then is a special case of any textword translation. It is, of course, related to the lexicon but transcends it. Having left the dictionary, monolingual and bilingual, behind, it becomes entirely a matter of the textual framework from which it has to be derived by the translator. Attempting to find a German title for 'Slippage' becomes almost impossible. The translator, rather, reconstructs it in retrospect according to what s/he has come up with in the course of rendering the whole story into German. With this textual overview in mind, for the German text, for that matter, titles such as *Abwärts, Abgleiten,* or *Anzeichen eines Niedergangs,* etc. suggest themselves. The last choice seems to be perhaps most opportune since it expresses, albeit more explicitly than the laconic 'Slippage', the many specific indications that are symptomatic of Professor Morison's pathetic experiences during one day at the end of term, his last term. It epitomises the relentless sequence of subtle but nevertheless relentless signs that all point to a downward trend in his life. Translating the English title word 'Slippage' into the German phrasal title *Anzeichen eines Niedergangs* is indeed a far cry from the dictionary equivalents though it is surely also informed by them as well as prompted by the translator's experience of Updike's storytelling.

Conclusion

Words and text, as we have seen, interact in inducing variable translation strategies. Perhaps it is a moot point to decide which of the two gains the upper hand. After all, the translation is a new text buzzing with words that relate to those of the original not only as individual items but also as pointers to a complex and total textual experience.

Notes

1. 'Between 1970 and 1980, he [Holub] was labelled a "non-person" in his own country and might be said to have been in the position of a moth that no one has seen, which he describes as beating against a window making a "non-sound".' (Redmond, 1997: 23.)
2. Elsewhere I have described the search for appropriate TL words as the 'imaginative' use of the bilingual dictionary. Based on or rather induced by the very few actually listed prototypical TL equivalents the knowledgeable dictionary user is challenged to go for 'better' words that alone will do in the particular case of the lexical equation (cf. Neubert, 1992b: 35).
3. Schmitt (1986) gives highly illuminating examples that describe the non-identity of technical terms across languages. Nevertheless, he leaves no doubt that the fiction of the non-ambiguity of scientific and technical writing can be solved by paraphrases based on recourse to technical knowledge, that is by transcending the word fixation of monolingual experts and dictionary-prone technical translators. Incidentally, this is also a criticism of the technical dictionary, or rather the disingenuous use to which it is often subjected. Unfortunately, it is typical of many technical dictionaries, even good ones, that they tend to favour sheer quantity of terms listed as against quality, i.e. giving syntagmatic examples for difficult and ambiguous terms so that not only the highly specialist expert in one particular field but also the technical translator, who has to be at home in a number of technical domains, can profit without having every meaning variant and their differential usage at their fingertips. And publishing houses try to outdo each other by priding themselves on the number of terms in their products instead of encouraging their authors to go for *meaning in context*, even if this means sacrificing part of the precious dictionary space in favour of discourse meanings.
4. This can also be the case when the text to be translated is very short, consisting of one sentence or even an elliptic sentence fragment functioning as a communicative whole. The wider context is then the non-linguistic situation in which the utterance is made. A trivial but telling case is the translation of notices such as *No Smoking* into *Rauchen verboten* or *Wet paint* into *Vorsicht frisch gestrichen*. This almost formulaic translation, which Newmark would accept as correct examples of *communicative translation* (Newmark, 1981: 54), is, incidentally, quite demanding with regard to the correct choice of individual words, which shows that a textual perspective can be just as nitpicking as a word-for- word translation. Thus a slight variant *angestrichen*, Newmark's rendering which is perfectly good German too, would not qualify because it violates the conventional German pattern. This problem of *user-determined* language use and, hence, translation approach was at the root of what we introduced into the translation studies of the sixties as *pragmatic* translation, with pragmatics denoting in Morris's tradition the semiotic relationship between language sign and language users (Neubert, 1968).
5. All quotations refer to a later collection of Updike's stories (Updike, 1988). The short story 'Slippage' was originally published in the *New Yorker* several years earlier.
6. Monolingual dictionaries usually give, at most, four sememes: '1. an act or instance of slipping. 2. an amount or extent of slipping. 3. failure to maintain an expected level, fulfil a goal, meet a deadline, etc.; loss, decline, or delay, a falling off. 4. (*Machinery*) the amount of work dissipated by slipping of parts, excess play, etc.' (*Random House Dictionary*, 1987: 1799). Bilingual ones do not manage more than a mere two, and mostly just the technical meanings, for that matter, such as *Schlupf*, *Spiel* and *Schlüpfungsverlust*, taking it tacitly for granted that the non-technical meaning of *slippage* ought to be deduced by the non-English users from the individual senses of the verb *to slip*, which actually run into quite more than four, which is indeed a far cry from the four sememes listed as systemic for the native speakers of English.

References

Agar, M. (1996) The slippery surface: Shifting between language and culture. Plenary talk given at the LAUD Symposium on The Cultural Context in Communication Across Languages: Duisburg, March 1996.

Aphek, E. and Tobin, Y. (1981) Problems in the translation of word systems. *Journal of Literary Semantics* 10/1, 32–43.

Beaugrande, R.A. de and Dressler, W. (1981) *Introduction to Text Linguistics*. London and New York: Longman.

Burgess, A. (1984) Is translation possible? *Translation: The Journal of Literary Translation* XII, 3–7.

Burgess, A. (1993) *A Mouthful of AIR: Language and Languages, Especially English*. London: Virago.

Catford, J.C. (1965) *A Linguistic Theory of Translation*. London: Oxford University Press.

Firth, J.R. (1968) Linguistics and translation. In F.R. Palmer (ed.) *Selected Papers of J.R. Firth 1952–59* (pp. 84–95). London and Harlow: Longman.

House, J. (1997) *Translation Quality Assessment: A Model Revisited*. Tübinger Beiträge zur Linguistik. Tübingen: Gunter Narr.

Lohnes, W.F. and Hopkins, E.A. (eds) (1982) *The Contrastive Grammar of English and German*. Ann Arbor, Michigan: Karoma.

Neubert, A. (1968) Pragmatische Aspekte der Übersetzung. In *Grundfragen der Übersetzungswissenschaft*. Beihefte zur Zeitschrift Fremdsprachen II (pp. 21–33). Leipzig: Enzyklopädie Verlag.

Neubert, A. (1979) Words and texts. In G. Graustein and A. Neubert (eds) *Trends in English Text Analysis*. Linguistische Studien, Reihe A (pp. 16–29). Berlin: Zentralinstitut für Sprachwissenschaft, Akademieverlag.

Neubert, A. (1992a) *Die Wörter in der Übersetzung*. Sitzungsberichte der Sächsischen Akademie der Wissenschaften zu Leipzig. Philogisch-historische Klasse, Band 131, Heft 4. Berlin: Akademie Verlag.

Neubert, A. (1992b) Fact and fiction of the bilingual dictionary. In *EURALEX 90: Proceedings IV International Congress* (pp. 28–42). Barcelona: Bibliograf.

Newmark, P. P. (1981) *Approaches to Translation*. Oxford: Pergamon Press.

Redmond, J. (1997) Neighbourly non-sounds. *The Times Literary Supplement*, March, No. 4904, 23

Schmitt, P. (1986) Die 'Eindeutigkeit' von Fachtexten: Bemerkungen zu einer Fiktion. In M. Snell Hornby (ed.) *Übersetzungswissenschaft — eine Neuorientierung* (pp. 252–82). Tübingen: Francke.

The Random House Dictionary of the English Language (1957) New York: Random House. 2nd edition.

Updike, J. (1988) 'Slippage'. In *Trust Me: Short Stories* (pp.179–89). New York: Fawcett Crest.

Vinay, J.P. and Darbelnet, J. (1972) *Stylistique comparée du francais et de l'anglais*. Paris: Didier.

Weaver, W. (1984) The start. *Translation: The Journal on Literary Translation* XII/17: 17–18.

Whorf, B.L. (1954) The relation of habitual thought and behavior to language. In L. Spier, A.I. Hallowell and S.S. Newman (eds) *Language, Culture and Personality: Essays in Memory of Eduard Sapir*. Menasha: Wisconsin University Press. Reprinted in S.I. Hayakawa (ed.) *Language, Meaning and Maturity*. New York: Harper.

Chapter 13

Translating the Introductory Paragraph of Boris Pasternak's Doctor Zhivago: A Case Study in Functional Sentence Perspective

Jan Firbas

> ... *the Prague School ... preserved the link between linguistics and literature*
>
> (Peter Newmark 1991: 163)

Introduction

By looking beneath the level of text in sentences and then in turn to clauses, phrases, words and even morphemes, a link is made between the lower levels of linguistic analysis with the high-level concept of a communicative purpose, thus providing a methodology for evaluating translations from a functional perspective. In *Functional Sentence Perspective in Written and Spoken Communication* (Firbas, 1992a: xii) I have gratefully acknowledged Peter Newmark's interest and should like to do so again in this contribution, which is a case study in FSP and concerns the short opening paragraph of Boris Pasternak's novel *Doctor Zhivago*. I propose to compare the Russian original with its English, Dutch, German and French translations in the light of the theory of FSP.

A detailed discussion of this theory can be found in Firbas (1992a). A sketchy outline of it is offered in Firbas (1995a), where comments on translations of the third paragraph of the opening chapter of *Doctor Zhivago* are also presented. Nevertheless, for the benefit of the readers who may not be acquainted with my approach, I shall recall some basic facts that are of particular relevance to the study in hand.

An Overview of Functional Sentence Perspective

According to different contextual conditions, one and the same syntactic and semantic sentence structure can function in different perspectives without any change in form. Different perspectives fulfil different communicative purposes. The sentence structure 'John has come into the dining room' can function, for instance, in the following perspectives. (i) Two friends, staying in the same hotel, are standing outside the glass door of the dining room. One of the two notices a newcomer entering the dining room. If the point of orientation is *John*, he says

129

perspectiving the structure to *John*, 'JOHN has come into the dining room.' (ii) The two friends are sitting in their hotel room and one asks the other about the whereabouts of John. The one asked looks at his watch and realises that it is noon and *perspectiving* the structure to *into the dining room*, he says, 'John/He has come into the DINING ROOM.' (iii) On another occasion, one of the two friends remarks that John will come into the dining room. The other, who happens to be better informed, corrects the remark. *Perspectiving* the structure to *has*, he says, 'John/He HAS come into the dining room.'

In each case the constituent to which the sentence structure is perspectived conveys the high point of the message. In doing so it completes the development of the communication offered, and proves to be the most dynamic constituent. It carries the highest degree of communicative dynamism (CD). By the degree of CD carried by a linguistic element of any rank I mean the relative extent to which this element contributes towards the further development of the communication. The distribution of degrees of CD determines the functional perspective of a sentence structure. The interpretative arrangements, which order the constituents in accordance with a gradual rise in CD, are the following: (i) *into the dining room — has — come — JOHN*, (ii) *John/He — has — come — into the DINING ROOM*, (iii) *John — come — into the dining room — HAS*. The distribution of degrees of CD is the outcome of an interplay of factors acting as formative forces in FSP. The following factors operate in both written and in spoken language: (a) the contextual factor, (b) the semantic factor and (c) linear modification. In spoken language they are joined in their interplay by (d) intonation. (For a detailed discussion of the interplay of signals yielded by these factors, cf. Firbas, 1992a: *passim*.) A sentence structure serving a particular communicative purpose functions in a definite perspective and acts as a sentence in the true sense of the word.

Enquiries into the distribution of degrees of CD have established that the verb shows a strong tendency to mediate between constituents carrying lower degrees of CD on the one hand, and constituents carrying higher degrees of CD on the other. In regard to the relationship between the subject and the verb, the enquiries have established that the verb participates in perspectiving the sentence either towards the subject, or away from it. These facts have led to the establishment of dynamic semantic functions. By a dynamic semantic function (DSF) I mean the role played by the semantic content of a constituent in the development of the communication when it serves as information participating in the fulfilment of a communicative purpose. Under different contextual conditions, one and the same constituent may perform different DSFs.

If the sentence structure 'John has come into the dining room' is perspectived towards *John*, the adverbial *into the dining room* conveys mere background information and performs the DSF of expressing a Setting (Set-function). On the other hand, if this sentence structure is perspectived away from *John*, the adverbial conveys an essential context-independent piece of information and performs the DSF of expressing a Specification (Sp-function). Different DSFs are also performed by the verb, *has come*, or rather its notional component, *come*, and the subject, *John*. Participating in perspectiving the structure towards the subject, *John*, the verb, *come*, performs the DSF of Presenting a phenomenon (Pr-function), and the subject the DSF of expressing the Phenomenon to be presented (Ph-function). If the verb participates in perspecting the sentence structure away from the subject, it says something about it; it performs the DSF of expressing a Quality (conceived of in a wide sense; Q-function) and the subject performs the DSF of expressing the Bearer of quality (B-function). On the basis of the DSFs, the theme and the non-theme can be delimited in the way presented in the following paragraph. The term 'context-dependent' is used there in reference to a constituent conveying information retrievable from the immediately relevant context (cf. Firbas, 1992a: 22–5, 29–31; 1995b).

The theme (or foundation) is constituted by (i) a context-dependent or context-independent Setting and/or (ii) a context-dependent or context-independent Bearer of quality and/or any other element that is context-dependent. (The last mentioned context-dependent elements are regarded as having had their dynamic semantic status reduced to that of a Setting.) The non-theme (the core which is built up during the development of the communication upon the foundation, i.e. the theme) is constituted by non-thematic constituents performing the Pr, Ph, Q, Sp and FSp-functions. (FSp stands for Further Specification. The non-theme may occasionally contain even more Further Specifications. The theme, on the other hand, may contain more Settings.)

The FSP function of the verb deserves a special note. Its notional component shows a strong tendency to start building up the non-theme and in this way mediate between the rest of the non-theme and the theme. The mediatory function creates a transition in the non-theme; the rest of the non-theme serves as rheme, the rhematic element completing the development of the communication serving as rheme proper. While the verbal notional component shows a strong tendency to perform the transitional function, the categorial exponents of the verb do so invariably. They do so through the temporal and modal exponents, the TMEs, which invariably perform the function of transition proper. (The categorial exponents, which are rich in information, can additionally perform thematic and/or rhematic functions; Firbas, 1992a: 70–3.) A distinction has therefore to be made between transition proper and ordinary transition, which can occasionally be performed by non-verbal elements, for instance, adjectives. The notional component of the verb serves as ordinary transition unless it is context-dependent and in consequence operates in the theme, or unless — in the absence of successful competitors — it itself completes the development of the communication and serves as rheme proper. It rarely performs the thematic function. (In regard to the development of the communication, any constituent induced by the interplay of FSP factors to carry a higher degree of CD than another constituent or other constituents is regarded as its or their successful competitor; Firbas, 1992a: 41–65.)

It is now possible to account for the functional perspective of the third contextual application of 'John has come into the dining room.' With the exception of two context-independent semantic features co-conveyed by the auxiliary *has* and the past participle form of *come* (showing vowel alteration in contrast with *came*), the entire semantic content of the sentence structure conveys context-dependent and hence thematic information. The two semantic features are not conveyed by the notional component, but by the categorial exponents of *has come.* One semantic feature is the temporal indication, and the other the establishment of the link between the information conveyed by the theme and that conveyed by the non-theme. Bearing in mind that the categorial exponents are formally welded together, we can say that the first feature is implemented by the temporal exponent (the TE) and the second predominantly by the exponents of tense and mood (the TMEs). Under the contextual conditions described, the TE serves as rheme proper and the TMEs (including the TE) as transition proper. Apart from being context-dependent, which in itself accounts for their thematicity, the other constituents can be regarded as thematic on the following grounds: the context-dependent subject performs the B-function and the adverbial *into the dining room*, which has been rendered context-dependent, has had its dynamic semantic status reduced to that of a Setting. It follows that the degree of context dependence of the sentence structure is extraordinarily high. The subject *John*, the notional component of *has come*, as well as the adverbial *into the dining room*, form an extensive theme. Under the circumstances, the high point of the message, i.e. the rheme proper, is expressed by the temporal indication conveyed by the TE. At the same time the TMEs function as transition proper, serving as a link between the extensive theme and the temporal indication serving as rheme proper: *John HAS come into the dining room.* (As has been pointed out above, the categorial exponents, which are rich in information, can additionally perform thematic and/or rhematic functions, Firbas, 1992a: 70–3.)

The Source Text

The opening paragraph of *Doctor Zhivago* starts with a description of the funeral of the boy Jurii Zhivago's mother. This is its original Russian version followed by an English gloss:

(1) *Shli,* (2) *i shli* (3) *i peli Vechnuyu pamyat',* (4) *i kogda ostanavlivalis', kazalos', chto ee po zalazhennomu prodolzhayut pet' nogi, loshadi, dunoveniya vetra.*

(1) *Shli* [They-went], (2) *i shli* [they-went] (3) *i* [and]*peli* [they-sang] *Vechnuyu* [Eternal] *pamyat'* [memory], (4) *i* [and] *kogda* [when] *ostanavlivalis'* [they-stopped], *kazalos'* [it-seemed], *chto* [that] *ee* [it; the dirge; object] *po zalazhennomu* [taking-up-the-repetition] *prodolzhayut* [they-continued] *pet'* [to sing] *nogi* [the-feet], *loshadi* [the-horses], *dunoveniya* [the-gusts] *vetra* [of-wind].

The slow continuous march of the funeral procession is indicated by the repetition of *shli* (1 and 2), the preterite *-li* signal (1, 2 and 3), the conjunction of *i* (2, 3 and 4), and the three noun items ending sentence (4). Rhythmic monotony is paradoxically even enhanced by the absence of *i* [and] before the last of the three items. Sentence (4) is of particular relevance. Its adverbial *kogda* [when]-clause acts as a Setting and constitutes its theme. As it is not the verb *kazalos'* [it-seemed], but the subject *chto* [that]-clause, that completes the development of the communication, the former performs the Pr-function of presenting a phenomenon and the latter the Ph-function, i.e. that of expressing the phenomenon. The former serves as transition and the latter as rheme proper.

The *chto* [that]-clause has its own functional perspective. Its theme is expressed by the context-dependent object *ee* [it], the context-dependent *pet'* [to sing] and the context-independent adverbial *po zalazhennomu* [taking-up-the-repetition]. All three act as Settings, the two context-dependent constituents showing reduced dynamic semantic status. Before naming the transitional and rhematic constituents, let me point out the following. The adverbial *po zalazhennomu* [taking-up-the-repetition] clearly suggests the notion of continuation, which is explicitly expressed by the verb *prodolzhayut* [they-continued]. Developing the information further, the verb turns attention to (presents) the phenomena that cause the continuation. These are expressed by the sequence of the three nouns, *nogi* [the-feet], *loshadi* [the-horses], *dunoveniya* [the-gusts] *vetra* [of-wind], which form the subject. The semantic pattern permits the verb *prodolzhayut* [they-continued] to be interpreted as implicitly suggesting appearance/existence on the scene. The verb takes part in depicting a situation in which non-human phenomena, expressed by the subject, *nogi* [the-feet], *loshadi* [the-horses], *dunoveniya* [the-gusts] *vetra* [of-wind], emerge on the scene as 'continuers' of the singing. Seen in the light of these facts, the subject proves to be a successful competitor of the verb. Whereas the verb performs the presentational Pr-function, the subject performs the expressive Ph-function and conveys the high point of the message. The verb *prodolzhhayut* [they-continued] serves as transition and the subject *nogi* [the-feet], *loshadi* [the-horses], *dunoveniya* [the-gusts] *vetra* [of-wind] as rheme proper. Like the context-independent verb *kazalos'* [it-seemed], the context-independent verb *prodolzhayut* [they-continued] precedes its context-independent subject, which occurs in final position. This permits linear modification (Firbas, 1992a: 10; 1996: *passim*) to come in and effectively co-signal the rhematicity of the subject.

As the subject is the rheme of the subordinate *chto* [that]-clause, which in its turn constitutes the rheme of sentence (4), it conveys a piece of information that is the high point of the message offered by this sentence. Under the circumstances, it is, in fact, this information to which the entire short opening paragraph of *Doctor Zhivago* is perspectived. I propose to examine to what extent the Dutch, English, German and French translations have succeeded in following suit. I shall first examine the Dutch translation.

The Dutch Translation

(1) *Zij liepen* (2) *en liepen maar door* (3) *en zongen 'Eeuwige herinnering',* (4) *en steeds als zij ophielden leek het, alsof hun benen, de paarden, de windvlagen op'hun eigen ritme doorgingen met zingen.*

The slow march of the funeral procession is indicated by the repetition of *liepen* (1 and 2), the conjunction *en* (2, 3 and 4), and the three nouns, *hun benen, de paarden, de windvlagen* (4), ending the paragraph. It is worth noticing that continuation, which is naturally implied in repetition, is explicitly mentioned earlier in the translation than in the original. While *maar door*, explicitly expressing continuation, is rhematised and occurs already in (2), *prodolzhayut* [they-continued] appears in the transition of (4). While the original links continuation explicitly with the non-human continuers (in 4), and in this way strengthens the contrast between them and the singers, the human mourners, the translation links it explicitly with the human mourners (in 2). To sum up: explicitly linking the non-human sound producers with continuation, the original presents them as the actual continuers. In doing so, it strengthens the contrast between them and the singers, the human mourners, who have stopped singing and, for the moment, are the 'discontinuers'.

Let me turn to the functional perspective of sentence (4). The impersonal *het* occurring there is not totally devoid of meaning. It refers to the immediately relevant situation (cf. Firbas, 1992a: 24) and acts as a B-element expressing the Bearer of quality. Together with the adverbial Setting, *steeds als zij ophielden*, it constitutes the theme. The verb, *leek*, does not complete the development of the communication. It performs the Q-function of expressing Quality and is transitional. Acting as a successful competitor of the verb, the subordinate *alsof*-clause serves as a Specification and constitutes the rheme. In its turn, it has a functional perspective of its own. It is the counterpart of the *chto* [that]-clause and its rheme proper will convey the information to which sentence (4) is perspectived.

What is the rheme proper of the *alsof*-clause? The *alsof*-clause can be perspectived neither to *doorgingen* nor to *met zingen*. The notional component of *doorgingen* is context-dependent and therefore thematic, and so is *met zingen*. The transition is implemented only through the TMEs of *doorgingen*, which serve as transition proper. It remains to decide whether to perspective the *alsof*-clause towards the subject, *hun benen, de paarden, de windvlagen*, or towards the adverbial *op hun eigen ritme*. It would have to be perspectived to the subject if the adverbial expressed mere background information and hence served as a Setting. The emphasis conveyed by *eigen*, however, turns *op hun eigen ritme* into a Specification, which has something important to say about the non-human continuers and serves as rheme proper. In consequence, the subject, *hun benen, de paarden, de windvlagen*, performs the B-function and is thematic. Being thematic, both the notion of 'the non-human continuers' and that of the 'singers' appear in the thematic layer of the paragraph. (The thematic layer is constituted by all the thematic elements occurring in a paragraph; Firbas, 1992a: 79; 1995a: 59–72.) This not only weakens the contrast discussed above, but results in putting (4) in a perspective different from that implemented by the original.

An additional note may be of interest. As has been indicated, both the original and the translation indicate repetition and continuation by non-lexical means. It is especially the original that powerfully evokes the impression of a rhythmic movement reflecting the regularity of the slow forward motion of the funeral procession. In contrast to the translation, however, it does not use a lexical item (cf. the word *ritme* in the translation) that explicitly refers to the rhythmic march of the procession. It is important to note that while under the circumstances the non-lexical means do not affect the perspective, the explicit mention of the rhythm (*ritme*) happens to do so; it appears in the rheme.

The English Translations

It is now possible to move on to two English translations, an earlier version and its revision:

(1–3) *On they went, singing 'Eternal Memory'*, (4) *and whenever they stopped, the sound of their feet, the horses and the gusts of wind seemed to carry on their singing.*

(1–3) *On they went, singing 'Eternal Memory'*, (4) *and whenever they stopped, their feet, the horses and the gusts of wind seemed to carry on their singing.*

With one exception, the opening paragraph is the same in both versions. The exception is the noun *sound*, which occurs only in the earlier version.

The notion of repetition is hardly indicated by (1–3). As for the notion of continuation, it is implied in the words *On [they] went*, but these words predominantly refer to the slow forward motion of the funeral procession. Continuation is explicitly expressed by *to carry on* of (4) and exclusively linked with the non-human sound producers. *To carry on* is, in fact, opposed to *stopped*: the mourners stop the singing and the non-human continuers take it up. In this way, the translation faithfully follows the original in retaining the contrast between the mourners and the non-human continuers. It must, however, be asked whether, like the original, the translation also rhematises the continuers. The answer is to attempt an interpretation of the functional perspective of (4).

Its adverbial clause *whenever they stopped*, serving as a Setting, and the context-dependent object, *their singing*, are thematic. *Seemed* serves as transition proper. It remains to determine the functions of the context-independent subject, *the sound of their feet, the horses and the gusts of wind*, and the context-independent notional component, *to carry on*, of the verbal constituent (*seemed to carry on*). Does the notional verbal component participate in perspecting sentence (4) towards the subject or away from it? Before answering this question, let me recall the conditions that must be taken into consideration.

Absolutely essential roles are played by the **context independence of the subject** and the **absence of any other successful competitor(s) of the verb**. With provisos or specifications to be adduced below, it applies that **the notional component of the verb** participates in perspecting the sentence (clause) to a context-independent subject and rendering it rhematic (i) if it is **context-dependent**; or (ii) if, **though context-independent**, it expresses **the notion of 'appearance/existence on the scene' explicitly or with sufficiently clear implicitness**. Let me recall the operation of *come*, which, in the second contextual application of 'John has come into the dining room' as discussed above, explicitly expresses appearance on the scene and concurs with a context-independent subject (*John*); and the operation of *kazalos'*, which expresses existence with sufficient implicitness and concurs with the context-independent subject *chto*-clause in sentence (4). In the absence of another successful competitor, each verb participates in perspecting the sentence towards the subject.

The provisos or specifications for deciding whether the notional part of the verb is participating in perspecting the sentence towards the subject or away from it are the following. (i) Insufficiently clear implicitness of appearance/existence on the scene may open the door to **potentiality**, that is the possibility of two interpretations, one tipping the scales towards the subject and viewing it as rhematic, the other tipping the scales away from the subject and viewing it as thematic. (ii) The strong tendency of the verb to perform the transitional function may participate in tipping the scales towards the context-independent subject and rendering it rhematic. (iii) Especially through the position of a context-independent subject after a context-independent notional verbal component, linear modification may participate in removing potentiality by participating in tipping the scales towards the context-independent subject. (iv) From the point of view of the immediately relevant following context, the interpreter's tipping the scales towards the subject is justified if the information conveyed by the subject is kept in the flow of the communication. In that case the information conveyed by the context-independent subject has been presented in order to be spoken about in the immediately relevant following context. (v) The presence of another successful competitor tips the scales away from the subject.

We can now continue the discussion of sentence (4). Standing in contrast to *stopped*, *to carry on* indicates an act performed by the non-human sound producers. In fact, the contrast so indicated is a piece of irretrievable information *sui generis*. Expressing it, *to carry on* becomes a conveyer of additional irretrievable information (cf. Firbas, 1995b: 23). Even if the notion of 'continuation' as suggested by *On [they] went* were taken into account and regarded as retrievable, all the irretrievable information conveyed by *to carry on* would predominate .

The non-predominance of the notion of 'appearance/existence on the scene' in the information conveyed by *to carry on* and the position of *to carry on* after the subject eventually perspective the sentence away from it. According to this interpretation, the subject performs the function of expressing the Bearer of quality — B-function — and is therefore thematic, whereas the verbal notional component *to carry on* says something about the subject — performing the Q-function — and serves as rheme proper. This interpretation cannot certainly be regarded as inapplicable. On what ground then could an interpreter perspective sentence (4) to the subject?

Enquiries into FSP have shown that the notional component of the verb shows a striking tendency to mediate between the theme and the rheme, in other words, to act as transition. This tendency is primarily reflected by the following facts. First, the notional verbal component can complete the development of the communication and convey the high point of the message, in other words, act as rheme proper, only in the absence of successful competitors. Second, it rarely conveys retrievable information and functions in the theme. The strength of this tendency may manifest itself even as follows. In the presence of a preposed context-independent subject and in the absence of any other possible successful competitor, a context-independent notional verbal component may potentially be regarded as receding into the background in spite of the fact that it does not express the notion of 'existence/appearance on the scene' explicitly or with sufficiently clear implicitness. In accordance with this interpretation, it presents something, i.e. performs the Pr-function, and, consequently, the context-independent subject expresses it, duly performing the Ph-function. If this potential interpretation is adopted with regard to sentence (4), its subject, *their feet, the horses and the gusts of wind*, is considered to complete the development of the communication and to perform the function of rheme proper. In any case, there is another signal that could potentially participate in tipping the scales towards the subject. This signal is provided by the contrast between the human singers, referred to by *they*, and the non-human producers of the sounds carrying on the singing, referred to by the subject. The word *sound* used in the non-revised version contributes to the creation of this contrast.

Under all the conditions stipulated, sentence (4) illustrates an interplay of FSP factors (reflected by the interplay of signals they yield) that is not unequivocal and opens the door to potentiality. Seen in the light of the present state of research, neither of the two interpretations offered can be rejected. In any case, potentiality is a linguistic fact. I will briefly take it up in my closing section.

The perspective of the original is unequivocal. The potentiality displayed by the two English versions would be removed if the passive were used and the notion of 'the non-human producers of the sounds carrying on the singing' were expressed by an adverbial of agency placed in final position:

> (1–3) *On they went, singing 'Eternal Memory', (4) and whenever they stopped, their singing seemed to be carried on by the sound of their feet, the horses and the gusts of wind*

> (1–3) *On they went, singing 'Eternal Memory', (4) and whenever they stopped, their singing seemed to be carried on by their feet, the horses and the gusts of wind.*

The German Translations

We can now turn our attention to two German versions. I shall first discuss the earlier of the two:

> (1) *Man ging (2) und ging (3) und sang 'Ewiges Gedenken'. (4) Und wenn die Stimmen verstummten, tönte der Trauergesang fort im Rhythmus der Schritte, im Geklapper der Pferdeschuhe und im Wehen des Windes.*

Interpreting this version, I shall first discuss the perspective of sentence (4). Serving as a Setting, the *wenn*-clause of (4) is thematic. Conveying retrievable information and hence being context-dependent, the subject, *der Trauergesang*, is thematic as well. This causes the verb, *tönte . . . fort*, to participate in perspectiving the sentence away from the subject, which performs the thematic B-function. As *tönen* and *Trauergesang* share the notion of 'tone/sound', it is especially through *fort* that the verb contributes towards the further development of the communication. As this is completed by a successful competitor, the verb performs the Q-function and is transitional. The successful competitor of the verb is the adverbial *im Rhythmus der Schritte, im Geklapper der Pferdeschuhe und im Wehen des Windes*. It serves as a Specification and acts as rheme proper. In this way, the translation faithfully reflects the rheme proper of the original.

The translator's faithfulness to the original can be demonstrated in a number of other ways. The continuation and repetition is indicated by the three *und*s in (2), (3) and (4), respectively, and the three *ng*s in *ging, ging* and *sang* in (1), (2) and (3), respectively. (Note the three *i*'s, and the three *–li*'s — sh*li*, sh*li* and pe*li* — in the original.) The *ng*-series is in fact expanded by the *nk* in *Gedenken* of (4). The rhythmic repetition is also conveyed by the three equally structured noun phrases of (4), *im Rhythmus der Schritte, im Geklapper der Pferdeschuhe und im Wehen des Windes*. Their equal structure and their end position in (4) enhance the effectiveness of the rheme proper they convey. The effect is further intensified by the suggestive alliteration in *Wehen des Windes*. (Note the *dunoveniya* [the-gusts] *vetra* [of-wind] of the original.) Unlike the original, the translation even explicitly refers to what is indicated by the repetitions and the measured flow of phrases. It places the expression *Rhythmus* in the rheme proper of (4); it does so, however, without making it the sole conveyer of rhematic information.

It is worth mentioning that another case of alliteration, *die Stimmen verstummten*, occurs in the *wenn*-clause, which has a perspective of its own. In the absence of a successful competitor the notional component of the verb *verstummten* acts as rheme proper. The alliteration, together with the repetition of the word base *Stimm-/-stumm-*, suggestively indicates the temporary end to which the singing has come. It is not without interest to note that the rhematic information proper is effectively conveyed by the prefix *ver-* and the vowel alteration implemented through the contrast of *i* and *u* (*Stimm-* versus *-stumm-*).

This first German version employs a different syntactic structure than the original, but preserves its perspective. It does so in an unequivocal way, and faithfully renders the author's communicative purpose.

The second German version can be analysed in the following way.

(1) *Sie gingen* (2) *und gingen* (3) *und sangen das 'Ewige Gedenken'*, (4) *und jedesmal, wenn sie innehielten, schienen die Füße, die Pferdeschuhe, die Windstöße den Gesang harmonisch fortzusetzen.*

Like its predecessor, this second German version conveys continuation and repetition with the three *und*s in (2), (3) and (4), respectively, and the three *ng*s in *ging, ging* and *sang* in (1), (2) and (3), respectively. The *ng*-series is expanded by the *nk* in *Gedenken* of (4). Unlike the earlier version, it does not make use of alliteration. Unlike the original, it has two expressions, *jedesmal* and *harmonisch*, which can be regarded as explicit references to the continuation and repetition, and the effect created by them.

As for the functional perspective of (4), the temporal adverbial constituent *jedesmal, wenn sie innehielten*, which serves as a Setting, and the context-dependent object, *den Gesang*, are thematic. The question arises whether the non-thematic subject, *die Füße, die Pferdeschuhe, die Windstöße*, performs the thematic B-function or the rhematic Ph-function; in other words, whether the sentence is perspectived towards or away from the subject. The answer depends on the functions performed by the verbal constituent of *schienen fortzusetzen* and the manner adverb *harmonisch*. The verbal notional component of the former is implemented by *fortzusetzen*. The function of *schienen* is to serve as transition proper. It remains to be determined what the functions of *fortzusetzen* and *harmonisch* are.

The very observation that, in spite of the mourners having stopped singing, the fact that the singing seemed to continue constitutes irretrievable information. It comes as an unexpected piece of news. In any case, *fortzusetzen* conveys predominantly irretrievable information and is therefore to be treated as context-independent. The subject is context-independent as well. The scales, however, are tipped away from it because of the presence of *harmonisch*. Expressing the manner in which the singing continued, it is to be regarded as a successful competitor both of the verb and of the subject. It serves as a Specification and acts as rheme proper. In consequence, the subject performs the B-function and co-constitutes the theme, and *fortzusetzen* performs the Q-function and acts as ordinary transition. Whereas the Russian original and the earlier German translation perspective (4) to the notion of 'the non-human sound producers' as rheme proper, the later German translation perspectives it solely to the notion of the manner in which the mournful singing seemed to continue.

The French Translation

The French version permits of the following analysis.

(1) *Ils allaient*, (2) *ils allaient toujours*, (4) *et lorsque cessait le chant funèbre, on croyait entendre, continuant sur leur lancée, chanter les chevaux et le souffle du vent.*

The French simplifies and shortens the original. The perspectives, however, tally and are signalled unequivocally. Repetition and the continuation are conveyed by the double use of *allaient* and by the adverbial *toujours*. The notional component of *allaient* in (1) serves as rheme proper. In (2) it is context-dependent and therefore thematic, *toujours* serving as rheme proper. The shortness of (1) and (2) quite effectively throws the rhemes proper into relief and enhances the indication of repetition and continuation. As for (4), its *lorsque*-clause serves as a Setting and is therefore thematic. Also thematic is the subject, the pronoun *on*, which is context-dependent on account of the permanent presence of its referent in the immediately relevant situational context (Firbas, 1992a: 24). It follows that the sentence is perspectived away from the subject. The pronoun *on* performs the B-function and the verb *croyait* the Q-function. In the presence of a successful competitor, i.e. the context-independent infinitival semi-clause, *continuant sur leur lancée, chanter les chevaux et le souffle du vent*, the verb does not complete the development of the communication. It operates as transition. Its successful competitor serves as a Specification and acts as rheme proper.

The semi-clause, serving as rheme proper of (4), has its own functional perspective. Its theme is constituted by the context-dependent notional component of the infinitive *chanter* (the notion of 'singing' has already been introduced) and by the participial construction, *continuant sur leur lancée*, expressing a concomitant circumstance and serving as a Setting. Under these circumstances, the categorial verbal exponent *-er* acts as transition proper and the constituent *les chevaux et le souffle du vent* as rheme proper. As the semi-clause serves as rheme proper of (4), its own rheme proper simultaneously expresses the high point of the message conveyed by (4). The French version of (4) shows a different syntactic structure than the original, but unequivocally functions in a perspective that tallies with that of the original.

Conclusion: Potentiality and Translation

By way of closing let me add a word on potentiality. As has been shown, this is created by an equivocal outcome of the interplay of FSP factors, reflected by an equivocal outcome of the interplay of signals yielded by these factors. The following comments concern written texts and their translations.

Generally speaking, the functional perspective of a written sentence conveys and reveals the communicative purpose of the writer. It can therefore be justly required that a translator should interpret the original perspective correctly and find adequate means to express it. This requirement can necessitate the use of grammatical structures different from those employed in the original. It is, however, an open question to what extent inadequate renderings of the original perspectives are tolerable. The truth is that in spite of such inadequate renderings, a translation may read well. Nevertheless, a failure to present the original functional perspective accurately can put important original information in a different light. Essential aspects of the message may become lost on the reader in this way. (For a discussion of such cases, see Firbas, 1992b, 1994, 1995a, 1996.) In any case, a misrepresentation of the original functional perspective occurs when the outcome of the interplay of the signals in the original is unequivocal, but its counterpart in the translation is equivocal, or unequivocal but producing a different perspective.

For the interpretation of FSP, the signals offered by the text are of paramount importance. Present in the text, they are either duly taken account of, or overlooked, by the interpreter. The laws of the interplay of the signals (reflecting the interplay of the factors yielding them) are binding both on the writer and on the reader. If the interplay is unequivocal, then naturally only one interpretation is possible.

Different interpretations caused by potentiality are due to different interpreters assigning the predominating role to different signals operating in the given case of interplay. Even an equivocal interplay, however, provides limits within which an interpretation remains acceptable. The different interpretations permitted by potentiality need not share the same likelihood of being chosen by the interpreter. All this follows from the fact that, like language itself, FSP constitutes a system which is not rigidly closed.

The present discussion has highlighted one point or area in the system where potentiality can be observed. Further enquiries may establish signals (cues) disambiguating some types of potentiality. For instance, investigations into the need for semantic homogeneity within layers, thematic or non-thematic, running through a stretch of text, could establish further cues. More attention could be paid to the immediately relevant following context. The written text allows the enquirer to move forwards and backwards through the thematic and non-thematic layers of the text.

Texts of different authors can be expected to show different frequencies of cases of potentiality. It can be assumed that, in order to enhance exactness and lucidity, a low frequency of potentiality is desirable in professional texts. Cases of potentiality can be expected to be lower in spoken language that in written language, the interplay of signals in the latter combining with those yielded by the FSP factor of intonation. It cannot, however, be claimed that spoken language is devoid of potentiality.

In producing a sentence, a language user invariably links it with a communicative purpose. In so doing, s/he consciously or subconsciously employs signals yielded by the FSP factors. Tension, however, may arise between the functional perspective objectively signalled and the language user's interpretation of it. A language user can even fail to handle the interplay of signals adequately. His or her use of the signals may produce an unequivocal interplay, but not adequately reflect his or her communicative purpose. Awareness of the presence of potentiality in FSP as well as of the tension mentioned assists the linguistic enquirer in accounting for the differences in the interpretations of the functional perspectives of sentences. As the interplay of the FSP signals (reflecting the interplay of FSP factors) conveys the communicative purpose which the sentence is to serve, a study of the operation of the FSP signals (yielded by the FSP factors) may throw revealing light on the way a sentence functions in the act of communication. As I see it, enquiries into FSP have their place both in the theory and in the practice of translation.

References

Firbas, J. (1992a) *Functional Sentence Perspective in Written and Spoken Communication.* Cambridge: Cambridge University Press.

Firbas, J. (1992b) Translation and functional sentence perspective (A case study of John 1: 1–2). In A. van Essen and E.I. Burkart (eds) *Homage to W.R. Lee* (pp. 221–31). Berlin and New York: Foris Publications.

Firbas, J. (1994) Communicative purpose as conveyed by functional sentence perspective (A case study of Psalm 111.10). In K. Carlton, K Davidse and B. Rudzka Ostyn (eds) *Perspectives on English* (pp. 203–12). Leuven and Paris: Peeters.

Firbas, J. (1995a) On the thematic and the rhematic layers of a text. In B. Wårvik, S.-K. Tanskanen and R. Hiltunen (eds) *Organization in Discourse* (pp. 59–72). Turku: University of Turku.

Firbas, J. (1995b) The retrievability span. *Brno Studies in English* 21, 17–45.

Firbas, J. (1996) A case study in linear modification (On translating Apoc. 21.6b). *Brno Studies in English* 22, 23–48.

Newmark, P.P. (1991) *About Translation.* Clevedon: Multilingual Matters.

Translations (in order of presentation)

Pasternak, B. (1961) *Doktor Zhivago.* Milan: Feltrinelli.

Pasternak, B. (1958) *Dokter Zjivago,* transl. by N. Scheepmaker. Utrecht and Antwerpen: Bruna and Zoon.

Pasternak, B. (1958) *Doctor Zhivago,* transl. by M. Hayward and M. Harari. London: Collins.

Pasternak, B. (1981) *Doctor Zhivago,* transl. by M. Hayward and M. Harari, authorised revision. New York: Ballantine Books.

Pasternak, B. (1958) *Doktor Schiwago,* transl. by R. von Walter. Frankfurt am Main: Fischer.

Pasternak, B. (1997) *Doktor Schiwago,* transl. by Th. Reschke. Frankfurt am Main: Fischer.

Pasternak, B. (1958) *Le Docteur Jivago* (translator's name not given). Paris: Gallimard.

Chapter 14

Translating Prismatic Poetry: Odysseus Elytis and The Oxopetra Elegies[1]

David Connolly

> *The more important the words and their order in the original, the more*
> *closely the original should be translated. Since the genre where words and*
> *their order are most important is poetry, you would expect the translation of*
> *poetry to be the closest form of translation. Far from it. This is not possible*
> *since the language of poetry includes so many additional factors — the kind*
> *of poem, poetic form, metre, connotations, rhythm, sound, including rhyme,*
> *alliteration, assonance, onomatopoeia, wordplay — which are missing or not*
> *so important in other types of writing. Nevertheless, poetry translation is*
> *always worth attempting, and I think the best poetry translations are*
> *miracles of closeness . . .*

(Peter Newmark, 1995: 13)

'Prismatic' versus 'Plane' Poetry

In his essay entitled 'Romanós O Melodós' (Elytis, 1992: 33–56), Elytis distinguishes and contrasts two types of poetry which he terms 'prismatic' (πρισματική) and 'plane' (επίπεδη). The terms are novel as is the classification of Greek poetry that is put forward.[2] I am not concerned here with the question of the objective validity of this distinction, but with its importance for understanding Elytis's poetics and its consequences for the aspiring translator of Elytis's poetry.

The features of these two types of poetry may be summarised as follows. In prismatic poetry, words are never on the same plane but *undulate*. The poetic text is organised around certain 'nuclei' (πυρήνες), which stand out like peaks within the poem and which, in retrospect, can be seen to hold the poem together. These 'nuclei' are not necessarily images, but are rather phrasal units with a self-generating radiance, in which the combination of word sound and form (i.e. the word's phonic and graphic effects[3]) coincides with the semantic content to such a degree that it is impossible to decide whether the poetic effect comes from *what* the poet says or the *way* it is said. The repetition of this feature gives a prismatic form to the poetic expression. Poems containing this feature affect the reader not only as a whole, but also in their parts, precisely because of these

142

peaks, these concentrated and laconic crystallisations of what Elytis calls 'the poetic spirit'. They are utterances in which the cast of the language and the images produced are fused and in which the formulation of a truth gives rise to another perception of the world seen through the imagination. The test of this type of poetry is to imagine that 90 per cent of the poetic text has been lost and to examine whether the fragments that remain still function as poetry as is the case, for example, with Sappho's poetry. Prismatic poetry, according to Elytis, is that feature which characterises the true Greek poetic tradition, and is a feature of Homer, Pindar, the ancient lyric poets, Romanós, Kálvos and, by inference, Elytis himself.

Plane poetry, on the other hand, is characterised by a flat, linear form of expression. It is narrative in style and has a poetic value only when taken as a whole. If such poetry is fragmented, all that remains is plain statements. He asserts that such poetry can be translated almost as easily as prose in contrast to the insurmountable translation problems in prismatic poetry, which is in keeping with many other statements by Elytis as to the virtual untranslatability of other poets in this latter tradition, such as Solomós (cf. Elytis, 1974: 29; 1975: 638), and of his own poetry in particular.[4] Without explicitly saying so, Elytis makes it clear that he throws in his lot with prismatic poetry, his description of which corresponds entirely to the features of his own poetry. As one critic (Dimou, 1986: 420) remarks: 'In this contrast [between prismatic and plane poetry], we find the clearest expression of his own poetics.'

Approaches to Translating Prismatic Poetry

The interest for the translator in this classification is twofold: firstly, it raises serious questions as to the translatability of prismatic — and of Elytis's — poetry and, secondly, it provides a clear statement of the peculiar features of this type of poetry, features which the aspiring translator of Elytis must somehow reproduce in the target language (TL). My work here arose from the need to establish an approach to the translation problems I encountered in my own translation of Elytis's most recent collection, *The Oxopetra Elegies* (1991), and all the examples cited are taken from this same collection. My aim is not to be in any way prescriptive; rather, I will discuss some of the factors involved in the process of translating a particular type of poetry, always with the hope of achieving a better translation product.[5]

What, then, would constitute a suitable approach to translating prismatic poetry and the poetry of Odysseus Elytis in particular? As with all translations of poetry, much depends on the translator's aims which should always be stated. Any approach to poetry translation (and evaluation for that matter) is insepara- ble from the translator's aims and the way he or she sees the translation as functioning in the TL.[6] If the aim here is to convey in the TL as accurate a presentation as possible of a major and original poetic voice, and a pre-eminently Greek one, and of all those features that characterise Elytis's poetry and distinguish it from that of other poets, then such factors have to be accounted for and the translator's approach must also be based on an interpretation of the poet's aims and of how his poetry functions in the source language (SL).

It is not my intention to attempt a critical analysis or evaluation of Elytis's poetry. I am concerned with his aims and techniques and with how he himself sees the function of poetry in so far as these directly affect the translation process. We are fortunate in that Elytis has explained his intentions and his views on poetry in several important essays (collected in Elytis, 1974; 1992), but also, and perhaps even more so, from within his poetry, in which he speaks about poetry through poetry (cf. Babiniotis, 1991).

Elytis's poetry exhibits the same features as those of prismatic poetry outlined above, namely: the presence, first of all, of 'nuclei' or phrasal units of self-generating radiance around which the poem is organised; secondly, within these units, the phonic and graphic effects of the word or unit coincide with the semantic content to such a degree that it is impossible to separate the poem's formal and semantic elements; thirdly, such utterances stimulate the intuitive power of the imagination and can lead to the apprehension of another reality, of the world not as it is but as it could be (which is the ultimate function of poetry for Elytis).[7]

Translating this type of poetry does not mean simply re-expressing the words' semantic content, their message or invariant core. This is not poetry that can be paraphrased. In a poetry that can be fragmented and still function as poetry, the words simply *are*, they do not *mean* something else. There is no logical conclusion to be drawn from juxtaposing two words or even two lines in prismatic poetry, as Elytis himself explains in his essay 'The method of "Therefore" ' (in Elytis, 1992: 163–84).

A common approach to such problems is that which sees the translation of poetry as 'αναδημιουργία', a 're-creation'. The idea underlying the 're-creation approach' to translating poetry is that both the poet and the translator are 'translators' of the poet's original vision, in the sense that the poet, too, is faced with the problem of finding a suitable form of expression in the SL in which to embody his vision. Consequently, the translator's task is somehow to recreate in the TL the poet's original vision which underlies the SL words. Such an approach is inapplicable here as the content of the poem is elicited by the very language in which it is conceived and, according to Elytis, the ideas are born at the same time as their verbal expression:

> I am one of those poets who work from within their language. This is not a detached attitude. I do not think of something and then 'translate' it into language. Writing is always an experiment, and often I am guided by language itself into saying certain things which I might otherwise not have thought of.
>
> [Elytis, 1975: 637]

Similarly, it is not valid here to ask how the poet would have expressed his vision in a particular word, phrase, or verse if, at the moment of composition, he had had the entire resources of the English language at his disposal (which, in any case, becomes how would I, the translator, have expressed it?) as this approach again assumes that somehow the semantic content precedes its verbal expression.

In prismatic poetry the phonic and graphic qualities of a word or phrasal unit cannot be understood as something separate from its semantic content; in other words, the letters and sounds are themselves semantically significant. What does this mean for the translator of Elytis? I would suggest that what is called for is equal if not greater attention on the part of the translator to the formal elements of the phrasal units (nuclei) than to the semantic content. With regard to the sound effects employed by Elytis, it has been noted (Beaton,1992: 9) that *The Oxopetra Elegies* exhibit a more pronounced use than in any of his previous collections of assonance and alliteration (and, I might add, of internal rhyming). The translation should reproduce these features where possible even at the expense of the semantic content. For example, in the line:

'Ασταλτα κι άπιαστα ορατά γίνονται τώρα [Elytis, 1991: 22]
[Unsent and ungrasped (things) visible become now]

the semantic content is that what was unsent and ungrasped (i.e. elusive) now becomes visible, but the line functions primarily as a result of its formal elements, in this instance, through the sound effects created by the assonance and alliteration (cf. underlined parts). Hence the translation:

Things un*classed* and un*grasped* at *last* become seen

where similar sound effects are retained and the semantic content is not greatly altered. An illustration of the difficulties faced by the translator of this kind of poetry is provided by the poem 'Ρήμα το Σκοτεινόν', 'The Obscure Verb' (Elytis, 1991: 35–7), which ends with the lines:

. . . Κι άλλοι άλλα σ' άλλες. Αλλ'
[. . . And other (people) other (things) in other (languages). But]
Η Αλήθεια μόνον έναντι θανάτου δίδεται.
[The Truth only in-return-for death is-given.]

The semantic content is: 'Other people say other things in other languages. But/The Truth is only given in return for death.' Yet what is the translator to do with the fivefold repetition of the sound [al] other than accept the loss of the formal elements in the translation? As Berlis (1992: 50) notes: 'what is the meaning of a line that focuses on itself, that refers to its own formulation to such a degree that its referential meaning recedes (or is reinforced?)'. In such cases, very little can be saved other than the referential meaning.

A useful translation device for dealing with such problems is that of compensation. Compensation as a concept in poetry translation expresses the idea that if poetry is what is lost in translation, it is also what is added. Baker (1992: 78) discusses compensation as a technique for dealing with 'any loss of meaning, emotional force, or stylistic effect which may not be possible to reproduce directly at a given point in the target text', which sees compensation as a possible strategy for dealing with translation problems on all three levels, i.e. semantic, stylistic and pragmatic. Similarly, Newmark (1988: 90) remarks that compensation 'is said to occur when loss of meaning, sound-effect, metaphor or pragmatic effect in one part of a sentence is compensated in another part, or in a contiguous sentence', thus giving it a widespread application. What is lacking in the discussion on compensation, however, as Harvey (1995) points out, is a descriptive framework for the processes it entails. He himself defines it as:

a technique for making up for the loss of a source text effect by recreating a similar effect in the target text through means that are specific to the target language and/or the target text. [1995: 66]

Harvey, quite rightly, finds existing definitions and usage of the term far too general and convincingly argues that the term should be retained for essentially stylistic, text-specific features and effects. Newmark's definition above also raises the issue of the location of compensation in relation to the instance of loss. For example, it rules out parallel compensation and displaced compensation. Following Harvey (1995: 82–4), a *parallel* relationship obtains where the compensation occurs at exactly the same place in the target text (TT) as the effect that has been lost in the source text (ST). A *contiguous* relationship obtains where the compensation occurs in the TT within a short distance from the lost effect of the ST. A relationship of *displaced* compensation obtains where the instance of compensation in the TT is a long distance from the ST loss. *Generalised* compensation occurs where the TT includes stylistic features that aim to naturalise the text for the target reader and that aim to achieve a comparable number and quality of effects, without these being tied to any specific instances of ST loss.

There are many cases in Elytis's poetry where very little can be saved in translation except the semantic content and where loss on the stylistic level is unavoidable. Often, however (depending on the translator's own creative talent), a greater or lesser degree of compensation is possible as in:

'Άβαφη κι από τις πολλές απαλές που πέρασαν παλάμες λεία!
[Elytis, 1991: 10]
[Unpainted and from the many soft that passed palms smooth!]
Paintbare and from the passing of so many soft palms smooth!

Here the alliteration of the [p] and [l] sounds in the Greek is reproduced in the same words in the same line through the [p] and [s] sounds in English, which in Harvey's terms would be an example of parallel compensation. In other cases, the stylistic features lost in one line may be gained in the following line (contiguous compensation) as in the lines:

Του βατόμουρου το βαποράκι μες στα βαθιά των φυλλωμάτων
[Of-the blackberry the tiny-steamboat in the deep of-the leafage]
Ρεύματα! Κι ο πρωραίος ιστός όλο σημαίες! [Elytis, 1991: 33]
[Currents! And the prow mast all flags!]
The blackberry's tiny steamboat in the deep currents
Of the leafage! And the foremast full of flags!

Here the alliteration of the first line in Greek in transferred to the second line in the English translation. Where reproduction of the alliteration in the same or a contiguous line is impossible, it may be reproduced in another line altogether as, for example:

Κι οι άλλες που απώλεσες παλαιές αισθήσεις επάνω στ' ουρανού την ύλη . . .
[And the other that you-lost old sensations on the sky's matter . . .]
Other sensations of old you spent upon the sky's substance

Here in Greek the alliteration is minimal, yet the English translation becomes a line with pronounced alliteration. This would be an example of displaced compensation, where the alliteration is added to compensate for loss elsewhere. Such instances of compensation are slightly more problematical than are instances of generalised compensation, as they are more difficult to justify as being instances of compensation for specific instances of loss in the ST. If, however, as sometimes occurs, a line in translation exhibits stylistic effects simply by a fortuitous accident of language, I would, in keeping with Harvey's category of generalised compensation, retain the effects in the case of Elytis as so much loss occurs elsewhere. It is worth noting that in the examples I have given, the original sounds are compensated for by using different sounds in English. This is an aspect of the concept of compensation not discussed in the literature. For example, does the substitution of the [s] sound for the [l] sound in the above example, in fact, constitute compensation? Particular sounds have their own qualities and associations. Tsekouras (1995: 23) notes in relation to Elytis's poetry that experimental studies show, for example, that [l] is associated with something pleasant and tender, and it might be added that [s] is often associated with something frightening or ominous. Can substituting the one for the other be considered, therefore, an instance of compensation? Friar (1973: 677) maintains that 'it is false to believe that any single sound in itself may denote some particular quality'. In the absence of further research, all the translator can do is to reproduce the repetition of sound (if possible) thereby conveying the stylistic device if not the pragmatic effect.

The same is true for sound effects produced by internal or approximate rhymes where the aesthetic function takes precedence over meaning. Sometimes the loss has to be accepted as in:

Περιπατούν τα κύματα στα σκοτεινά. Οι ασφόδελοι
[Walk the waves in-the dark. The asphodels]
Και οι νάρκισσοι κι εκείνοι αποκυήματα
[And the narcissi also these figments]
Της φαντασίας . . . [Elytis, 1991: 9]
[Of the imagination . . .]

where in the TL there can be no corresponding effect between *waves* (κύματα) and *figments of the imagination* (αποκυήματα).

In other cases the formal elements can be accounted for without great alteration to the semantic content, as, for example, the internal rhyming in:

Το νου του ανθρώπου και τον ρου στης Σουαβίας τα ύδατα [Elytis, 1991: 11]
[The mind of man and the flow in Swabia the waters]
Man's *mind* and the *wind*ing of Swabia's waters

Πέρ' απ' τα πάθη περ' απ' τα λάθη των ανθρώπων [Elytis, 1991: 31]
[Beyond the passions beyond the mistakes of men]
Beyond the *sorrows* beyond the *errors* of men

Just as the sound effects of the nuclei in prismatic poetry should not be sacrificed to the semantic content, so too the images created by the nuclei should be scrupulously translated in that the aesthetic function of the image is often of greater significance than any referential meaning. The poetic image is the picture created by use of metaphor. Metaphor, as Newmark (1988: 104) notes, 'demonstrates a resemblance, a common semantic area between two (more or less) similar things — the image and the object'. He further explains:

> The purpose of metaphor is basically twofold: its referential purpose is to describe a mental process or state, a concept, a person, an object, a quality or an action more comprehensively and concisely than is possible in literal or physical language; its pragmatic purpose, which is simultaneous, is to appeal to the senses, to interest, to clarify 'graphically', to please, to delight, to surprise. The first purpose is cognitive, the second aesthetic. In a good metaphor, the two purposes fuse . . . [1988: 104]

What Elytis took from surrealist poetry was the mechanism for creating metaphors in which it is not the resemblance but the dissimilarity and unexpected identification of these two objects or concepts that creates the force of the image. Formal simile, which uses analogy and is based on the word 'like' (this is *like* that) seems to him (cf. Elytis, 1974: 147) to remind the reader that someone is speaking, to underline the fact that some contract is being made at that moment between the poet and the reader, according to which the latter undertakes to believe whatever the former concocts. He goes on to explain that, in poems today (and he is referring to post-surrealist poetry), the world bursts out triumphantly and *is* what it wants to be each time. Analogy gives way to identification. This *is* that. The surprise, whether big or small, leaves no time to anyone to think whether a thing can be or not be this way. And Elytis (1974: 148) explains: 'There's no room for discussion; what the poet says, that's the way it is.'

In Elytis, we find a relative absence then of formal simile with 'like' and 'as', which has to do with his view of the function of poetry and of the analogies that exist between the senses and the spirit. As he points out:

> I have never picked up a pencil to write that something was like this or that! I have always been preoccupied with finding the analogies between nature and language in the realm of the imagination. [Elytis, 1975: 637]

Original metaphor is among the most frequent stylistic devices used by Elytis.[8] Apart from his use of metaphorical compounds, particularly in his early period, what we commonly find throughout his work are metaphors dependent on the genitive:

> Του ήλιου η λόγχη [Elytis, 1991: 17]
> The sun's spear

> με τη νοημοσύνη ανέμου [1991: 34]
> with the wind's intellect

juxtaposed metaphors:

> . . . οι βράχοι πιό ιερείς [1991: 14]
> . . . rocks more priests

> . . . τα δέντρα πιό πουλιά [1991: 14]
> . . . trees more birds

and appositional metaphors:

> Μικρά χρυσά πετούμενα μωράκια της αναπνοής σου . . . [Elytis, 1991: 14]
> Tiny golden wings offspring of your breath . . .

> . . . η μακριά μακριά ζωή των αγνώστων η άγνωστη [1991: 33]
> . . . long long life of unknowns the unknown

In terms of his view of poetry and the feature of prismatic poetry that stimulates the imagination so that it might apprehend a second reality through the analogy of the effect of the senses on the spirit, all metaphors are of the utmost importance and must be accurately rendered in terms of image,[9] even if this produces what might be referred to as a 'cultural shock'. A shock to the senses is exactly what Elytis's metaphors are intended to produce, as is his language in general:

> The success of a poem's language depends on the way in which it combines certain words . . . In a poem one should have the surprise of expression . . . Your reaction should be 'Look no one has thought before of juxtaposing these two particular words!' Suddenly, we feel as if an electric current had passed through us. [Elytis, 1975: 638]

Elytis's poetry also functions in a third way, as does all poetry. That is to say, poems do not only function on a semantic level in terms of their referential meaning and on a stylistic level in terms of their sounds and formal qualities; they also have an emotional and overall communicative effect on the reader. In other words, poems comprise not only thoughts, sounds and images, but also sentiments (for which reason poetry is able to elevate the reader's understanding beyond the confines of the usual rational processes and bring about the imaginative leaps of perception that Elytis sees as being the ultimate aim of poetry). Even if equivalence between languages were possible, and even if the peculiar formal aspects of one language could be compensated for in another, the pragmatic effect, that is, the emotive and communicative impact on the reader, will rarely coincide. This is because translation involves not just two languages, but transfer from one culture to another. As Newmark points out:

> The principle of equivalent effect or (Nida's) dynamic equivalence is usually defined as producing the same effect on the target readership in translation as was produced by the original text on the source language readership. The effect is assumed to be mainly emotive, rather than cognitive, since the effect of acquiring new information is not particularly emotionally important. It is usually agreed that national cultures are the biggest barriers to equivalent effect . . . [Newmark, 1994: 137]

What then of the translation problems that arise because of cultural differences where meaning is generated through culturally-specific references and allusions of a social, historical or political nature? Even the simplest word never has an exact equivalent in all aspects of its meaning and, in addition, will usually have different cultural significance and associations and, consequently, a different emotive and communicative impact. I refer here to ostensibly simple words (yet, with a high frequency in Elytis's poetry) such as 'sun', 'sea', 'light', 'bread' and 'olive tree', with their very different connotations for Greek and English readers.[10] Elytis is aware of this when he says:

> You would assume that at least the content and the thematics of my poetry, that which we perceive through our senses, would be more accessible [to the foreign reader]. But is it? If I say in Greek, for example, 'olive tree' or 'sea', these words have completely different connotations for us than, say, for an American. [1975: 637]

There are also words with less than even approximate equivalence; words, that is, that are more or less completely culturally specific with no exactly corresponding concept in the TL culture, such as λεβεντιά (upstandingness, 'dash', gallantry), φιλότιμο (sense of honour, self-esteem), etc. Recourse can always be made to the use of a compound of several elements, but this is a rather clumsy method in poetry translation.

A common translation approach to these problems is that which has as its overriding aim to produce a corresponding or equivalent effect in the TL. According to Vayenas (1989: 22), this approach to translation attempts to reproduce a lexical and emotional harmony corresponding to that of the original. He cites as an example two different Greek translations of a line by T.S. Eliot which contains the word 'oakleaves' and expresses his preference not for the literal translation of 'βαλανιδόφυλλα' but for the corresponding Greek translation 'φύλλα δάφνης' (laurel leaves) on the grounds that the laurel for the Greek reader corresponds culturally to what the oak means to the English reader and, therefore, has corresponding associations and a similar pragmatic effect.

To what extent, however, should the translator search for cultural equivalence of this kind? In Elytis, should olive trees become apple trees? Should St Demetrius become St George? Should Mesolonghi become The Alamo? In translating the first poem in *The Oxopetra Elegies* which is entitled 'Ακινδύνου, Ελπιδοφόρου, Ανεμποδίστου '(Akyndinou, Elpidophorou, Anembodistou), the names of the three martyrs celebrated in the Orthodox calendar on 2 November, which is Elytis's birthday, I was tempted to use the corresponding date in the Western Church calendar, namely, 'All Souls' Day', which by a happy coincidence is not far removed in associations from the theme of the poem. I resisted the temptation and opted for a very useful device to which the translator can always have recourse in cases of unbridgeable cultural gaps: the explanatory note.

There are other cases, however, where the poetic units have no referential meaning even in the SL, yet where the words function pragmatically in terms of their connotations. In the poem entitled 'Τα Εισόδια Του Προθανατισμένου (Presentation of A Prefigured Death), Elytis lists the names of stars, islands in the celestial archipelago, all of them fictitious, but all with connotations for the Greek reader. To transliterate these words would be to deprive them of any function whatsoever. Instead, I attempted to reproduce the associations in English through recourse to Latin roots and the word-forms of well-known stars, endeavouring also to retain the word's gender. So, for example, Το Λιγινό (neuter with connotations of 'small') becomes 'Minorion' , Ο Αντύπνος (masculine with connotations of 'instead of sleep') becomes 'Prosomnes', Ο Αλογάρης (masculine with connotations of 'horse') becomes 'Hippirius', *Η Ευβλωπούσα* (feminine with connotations of 'seeing well') becomes 'Benvidora' , *Η Μάισσα* (feminine with connotations of 'sorceress') becomes 'Sorcera', etc.

This is a special case. In general, we read foreign poetry to become acquainted with the particular poet and the SL culture. If we require the translation of a foreign poem to function as an English poem in terms of equivalent effect, there would seem to be little point in reading foreign poetry in translation. I think we have to accept that in all translations of poetry, there will be pragmatic loss as the translator's duty (though this depends on his aims) is above all to the author and the SL culture rather than to the TL reader and the TL culture. We have to assume a sensitive and imaginative reader with some awareness of the SL culture rather than make concessions to the TL reader. Here, I would refer to Newmark's comment (1988: 48) that the concept of equivalent effect is more a desirable result of translation than an aim, and as such, it cannot really be included as a factor in the translation process.

To the semantic, stylistic and pragmatic functions discussed above of the phrasal units or 'nuclei' in prismatic poetry, another must be added; one which I choose to call the 'incantatory' function, not in the sense of the ritual recitation of magical words and sounds, but rather the ability of these nuclei to stimulate the imagination leading to the revelation and apprehension of another reality, a function of language referred to by Elytis as a contemporary form of magic:

> I consider poetry a source of innocence, full of revolutionary forces. It is my mission to direct these forces against a world my conscience cannot accept, precisely so as to bring that world through continual metamorphoses more into harmony with my dreams. I am referring here to a contemporary kind of magic whose mechanism leads to the discovery of our true reality.
>
> [Elytis, 1975: 643]

Magic for Elytis is the art of transforming (cf. Elytis, 1992: 137) and the kind of poetry that functions in this way is a 'mechanism that demechanises man from his relationship with things' (Elytis, 1974: 261). Poetry's function is to lift the curtain (Elytis, 1992: 177), open the door leading to another reality. *Katarkyth-mévo*, the verb fashioned by Elytis in the poem entitled 'The Obscure Verb' (Elytis, 1991: 35–7), is the key to this door, just as 'The Obscure Verb' is the key to his poetry of the later period.

The obscure verb *Katarkythmévo* has no intended function in terms of the three functions already mentioned. It has no referential meaning, is stylistically indifferent and has no obvious connotations or emotional impact. Yet it is far from being a nonsense word. The verb has another function. It is intended to 'obscure your one side until / Your other side appears'; to serve as a key to open 'the great portals' *(οι μεγάλες θύρες)*, so that 'our nature the third may be revealed' *(η φύση μας η τρίτη να φανερωθεί)*. It is intended to function in the same way as words such as 'abracadabra' and 'open sesame'.

The verb fashioned by Elytis obviously cannot be translated in terms of its semantic content, nor is its stylistic or pragmatic effect immediately obvious. It could of course be simply transliterated, yet a transliteration of this word into English would have no meaning for the TL reader and also the added disadvantage of being foreign to the linguistic system. (The verb in Greek contains a common prefix and verb-ending and has been fashioned by Elytis in keeping with the norms of the Greek linguistic system). The translation follows the rules laid down in the poem for a verb with harsh sounds, bearing in mind that the verb is meant to function as a key opening the door to a second and third reality. Elytis says in the poem (1991: 35–6):

Ένα ρήμα τώρα μηχανεύομαι όπως ο διαρρήκτης το αντικλείδι του
Ένα ρήμα σε –άγω ή –άλλω ή –εύω
Κάτι που να σε σκοτεινιάζει από τη μία εωσότου
Η άλλη σου φανεί. Ένα ρήμα μ' ελάχιστα φωνήεντα όμως
Πολλά σύμφωνα κατασκουριασμένα κάππα ή θήτα ή ταυ
. . . Ώρα να δοκιμάσω το κλειδί. Λέω:
     καταρκυθμεύω

And the translation (Connolly, 1996: 65–7):

Now I'm fashioning a verb; like a burglar his pass-key
A verb ending in -ate or -age or -ise
One to obscure your one side until
Your other side appears. A verb with few vowels yet
Numerous consonants deep-rusted d's or c's or t's
. . . Time to test the key. So saying I:
     decrasticate

'Decrasticate', a verb fashioned in accordance with Elytis's specifications and in keeping with the norms of the English linguistic system, reproducing the harsh, rusty sounds of the key turning in a lock, hopefully retains something of the incantatory function of the original, though in the end, this comes down to a matter of taste.

There are two more features of Elytis's poetry that function in a similar way; his use of rare words or common words used in an unusual way, and his use of what might be called 'presocratic' utterances. He is aware of the criticisms regarding his use of rare words or words used in an unusual way (with its obvious consequences for the translator), but, as he says (1975: 637): 'I want the text to be completely virginal and far removed from the everyday usage of words. I would go so far as to say, I want it to be contrary to colloquial usage.' This is not to say that he simply plays with words (cf. Elytis, 1985: 53). The aim is to effect a different view of the world; a vision of a different reality, not the world as it is but the world as it could be (cf. Elytis, 1974: 18), so that poetry becomes a means of reshaping the world through the senses (Elytis, 1992: 116), or as Shelley (1966: 445) puts it: 'a poetry that would create anew the universe'. Such words are intended to function in another way; in the way already explained, as a contemporary form of magic.[11]

Another feature of the incantatory function of Elytis's poetry is the 'presocratic' utterances that are intended to startle, to mystify. Just as 'ο άναξ ου το μαντείον εστί το εν Δελφοίς ούτε λέγει ούτε κρύπτει αλλά σημαίνει ', 'The lord whose oracle is in Delphi neither speaks out nor conceals, but gives a sign' (Heraclitus, fr. 93) so too, for Elytis ' Ο ποιητής δείχνει '; 'The poet indicates'

(Elytis, 1992: 181). The epithet σκοτεινός (*obscurus* in Latin) attributed to Heraclitus in antiquity (cf. Cicero, *de finibus* II, 5, 15) is equally applicable to Elytis in some of his utterances (cf. Georgousopoulos, 1991: 753). Characteristic examples from *The Oxopetra Elegies* include:

Λάμπει μέσα μου κείνο που αγνοώ. Μα ωστόσο λάμπει [Elytis, 1991: 7]
What I know not glows within me. And yet it glows

Από μικρό το θαύμα είναι λουλούδι και άμα μεγαλώσει θάνατος [1991: 8]
In infancy the marvel is a flower and when grown old is death

What this means for the translator is that no attempt should be made here to explain or interpret through the translation. The dense opaqueness of the language must be allowed to perform its intended function. As Elytis notes:

Βέβαια, υπάρχει το αίνιγμα. Βέβαια, υπάρχει το μυστήριο. Αλλά το μυστήριο δεν είναι μιά σκηνοθεσία που επωφελείται από τα παιχνίδια της σκιάς και του σκότους για να μας εντυπωσιάσει απλώς· είναι αυτό που εξακολουθεί να παραμένει μυστήριο και μέσα στο απόλυτο φως. Είναι τότε που προσλαμβάνει την αίγλη εκείνη που ελκύει και που την ονομάζουμε Ομορφιά. Την Ομορφιά που είναι ίσως μιά οδός – η μόνη ίσως οδός – προς το άγνωστο μέρος του εαυτού μας, προς αυτό που μας υπερβαίνει. Επειδή αυτό είναι στο βάθος η ποίηση: η τέχνη να οδηγείσαι και να φτάνεις προς αυτό που σε υπερβαίνει.

Of course there's enigma. Of course there's mystery. But the mystery isn't a stage-setting that takes advantage of the play of shadow and darkness so as to simply impress us. It is that which continues to remain a mystery even in total light. It is then that it acquires that lustre that attracts and that we call beauty; the beauty that is a path — perhaps the only one — towards the unknown part of ourselves, towards that which transcends us. And this is what poetry is after all: the art of being led and of reaching towards that which transcends you. [Elytis, 1992: 319]

It is a constant temptation for the translator of poetry to clarify or explain in the translation. All translation, it is true, is to some extent an interpretation, but it should not preclude other possible interpretations. The TL reader must be allowed access to the various levels of meaning and possible interpretations contained in the original where the original remains intentionally allusive.

Conclusion

To summarise, I have attempted to discuss some of the factors involved in the process of translating a particular type of poetry and one of its main exponents, Odysseus Elytis, who has expressed doubts as to the translatability of this poetry. We may not accept the assertion attributed to Frost that poetry is what is lost in translation, but we have to accept that much of what we call poetry is lost in translation. From this humble starting point, the aim should be to save as much as possible. Elytis's belief is that only 20–30 per cent of his poetry is retained in translation. My aim in translating *The Oxopetra Elegies* was simply to improve on that percentage.

My implicit argument is for an approach not to translating *poetry*, but to translating *poets*. Just as we accept that the problems involved in literary translation differ from those of other types of translation (technical, economic, etc.), so too, within literary translation, different factors are involved in the translation of poetry, prose and drama. But even within the separate category of poetry, we cannot approach all poets in the same way. Discussions of approaches to translating poetry often tacitly assume that all poetry is the same and no distinction is made between different types of poetry and the different translation problems that each type involves. A more useful approach, in my opinion, is to establish the characteristic features of a particular type of poetry or poet before deciding on a suitable translation method.

What I have argued for as an approach to translating Elytis is a closer correspondence to what Elytis calls the 'poetic nucleus' (the word or phrasal unit), an approach I abandoned in my own translations only when the result was clearly unnatural in terms of utterance in the TL or unsatisfactory in terms of poetic effect. And this, in contrast to the approach that sees poetry translation as the re-creation of the poet's vision, or as the creation of a new and 'equivalent' poem in the TL, mainly because I see as the translator's aim to make Elytis available to the English reader, but not to Anglicise him.

Of course, the translator has to accept that there are limits; these have to do with the capacities of the TL but also with the translator's skill. Similarly, the translation must, in the end, function as a poem in the TL and perhaps the ultimate criterion for the success of translations of prismatic poetry is the same as for the original poem: if fragmented, would the fragments still function as poetry?

As a conclusion, I would like to end with Elytis's own words on the subject of poetry translation:

> Όλα γίνεται να τα λύσεις και να τα επανασυνδέσεις, εκτός από τα λόγια που έγραψε ο ποιητής. Κάποια βίδα στο τέλος θα σε μπερδέψει. Μήτε που θα εφαρμόζει πουθενά, μήτε που χωρίς αυτήν θα λειτουργεί το μηχάνημα.

> Everything can be taken apart and put back together again except a poet's words. Eventually you'll come across a tiny screw that won't fit anywhere, but without which the machine won't work. [Elytis, 1992: 165–6]

This is the aspect of poetry that remains a mystery, that defies analysis, and which perhaps accounts for the fascination and endless discourse that poetry translation generates.

Notes
1. Revised text of a paper delivered at the International Conference: 'Translation: Means of Communication and Creation', Corfu, 7–9 April 1993, and attended by Peter Newmark.
2. Although it is not until 'Romanós O Melodós', written in 1975, that these terms first appear, the view of poetry on which they are based is expressed in earlier essays and can, therefore, be regarded as a constant feature of Elytis's poetry. Cf., for example, Elytis (1974: 150, 353–4; 1992: 217).

3. Cf. Hervey and Higgins (1992: 74–80).
4. Cf. Elytis (1992: 329): 'We know you and you us from the twenty or at most thirty per cent that remains after translation. And we, especially, who belong to a particular tradition and have as our aim the miracles of the written word, the spark that flies out each time that two words are appropriately placed, remain silent and *incommunicable.'
5. Of course, I am aware that the word 'better' implies criteria on which to base an evaluation of poetry translations. The difficult question of evaluation is outside the scope of this essay, though a number of the points raised have direct bearing on this question.
6. For example, we may choose to translate because we wish to test the capacities of the TL to express a certain kind of poetry, perhaps enriching and renewing the TL at the same time (as with Seferis and his translations of Yeats and Eliot into Greek). We may translate because we are commissioned by either poet or publisher to do so (financial or other reward). We may translate because we feel an affinity with the poet and are inspired to want to appropriate the poem in the TL (personal reasons). We may use the poem as a starting point for creating a new poem in the TL, through emulation, imitation, adaptation, and all the other extreme forms of free translation (e.g. Pound and Lowell). Or, our aim may be to make the poet known in the TL culture because we are dealing with a major and original poetic voice that is worth the 'thankless efforts' (according to both Elytis and Seferis) involved in poetry translation.
7. Cf. Elytis (1975: 641): 'There is a search for paradise in my poetry . . . It is another world which is incorporated into our own, and it is our fault that we are unable to grasp it.'
8. On Elytis's use of metaphor, cf. Tsotsorou (1986) and Rotolo (1975: 694).
9. Cf. Newmark (1988: 112, 164) on the translation of original metaphors.
10. Hervey and Higgins (1992: 102–9) list and discuss six major types of connotative meaning, which they term attitudinal, associative, affective, reflected, collocative and allusive.
11. Such words from *The Oxopetra Elegies* include: *ιουλίζει* (a verb fashioned from the noun 'July'); *Τιμαριώτης τ' ουρανο ύ* 'feudatory of the sky'; *κατακυμάτων* 'against the waves'; *ύσγινη* (according to Liddell and Scott, a vegetable dye of scarlet colour, though the meaning here is 'red-hot' or 'glowing with heat'. I translated it as 'candescent' i.e. white hot, a lower-frequency and higher register word, as having a closer functional correspondence to the Greek word); *στρειδόφλουντζα* (a word found in Solomos, 'oysterskin') and the rare words for flowers *ανεμοκλείτια* 'Parietaria Officinalis' and *διατσέντα* 'Polyanthes Tuberosa', a less common Greek word for hyacinth.
12. Throughout this chapter all necessary translations from Greek into English are my own.

References

Babiniotis, G. (1991) Ποιητική Μεταγλώσσα και Μεταγλωσσική Ποίηση (Poetic metalanguage and metalingual poetry). *I lexi* 106, 733–49.

Beaton, R. (1992) Nearing the reef. *TLS* 7 August 1992, 9.

Berlis, A. (1992) *5(+2) Δοκίμια για τον Ελύτη (5(+2) Essays on Elytis)*. Athens: Ypsilon.

Connolly, D. (tr.) (1996) *Odysseus Elytis. The Oxopetra Elegies*. Amsterdam: Harwood Academic Publishers.

Dimou, N. (1986) Πρισματική και Επίπεδη Ποίηση (Prismatic and plane poetry). *Hartis* 21(3), 420–7.

Eliot, T.S. (1957) *On Poetry and Poets*. London: Faber.

Elytis, O. (1974) *Ανοιχτά Χαρτιά (Open Book)*. Athens: Asterias.

Elytis, O. (1975) Odysseus Elytis on his poetry. From an interview with Ivar Ivask. *Books Abroad* 49(4), 631–43.

Elytis, O. (1984) Σαπφώ. Ανασύνθεση και Απόδοση (Sappho. Recomposition and Rendition). Athens: Ikaros.
Elytis, O. (1985) Ο Μικρός Ναυτίλος (The Little Mariner). Athens: Ikaros.
Elytis, O. (1990) Newspaper interview. Ta Nea 3 February 1990.
Elytis, O. (1991) Τα Ελεγεία της Οξώπετρας (The Oxopetra Elegies). Athens: Ikaros.
Elytis, O. (1992) Εν Λευκώ (Carte Blanche). Athens: Ikaros.
Friar, K. (1973) Modern Greek Poetry. From Cavafis to Elytis. New York: Simon & Schuster.
Georgousopoulos, K. (1991) Ο Προσωκρατικός (The presocratic). I lexi 106, 750–4.
Harvey, K. (1995) A descriptive framework for compensation. The Translator: Studies in Intercultural Communication 1(1), 65–86.
Hervey, S. and Higgins, I. (1992) Thinking Translation. A Course in Translation Method: French to English. London and New York: Routledge.
Newmark, P.P. (1988) A Textbook of Translation. London and New York: Prentice Hall.
Newmark, P.P. (1994) Paragraphs on translation — 32. The Linguist 33(4), 136–41.
Newmark, P.P. (1995) Paragraphs on translation — 37. The Linguist 34(3), 112–13.
Rotolo, V. (1975) The 'Heroic and Elegeiac Song for the Lost Second Lieutenant of the Albanian Campaign': The transition from the early to the later Elytis. Books Abroad 49(4), 690–5.
Shelley, P.B. (1966) A defence of poetry. In H. Bloom (ed.) The Selected Poetry and Prose of Shelley (pp. 415–48). London: The New English Library Ltd.
Tsekouras, D.I. (1995) Γλωσσικές Ανιχνεύσεις στα 'Ελεγεία της Οξώπετρας ' (Linguistic explorations in 'The Oxopetra Elegies'). Porphyrus 71(2), 21–5.
Tsotsorou, A. (1986) Μεταφορές στο 'Ημερολόγιο ενός Αθέατου Απριλίου' (Metaphors in 'Journal of an Unseen April'). Hartis 21(3), 368–86.
Vayenas, N. (1989) Ποίηση και Μετάφραση (Poetry and Translation). Athens: Stigmi.

Chapter 15

How Come the Translation of a Limerick Can Have Four Lines (or Can It)?

Gideon Toury

... a text is to be translated like a particle in an electric field attracted by the opposing forces of the two cultures ...

(Peter Newmark, 1981: 20)

An Introductory Note

A recurring claim is that translation involves texts and nothing but texts. These texts may be approached differently, but it is always a text that is submitted for translation, and it is always a text which comes out of it. This problematic claim notwithstanding, the present discussion will not revolve around texts at all. Rather, its key notion will be that of MODELS, those hypothesised entities which underlie the way texts are created, classified and assessed within a particular cultural set-up (cf. Sheffy, 1997). The notion of model itself will be used first and foremost in its *generative sense*. It will thus be conceived of as a set of guidelines for the production of an infinite number of texts recognised as belonging to one and the same type, whether these texts (or the model they supposedly embody) have also been given a collective name or not. Naming is, of course, an important indicator of the institutionalisation of a model within a particular culture, but it is far from necessary for its generative capacity.

A model as a set of guidelines for text production should always be seen as *hierarchically ordered:* not every principle derived from it is equally essential to the text-type in question, and hence to individual acts of performance pertaining to it. What we will in fact be doing is to isolate for closer inspection one feature of the model of the English limerick. However, in order to enhance the significance of our discussion, not just *any* feature will be singled out but one of the most salient ones. The claim that what applies to a high-level generative principle is also applicable to lower-level principles is, of course, much easier to maintain than its opposite.

Something about the English Limerick

In many respects, the following text (Lear, 1965) could be regarded as a prototypical limerick:

> There was an old man with a beard,
> Who said, 'It is just as I feared!
> Two owls and a hen,
> Four larks and a wren,
> Have all built their nests in my beard!'

Like all English texts which embody the model underlying this text, thus pertaining to what has come to be known as the limerick,[1] this text comprises one stanza occupying exactly five lines which also rhyme, using the *aabba* scheme. It is the omnipresence of BEING A FIVE-LINER which renders this feature the most salient single generative and classificatory principle of the English limerick: a texter failing to subscribe to it would hardly be said to have produced a limerick.

To be more precise, what we have here is more like five PROSODIC UNITS: two of the lines, the third and fourth, which are shorter than the rest (dimeters versus trimeters), can be, and have indeed sometimes been, joined together in print to form the visually longest line of a seeming four-liner, thus partly normalising the limerick even for the English reader, accustomed to considering rhyming verses in pairs. However, the resulting typographic tetrameter always featured an internal rhyme, and at its exact middle at that. It thus fell into two equal, and rhyming parts (the *b*s in the scheme), which still permits us to regard the English limerick as a five-liner throughout.

A prototypical limerick is also basically ANAPAESTIC in metre, even though not all that piously: quite often, metrical irregularities may occur. It also tends to be COMIC, bordering on complete nonsense. To a substantial extent, this comic-to-nonsensical impact hinges on the limerick's CLOSING LINE, especially the way it ties in with the rest of the text, which renders it a kind of punchline. The OPENING LINE enjoys special status too, the more so as it often imitates the beginning of an English fairy tale. Finally, the final line is often a repetition, or varied repetition, of the first.

The following text constitutes another prototypical realisation of the model, the enumeration of whose features has far from been exhausted:

> There was an Old Man of the Dee,
> Who was sadly annoyed by a Flea;
> When he said, 'I will scratch it,'
> They gave him a hatchet,
> Which grieved that Old Man of the Dee.

Most readers have probably known all along what I have been driving at. On the other hand, I suspect that, even among experienced readers of English, there would be some who have just encountered their first (and second) limericks. Then there would be those who may never have come across the *word* 'limerick' before, even though they might have encountered texts manifesting the aforementioned features, or — if they have — would have been hard put to specify the *generative rules* of the limerick, or even differentiate between better- and worse-formed texts embodying the model. The requirement seems obvious: acquaintance with a particular cultural tradition rather than mere knowledge of a language.

Thus, it would hardly be surprising if it were to emerge that readers who have never encountered the word 'limerick', or who would run into difficulties trying to account for its contents, were found to have had limited exposure to English culture — or to any other culture which has had close contacts with it, especially contacts leading to the appropriation of the limerick by that other culture — whether lack of exposure to the English culture was merely accidental or typical of the reader's culture as a whole. In the latter, more significant case, it is quite safe to assume that no limerick-like texts, or only very few, would have figured in that culture, whether translated or original, or — if they had — that the products, and especially the model they realise, have settled down somewhere in the periphery.[2] To be sure, if limerick-like texts were to have been produced in the reader's culture, they would not necessarily bear a generic label of any kind, much less so the label 'limerick'.[3] Finally, even if they were to have been called limericks, the features of what is referred to by that name in this other culture need not be identical to those expected of an English limerick, in either quantity or salience (i.e. in terms of sheer number of features or their position in the hierarchy of the text-type model).

Which brings us directly to our Title Question:

> if an English limerick is indeed characterised first and foremost by its being a five-liner, how come the translation of a limerick into the language of another culture can have four lines?

This question has both theoretical and descriptive aspects. On the one hand, its formulation suggests a mere *possibility*; and questions of possibility, while definitely theoretical in nature, are obviously located in a most elementary kind of theory. On the other hand, if and when a possibility is realised, the choice underlying it cannot remain unexplained, namely, in terms of the circumstances which can be said to have motivated such a decision. Whatever the explanation, it would be applied to an *empirical* finding, a real-life instance of behaviour, within a descriptive kind of approach. However, its terms of reference would necessarily be theoretical again, only this time taken from a much more elaborate kind of theory which had already taken into account previous instances of actual behaviour. (This spiral mode of progression in Translation Studies is described in Toury, 1995a: 14–17.)

Before dealing with these issues in connection with the English limerick, some basic assumptions concerning translation as an object for study will be sketched. These are the assumptions underlying my *Descriptive Translation Studies and Beyond* (Toury, 1995a). The interested reader is referred especially to the methodological sections comprising Part Two of the book.

Assumed Translations and the Limerick

For descriptive-explanatory purposes, any text which is assumed to be a translation, no matter on what grounds, will be taken into consideration. This notion of ASSUMED TRANSLATION implies at least three interdependent postulates:

(1) There is another text, in another culture/language, which has both chrono-
     logical and logical priority over it and which can be assumed to have served
     as its immediate source (The Source Text (ST) Postulate);
(2) The process whereby the assumed translation came into being involved the
     transference of certain features from the corresponding assumed ST (The
     Transfer Postulate);
(3) There are accountable relationships which tie the assumed translation to its
     assumed original, an obvious function of the transferred features that the
     two now share in the context of the differences that exist between them (The
     Relationship Postulate).

How these postulates are realised in any particular situation constitutes an open
question rather than a precondition for regarding a textual entity, or the act in
which it came into being, as a translation within the culture in question.[4]

In fact, there is a whole list of open questions here which will have to be
answered during the execution of the descriptive-explanatory study; for instance:

- Was there indeed an ST?
- Was there just one such text, or more than one?
- Was the assumed ST the ultimate original (the first in the line, so to speak)
  or another text, notably a mediating translation?
- And what are the relationships actually tying the two textual entities (or
  parts thereof) to each other?
- To what extent and in what way do these observed relationships realise the
  norm of appropriateness as it is held by the culture in question?
- And what was the reconstructable process of translation like? What
  strategies did the translator have recourse to? (And if there was more than
  one pair of hands involved in the passage from the assumed ST to the
  assumed target text (TT) — for instance, a translator and a reviser, or editor
  — what exactly did each one of them do?)

The starting point for any attempt to account for an assumed translation as the
translation it assumedly is is the assumption that it was designed to fulfil a need
of the culture that hosts it, or rather to fulfil what that need was taken to be by
the translator. However, individual translators are always products of a given
societal group, and therefore they are bound to make their decisions with
reference to a culturally-determined normative framework, whether they are
fully aware of it or not and whether they wish to enhance or undermine that
framework.

Whatever the need, translating satisfies it in a way of its own which is different
from any other way of satisfying that need, namely, by introducing into the
culture in question a version of something which has already been in existence
elsewhere and which is deemed worthy of introduction into it. This worthiness
too is established within the receiving culture and on its own terms, even if the
status which that something enjoyed in the source culture is being heeded. After
all, the decision to take such a status into account can only be made in the culture
in and for which the translator is operating.

The introduced entity itself, the way it enters the target culture, is something which has never been there before: even in the case of *re*translation, what is actually incorporated in that culture will definitely *not* have been there before, no matter how many translations preceded it. Needless to say, the decision to retranslate itself (rather than reprint, submit to editing, or simply ignore) is another matter determined by the recipient culture.

At the same time, what is introduced through translation is never completely new either, never alien to the receiving culture on all possible counts, otherwise there would be little sense in saying that it has been introduced into that culture, let alone incorporated in it. To quote an analogy from medicine: to prevent immediate rejection, transplantation always requires some measure of *matching* between the transplanted organ and the recipient's system. Moreover, even if initial matching exists, it will have to be backed up and enhanced through constant *medication* to safeguard against alienation and delayed rejection.

Thus, much as translation always entails the *retention* of aspects of an ST (which forms a basis for many of the novelties it may introduce into the receiving culture), it also involves an element of *adjustment* of its requirements, and not necessarily in terms of language alone: alien models, and especially their most deviant features (from the point of view of the prospective target system), if retained, may be grounds enough for rejection.

Obviously, the greater the proximity of the model embodied by an ST to models which are already included in the repertoire of the target culture, or the 'tool kit' at the disposal of its texters (Swidler, 1986), the greater the initial possibility of constituting a suitable match, whether this proximity (and match) are then brought to bear on particular acts of translation or not. By contrast, the greater the distance between the systemic constellations of the two cultures involved in the contact, the greater the need to make adjustments and allowances — to the extent that the act of translation is governed by an initial norm of acceptability.

Once the focus is on the behaviour of flesh-and-blood translators within definable sociocultural conditions rather than on any ideal(ised) notion of translation, there is no way of taking for granted any kind of balance between retention and adjustment — not even when the opening conditions of the game have been established. Rather, the realisation of this crucial balance constitutes a question, namely, of the kind we have just been posing.

In the simplest of cases, the only thing which is added to the recipient culture by means of translation seems to be an individual text. In more complex cases, however, fully-fledged models (or elements thereof) may also be imported, normally with groups of texts which either embody recurring patterns or else are translated in a way which unifies the end-products. Nor is the novelty an immediate function of what the ST itself manifests in view of the options offered by the recipient culture, however striking the incongruity between the two. Rather, any novelty is a matter of what the target culture is willing (or allowed) to accept versus what it feels obliged to submit to modification, or occasionally even reject.

It is precisely for this reason that an act of translation performed on an English limerick can yield a four-line entity. Thus, not only is there nothing in principle to exclude this possibility (which would have been reason enough to retain it in any *theoretical* account), but there may also be circumstances in the recipient culture which would reduce the acceptability of a translated limerick, if transferred in an *un*modified fashion, to the verge of total rejection.

Under such unfavourable circumstances, a target language (TL) five-liner may well constitute an *irregular* textual entity, unrecognisable as a poem, or even as a literary text. If such an entity exists at all, it may be reserved for other uses and hence regarded as unfit for the recasting of an English limerick. If a translated limerick is recast in five lines nevertheless, the result is likely to look strange, at best.

Of course, no translation of a limerick can be expected to reflect *all* the features of the English model, let alone all the characteristics attributed to the immediate ST as an act of verbal performance. This is precisely why I have chosen to single out the most salient feature of the underlying model. Needless to say, a culture rejecting certain features of an alien model, or even the model as a whole, may still have its reasons for wishing to possess a version of a text pertaining to this model, and a version which would not be rejected too readily either. Under such circumstances, it may well favour, even encourage, the adoption of any number of solutions, among them the four-line option.

To be sure, there was good reason to select the number four, in this connection, even though any number other than five would have done: in most Western literatures, four-liners have been regarded as highly regular poetic entities. Texts couched in four lines thus come closer to the target culture's conventions, making this number a paradigmatic representation of the 'adjustment' option. (It might be recalled that, even in the English culture itself, limericks have sometimes been partly 'normalised' by being printed as four-liners.)

In Search of Explanations

Claiming that the translational replacement of an English limerick *may* have four lines is, of course, a far cry from claiming that it *will* in fact have them, under all or any circumstances. Having agreed on the theoretical claim, the next step should be to proceed descriptively and try to find out:

(1) whether a limerick has indeed been replaced by a four-liner which has then been presented and/or regarded as its translation; and if so —
(2) under what circumstances this kind of replacement and presentation occurred; and finally,
(3) how the correlation between the circumstances (2) and a specific type of behaviour (1) could be accounted for.

The first question is easy enough to answer. All that is needed for a *positive* reply is a single instance of behaviour of the required type, and since such an instance can always be produced at will, potentiality is proof enough of existence. By contrast, a truly *negative* answer could be given only after all assumed translations, past, present and future, have been scanned — to no avail. For all practical purposes, this is tantamount to never, which reinforces the positive answer yet again.

A descriptivist pursuing regularities of behaviour would, however, welcome more than a single instance of any type; many more, in fact, and contextualisable instances, at that. Only a significant volume of material can attest to the real weight of a particular mode of behaviour, and it is only recurrent patterns of behaviour under definable circumstances that make it possible to extract the relevant variables and determine their role as conditioning factors of that behaviour.

Nor would anything be solved by calling a practice such as the substitution of a TL four-liner for a source language (SL) five-liner 'adaptation'. It is not that adaptation is inferior in any way. It is only that the distinction implied by the term is not necessarily in keeping with the culturally pertinent one. Any use of such a label would therefore blur the issue. Above all, it would make it all the more difficult to establish the circumstances under which a particular strategy, such as the substitution of a four-liner for a five-liner, tends to be operative, which can be achieved with no recourse to any misleading, non-cultural and a-historical distinctions and labels.

As already indicated, a similar set of questions could be directed to any feature of the limerick and its behaviour under translation. For instance:

- Under what circumstances would a TT be produced which rhymes according to a scheme other than *aabba*? What rhyme scheme would tend to replace it, and where would it be taken from? And under what circumstances would completely *non*-rhymed entities (for example, jokes in prose) come into being, in preference, perhaps, to rhymed ones?
- Under what circumstances would the first, second and fifth lines of an assumed translation which is a five-liner be anything but trimeters and/or its third and fourth lines anything but dimeters?
- Under what circumstances would that text be non-anapaestic? Non-metrical? Non-comical?
- Under what circumstances would its closing verse not act as a kind of punchline?
- And so on and so forth.

However, once a positively-oriented answer has been given to the most *extreme* question, there should be no problem in extending that same answer to less extreme ones, applying it to less central features of the original model and its realisation in individual texts, on the way to establishing the correlations between them.

To be sure, in spite of the claim that translational considerations and decisions are basically governed by the needs of a *recipient* culture, the ST — and sometimes the tradition underlying it as well — still has an impact on the way the act of translation is performed. It is, however, the case that the way these are taken to bear on translation will (again) only be determined at the target end of the process.

In this vein, it would be interesting to find out to what extent the rejection of features in translational practice runs parallel to their relative position in the hierarchical organisation of the *original* model, to the effect that — as many a wishful thinker would have it — it is the less important ones which are the first to be obliterated. My experience with various case studies makes me doubt the generalisability of such a parallelism.

Thus, for instance, 'having seventeen syllables' was one of the first features to be obliterated when Japanese *haiku* poems were first translated into various European languages, even though it is no doubt one of the most important single features of the original model (cf. Toury, 1995a: 176–80). A similar conclusion arises from my attempt to establish the circumstances under which Shakespearean sonnets translated into Hebrew lost their most distinctive features and became Italian-like (Toury, 1995a: 114–22), and especially the detailed analysis of the reasons why the model underlying a German text of the *Schlaraffenland* tradition was not only rejected in its translation into Hebrew, but also replaced by a (mediating) Russian model (Toury, 1995a: 147–65).

The overall question as to what features of an ST (and model) are the first to be obliterated will certainly have to be tackled on its own terms, and answered on the basis of a series of well-targeted studies. There may be laws here, but one should resist the temptation to formulate them until ample data has been collected and analysed.

Translating Literary Texts versus Literary Translation

It is numerous observations of this kind, and attempts to account for them *within* Translation Studies rather than having the cases they involve dismissed as simply non-pertinent (in terms of an a priori, inevitably idealised concept of translation of whatever kind), which has led me to climb higher up the ladder of generalisation and question the notion of LITERARY TRANSLATION as a whole.

I soon came to the conclusion that the term 'literary translation' — as it had come to be used — was afflicted with ambiguity, referring as it does to two different things:

(a) the translation of STs which function[5] as literary texts in their home culture: in an extreme formulation, which has become rather obsolete, any translation of such texts; in a modified version, a translation where the focus is on the reconstruction of the ST's internal 'web of relationships', the one which makes that text a unique instance of performance (for example, Snell-Hornby, 1988: 69ff.);

(b) the translation of a text (in principle, at least, any text, of any type whatsoever) in such a way that the product is acceptable as literary to the recipient culture.

The manifestations of the two senses of 'literary translation' may, of course, overlap: there may be circumstances under which a close reconstruction of a text's web of relationships would indeed override any problems of acceptability. This may occur, for instance, when the two cultures involved have had very similar literary traditions anyway, often as a result of continuous contact between them, or else when the recipient system is considerably weaker *vis-à-vis* the source system in question, and is hence willing to use it as a source of enrichment in ways which transcend the individual piece of text, or, finally, when the translator him/herself has gained a position in his/her culture which allows him/her to deviate from sanctioned behavioural patterns and get away with it, sometimes to the point of being permitted to introduce changes into that culture. What differentiates the two senses of 'literary translation' is not that they can never coincide, then, but the fact that there is no inherent need for them to do so: even though reality may bring them together, they still remain different in essence, namely, source-oriented and target-oriented, respectively.

Thus, neither the literariness of the ST, nor even the careful embodiment of its web of relationships within a textual entity in the TL, would secure a position for the end product in the recipient literature, much less a position parallel to that which the ST has enjoyed in its own setting. As we have seen, a translation may well be eligible for rejection, precisely on the grounds that it reflects its source too closely, thus constituting an irregular entity within the receiving literature, according to its own norms.

Nor is the distinction between the mere 'translation of texts of a particular kind' and 'a kind of translation designed to fulfil a particular function' a peculiarity of literature alone. One could easily draw an analogical distinction between, say, the translation of legal documents (the products of which would, for instance, be incorporated in a TL history book and serve as a source of detailed information *about* the original document) and strictly legal translation (where the products are designed to serve downright legal purposes, whether similar to, or different from, those served by the STs). By the same token, there are translated versions of many national anthems yet few of these versions also *function* as anthems. Moreover, those that do (for example, in bilingual countries such as Canada or Belgium), do not necessarily reflect the most salient features of the texts in the other language, from which they were derived. (Cf., for example, Harris, 1983.)

Similar things can be said of the translation of a text such as the Hebrew Bible, which, at one point, was canonised as a Jewish religious text: of the many possible options only one would be for the translated version to represent the original Bible in this particular function (let alone replace it), and even then, there would still be a difference between functioning as a Jewish and a non-Jewish religious text. In this sense, not just any translation of the Bible, nor even necessarily one particular mode of translation, would amount to biblical translation. Needless to say, the Bible, or a national anthem, or sometimes even a legal document, can also undergo literary translation in sense (b) above, to the extent that attempts are made to have the end products incorporated in the *literary* system of the target culture.

Literature is just an example of a general phenomenon, then. It is, however, a very convenient one for a critical discussion of the concept of translation, precisely because, on the one hand, it is not normally regarded as so obvious a case as, say, the translation of legal texts, and, on the other hand, it evades many of the ideology-laden reservations which any discussion of the translation of national anthems, let alone the Bible, is bound to entail. By the same token, the limerick is just a convenient example for discussing literature under translation without sliding into too many issues involving value judgement.

The difference between the two senses of 'literary translation' stems from the fact that literature does not boil down to a body of texts, or even a repertoire of features which have something inherently literary about them. Rather, literature is first and foremost a CULTURAL INSTITUTION. Thus, in every culture, certain features, models, techniques (including modes of translation), and — by extension — texts utilising them, are *perceived as*, rather than *being*, literary, in any essentialistic sense. What lends a phenomenon or a text its position, as what Jurij Tynjanov called a 'literary fact', is a *systemic constellation* — a network of relationships into which it enters and by virtue of which it functions. Its literariness is thus established in terms of a given cultural system, and never in isolation. And, indeed, features, models and techniques, as well as texts utilising them, may both *become* literary or *lose* their literariness in the course of time without undergoing any change of textual organisation or linguistic formulation. It is thus clear that it is the systemic position which makes the difference, not any of the surface realisations.

Obviously, only rarely would two different cultural or literary systems fully concur; and since the (functional) identity of a phenomenon is governed first and foremost by the internal organisation of the system which hosts it, the literariness of an act of translation and/or its result can be said to be determined by the way the requirements of the *target* literature are brought to bear on it. Of course, these requirements can bear on an act of translation to various extents too, which makes 'literary translation' in sense (b) a *graded* notion rather than a matter of either/or. It is in fact no less graded than the possibility of reconstructing an ST's features, and, as we have already noted, very often the two stand in *inverse proportion*.

'Literary' as a qualifier of 'translation' can of course be added to 'linguistic' and 'textual', to form a series which is hierarchically ordered in terms of the specificity of the conditions imposed on the act, while also presenting basic homology. Thus, with respect to an ST which, institutionally speaking, is literary itself (as is the case we have been dealing with here), the following would apply:

- LINGUISTIC TRANSLATION would be any act yielding a product which is *linguistically well-formed*, even if it does not conform to any model of text formation within the repertoire of the target culture. In this case, at least partial interference of the model underlying the ST is to be expected.
- TEXTUAL TRANSLATION would, in turn, yield products which are well-formed in terms of *general conventions of text formation* pertinent to the target culture, even if they do not conform to any recognised literary model within it. Interference of the model underlying the ST may still be expected, namely, in terms of its literary-specific features.
- Finally, LITERARY TRANSLATION would involve the imposition of conformity conditions beyond the linguistic and/or general textual ones, namely, *to models and norms which are deemed literary at the target end*. It thus yields more or less well-formed texts from the point of view of the literary requirements of the target culture, at various possible costs in the realm of the reconstruction of the ST's own features.[6]

Subjugation to target literary models and norms may thus involve the suppression of some of the ST's features, sometimes even those which have marked it as literary, or as truly representative of a specific literary model, in the first place (such as the five-line structure of an English limerick, or the features which are unique to a Shakespearean sonnet, or the paratactic nature of a German *Schlaraffenland* text). It may also entail the reshuffling of features, not to mention the introduction of new ones, in an attempt to enhance the acceptability of the translation as a target literary text, or even one of a particular literary type. The added features may go so far as to occupy central positions within the translation (when considered as a text in its own right), or even serve as markers of its own literariness within the target culture, despite their having no basis in the original.

Completing the Circle

For all these reasons, it is easy to see how, conversely, a *non*-limerick-like text could be filtered through the limerick model when translated into English; and it is easy to see how the resulting entity could have five lines even if the original had, say, four. The translation of a tetrametric entity *can be* a five-liner, then; the question is, again, under what circumstances it would *tend to be* one, which is where the circle I have tried to outline closes, namely, with the beginning of another loop. I trust we can now trace this new loop from a more enlightened vantage point.

Notes

1. The history of the English limerick itself is of course different from the history of the use of 'limerick' as a label. Not surprisingly, it is much longer too. Even the classification of limerick-like texts as pertaining to one and the same type precedes the introduction of the label, which seems to have occurred towards the end of the 19th century. For both histories cf. e.g. Legman, 1964 v. Belknap, 1981.
2. And cf. for example, what Alfred Liede (1963: 266) has to say about the attempts to domesticate the limerick in the German-speaking world, which came to naught in spite of the existence of thousands of texts, including a substantial number of books, competitions for the composition of limericks (or for supplying them with the missing punchline), etc.
3. For instance, in the fifties, when the first Hebrew texts were produced which were based on the English limerick model, often directly on actual texts pertaining to it, they were usually referred to simply as *shirim* (= poems). When they were addressed to children, an attempt was made to introduce a new word as a label; namely, *lahadamim* (a plural form of the acronym *lahadam* — = completely false; or even: fully nonsensical). Later on the word *xamshir* was invented, a portmanteau word made out of *xamesh* (= five) and *shir* (= poem). This word caught on and gradually became the umbrella term for all sorts of texts, including English limericks, all sharing the use of a five-line stanza.
4. For a fuller discussion of the rationale underlying these claims cf. Toury, 1995b.
5. It should be clear that the term 'function' is used here in its *semiotic* sense, as the 'value' assigned to an item belonging in a certain system by virtue of the network of relations it enters into. (Cf. e.g. Even-Zohar, 1990: 10.) As such, it is not tantamount to the mere 'use' of the end product, as seems to be the case with other uses of the term, most notably in the so-called *Skopostheorie*.
6. In this connection, see also Roda Roberts's discussion of the differences between functions of language, functions of (source) text and functions of translation (Roberts, 1992), even though she uses the term 'function' within a different frame of reference (see note 5).

References

Belknap, G.N. (1981) History of the limerick. *The Papers of the Bibliographical Society of America* 75 (1), 1–32.
Even-Zohar, I. (1990) *Polysystem Studies*. (*Poetics Today* 11 (1).) Tel Aviv: The Porter Institute for Poetics and Semiotics, and Durham: Duke University Press.

Harris, B. (1983) Co-writing: A Canadian technique for communicative equivalence. In G. Jäger and A. Neubert (eds) *Semantik und Übersetzungswissenschaft: Materialien der III. Internationalen Konferenz 'Grundfragen der Übersetzungswissenschaft'* (pp. 121–32). Leipzig: VEB Verlag Enzyklopädie.

Lear, E. (1965) *The Complete Nonsense of Edward Lear*, ed. H. Jackson. London: Faber and Faber.

Legman, G. (1964) The limerick: A history in brief. In G. Legman *The Horn Book: Studies in Erotic Folklore and Bibliography* (pp. 427–53). New Hyde Park, New York: University Books.

Liede, A. (1963) *Dichtung als Spiel: Studien zur Unsinnpoesie und der Grenzen der Sprache 2.* Berlin: de Gruyter.

Newmark, P.P. (1981) *Approaches to Translation*. Oxford: Pergamon Press.

Roberts, R.P. (1992) The concept of function of translation and its application to literary texts. *Target* 4 (1), 1–16.

Sheffy, R. (1997) Models and habituses: Problems in the idea of cultural repertoires. *Canadian Review of Comparative Literature* 24 (1), 35–47.

Snell-Hornby, M. (1988) *Translation Studies: An Integrated Approach*. Amsterdam-Philadelphia: John Benjamins.

Swidler, A. (1986) Culture in action: Symbols and strategies. *American Sociological Review* 51 (2), 273–86.

Toury, G. (1995a) *Descriptive Translation Studies and Beyond*. Amsterdam-Philadelphia: John Benjamins.

Toury, G. (1995b) The notion of 'assumed translation': An invitation to a new discussion. In H. Bloemen, E. Hertog and W. Segers (eds) *Letterlijkheid/Woordelijkheid: Literality/Verbality* (pp. 135–47). Antwerpen-Hermelen: Fantom.

Tynjanov, J. (1967) Das literarische Faktum. In J. Tynjanov *Die literarischen Kunstmittel und die Evolution in der Literatur* (pp. 7–36), from Russian original by A. Kaempfe. Frankfurt am Main: Suhrkamp.

Chapter 16

The Source Text in Translation Assessment

Gerard McAlester

A good translation fulfils its intention
(Peter Newmark, 1988: 192)

This chapter deals with the subject of translation assessment from the point of view of translator education and accreditation. Within this context, I should like to distinguish between translation evaluation, criticism, analysis and assessment. These four words are often used interchangeably and confusingly in the relevant literature. In this chapter I shall use *translation evaluation* in the sense of placing a value on a translation (i.e. in terms of a grade or pass mark); *translation criticism* involves stating the appropriateness of a translation, which naturally also implies a value judgement, though it need not be quantified or even made explicit; *translation analysis* is used to mean the explication of the relationship between the target text (TT) and the factors involved in its production, including the source text (ST), but without implying any value judgement. The word *assessment* is used here as a cover term to include all three procedures. The related verbs (*evaluate, criticise, analyse, assess*) and agent nouns (*evaluator*, etc.) are used in the same way. Evaluation is naturally macrotextual, while criticism and analysis may be carried out at any level from the word to the whole text. Naturally, the boundaries between the three procedures may be fuzzy, but they can, and should, be distinguished in principle. There is also a directionality obtaining between them: evaluation presupposes criticism, and criticism analysis. Each may also be a valid procedure in its own right, and each has its own place in the academic training of translators: analysis would, for example, be involved in diagnostic studies of the way students translate with a view to improving their methods; criticism would be the main procedure for giving feedback to students concerning the translations they have produced; and awarding grades or marks to translations (and ultimately translators) is a process of evaluation.

Since in many countries a university training in itself constitutes a professional qualification, a training programme should be capable of evaluating the work of students so as to have predictive value with regard to their professional competence. The methods used for this evaluation should be reliable, realistic, objective and practicable. This last criterion has frequently been forgotten by theoretical approaches to assessment, with the result that the methods proposed have not generally been applied extensively in practice. It is debatable to what extent all four criteria can be satisfactorily met. Although it is future translators rather than their products (translations) that we wish to evaluate, we can only do the former through the latter if the criterion of objectivity is to be preserved (cf. Chesterman, 1997: 137–8). An outsider might expect the methods used by university departments and other accrediting bodies in evaluating translation quality to:

(1) show considerable agreement with one another as to the most suitable procedures employed;
(2) be elucidated in highly explicit terms;
(3) be based on the findings of a solid body of research on the subject.

In fact, the actual situation is very different: methods sometimes vary considerably even between colleagues working in the same department, let alone different universities. Moreover, the methods used are often not based on any scientifically elucidated principles, but follow fairly rough guidelines based, in the best cases, on experience and common sense, in the worst on purely subjective impressions.

Unfortunately, there is as yet no broad body of research providing a basis for suitable evaluation procedures. This is somewhat surprising considering the vast amount of prescriptive translation theory, in which the question of translation quality is constantly implicit, not to mention the wealth of criticisms of actual translations in existence. Notable contributions to the subject have been made by Reiss (1971), House (1981; 1997), Wilss (1982), Sager (1983), Nord (1991), Newmark (1988) and Chesterman (1997), among others. House's book *A Model for Translation Quality Assessment* (1981) has become a classic in the field, but it has not led to significant developments in translation assessment. Indeed, it is perhaps more often cited for its translation-theoretical concepts of overt and covert translation and its distinction between translations and versions than for its suggested assessment procedures.

The earlier pre-functionalist German tradition strove towards an approach that sought to be explicit and scientific, and as a result, despite frequent protestations to the contrary, tended to work on an analytical, atomistic or microtextual level. This, at least, is the impression gained from the actual examples of translation criticism cited in House, Wilss and to some extent even Nord. Similarly, there is a strong emphasis on comparison between the source and target texts as the basis for translation evaluation, to the extent that Koller, for example, states categorically: ' . . . eine Übersetzung nur im Vergleich mit dem Original analysiert und beurteilt werden kann'[1] (Koller, 1979: 206). In order to permit such a comparison to work, House's 1981 model excludes transfers between language pairs representing incompatible cultures, and those in which there is a change of function between the ST and the TT, dismissing them as versions. The effect of this is to omit from the evaluation model a lot of the activity that we would normally take to be a part of translation, and which certainly constitutes much of the daily bread-and-butter work of professional translators. In the approaches of House and Koller, the ST is assumed as the functional standard against which mismatches in the TT are taken as evidence of inadequacy. Yet professional translators frequently handle texts that are far from being functionally perfect, and being responsible professionals and not adhering to the 'garbage in, garbage out' principle (cf. Kussmaul, 1995: 146), they may well produce TTs in which there are indeed mismatches, but mismatches which represent functional improvements.

Both Katharina Reiss (1971) and Christiane Nord (1991) adopt a more functionally-oriented approach. Reiss's model is based on the concept of the text type of the TT, while Nord's model integrates the concept of the skopos into criticism. Her approach consists in creating a TT profile from a combination of the skopos and the ST, against which the adequacy of the TT is then assessed. She also points out that assessment (= evaluation?) is a matter not only of locating and marking errors (which she defines as a deviation from a selected, or rather prescribed, model of action, or a frustration of the recipient's expectations) but also of their grading (1991: 170). She suggests a hierarchy of errors dependent on the text function, with extratextual (pragmatic and cultural) errors generally being given more weight than intratextual (linguistic) ones. A major drawback to her approach is its laboriousness: an assessment of English and German translations of an extract of 105 words from a Spanish novel takes some eighteen pages, i.e. at least nine pages per language pair. While this might be an excellent project for an advanced seminar, it is hardly practicable for the translation evaluator who has a bundle of exams to mark for next week.

Nord (1991: 171) also sketches a possible method of positive evaluation whereby the transfer competence of a student might be stated in the form of a percentage calculated according to the number of adequate solutions to identified problems (which are weighted according to the above-mentioned hierarchies). Similar suggestions for positive evaluation are made by Gouadec (1989: 46–8) and Hatim and Mason (1997: 208–9), among others. While one agrees with Nord that it might be more encouraging for students to learn from their successes than their failures, in practice the system seems awkward to apply; it is often difficult to predict in advance just what will prove difficult and what not, particularly at the level of target language (TL) norms when the translation takes place into a non-mother tongue. And what happens where no problem has been identified, but the translator still makes a mistake? The major problem with these approaches, however, is that what is regarded as an adequate solution is simply the inverse of an inadequate one — indeed one could paraphrase Gouadec's proposal as 'What you don't get wrong, you get right'. As even 'incompetent' translators tend to get far more right than they get wrong, positive evaluation seems to involve an inordinate increase in the workload of the evaluator. I would also maintain that it is counter-intuitive; usually a translation is only noticed by its faults — some of which admittedly may not be apparent or even relevant to the end-user (see below). None of these proposals for positive evaluation is naturally able to specify just what proportion of successful solutions constitutes an adequate translation.

However, the majority of approaches to translation assessment depend heavily on the concept of error. But here, too, the same problem persists: in no case is any suggestion made concerning the amount and gravity of errors that can be tolerated for the total translation to be considered adequate. Some scholars have even hinted at the impossibility of arriving at any objective means of evaluating translations (for example Newmark, 1982: x; Sager, 1983: 121). Indeed, it may well be that it is in principle impossible to specify generally applicable norms of adequacy in view of the wide range of parameters involved in the translation process. However, this is exactly what we are required to estimate in evaluating the competence of students or examination candidates for a qualification as professional translators. National accreditation bodies that hold examinations to ascertain the translation competence of candidates are faced with the same task. Many of these use evaluation methods based on a summation of points deducted for mistakes, with certain kinds of mistakes being more heavily penalised than others, and what appears to be an arbitrarily fixed maximum of minus points for a pass. The evaluation of the exams conducted by the Institute of Linguists in Britain is, however, more holistic in its approach, in that it awards points for various aspects of the whole text, such as comprehension of the ST; accuracy and appropriateness of rendering (lexis and register); cohesion, coherence and organisation; grammar, punctuation, spelling, etc.

The notion of error that pervades these approaches to assessment can be roughly divided into two categories: errors violating the norms of the TL (mistakes in grammar, usage, vocabulary, register, etc.), and errors in representing the ST (for example omissions, mistranslations, unjustified additions). The latter are usually considered more serious than the former. Such a basis for evaluation inevitably requires a detailed comparison between the ST and the TT. Even where the schemes referred to above take other factors than correspondence with the ST into consideration, the examples of analysis that they present mostly start from a comparison of the TT with the ST.

To what extent is such a procedure justified? Certainly, the comparative method of evaluation does not correspond to the way an end-user typically reacts to translation. Even when the monolingual reader, for whom the translation is, one assumes, primarily written, is aware that the text is a translation — and this is not always the case — he[2] will normally judge the translation from the point of view of its communicative effectiveness for its purpose in his language, in other words by the same criteria as an original text. He will not normally have any explicit information about the skopos (of which he himself is, of course, a part), unless there is a translator's commentary or a publisher's statement of intent. If he finds the TT lacking in some respect, he may condemn it and put the fault down to the fact that it is a translation (providing he is aware of the fact), or he may tolerate the deficiencies as being irrelevant to his needs. But lacking the original text and/or the ability to use it, he can normally go no further. If part of the skopos is that the TT render the ST fully and truly (as, for example, with many literary or authoritative texts), he will have to accept in good faith that this has been done. In the rarer case where the end-user is familiar with the language of the ST, he has more options available to him. He may choose to ignore the ST. This would normally be the case if it was not easily available, or if it does not seem necessary to refer to it because the TT is adequate for his purposes. He will normally only refer to the ST to check on, and compensate for, any deficiencies (omissions, obscurities, infelicities, etc.)

that he finds in the TT. He may also be familiar with the ST (for example, if it belongs to the literary canon) and refer to it in order to compare the TT with it when he suspects a mistranslation. Finally, he may just be interested to see how the ST or parts of it have been translated, in which case he becomes a translation analyst. Only in rare cases, however, will the end-user engage in a detailed comparison between the ST and the TT; this might happen when the roles of the translation initiator and the end-user converge — a typical example would be the translation of a contract, which the initiator wishes to verify as an exact rendering of the original document before he signs it. To what extent then should a translation assessor place herself in the position of the end-user? This is a question to which I shall return below.

It is a fact that in both the academic context and particularly in accreditation, the translation tasks that are set in examinations have predominantly been of the kind that require a fairly faithful rendering of the ST . The evaluation of such transfer tasks requires a detailed comparison of the ST and the TT. Since such tasks certainly do not constitute the only type, and maybe not even the majority, of translations that professional translators deal with in real life, the reasons for their overwhelming predominance in translation examinations is worth considering. One reason might be that those who set the papers believe that only such tasks as require a faithful rendering of the ST by the TT are really translations, and that these should be given priority over various kinds of adaptation. The view is analogous to that of linguists who consider that the primary function of language is the informative or referential one, dismissing other functions as secondary. As we have noted above, such a view of translation can be found among translation theorists (House, 1981; Koller, 1979; etc.). However, there may be a more practical reason: ease of evaluation. If the function of a translation is to produce a linguistically correct rendering that is faithful in form and content to the original (as well as conforming to the linguistic norms of the TL), then the evaluation can be reasonably objective and even quantifiable in terms of points deducted for errors of language and equivalence combined with weightings to cover various degrees of gravity of error. It is notoriously more difficult to evaluate, particularly in a way that is quantifiable, the communicative success of a text which is not mainly dependent on linguistic accuracy and equivalence. A variety of schemes have been proposed for doing this — cf. Chesterman (1997: 31) for a discussion of some of them. They are mainly applicable to experimental use and often only test one aspect of communication, for example readability or accuracy. They are often totally unsuitable for practical evaluation — surely I must not wait to see how many end-users of a translation of instructions for connecting an electrical appliance actually electrocute themselves before I decide whether it is functionally adequate!

While several of the scholars mentioned above (e.g. Nord) do take other factors into account in their analyses and criticisms, they do not offer a practical way of evaluating and quantifying the success of such texts. However, if we wish the tasks by which we evaluate and accredit future translators to reflect the reality of the profession, it is patently obvious that we cannot confine ourselves to those kinds of translation tasks that only or predominantly involve content equivalence. Here, the academic world, which has the luxury of continuous assessment (i.e. evaluation) and can thus use a variety of translation tasks, has an advantage over accreditation bodies, which for logistic reasons are usually limited to two or three papers. In order to permit this wider variety of translation tasks, however, it is necessary to evolve practical objective evaluation procedures for the communicative success of translations as well as their transfer and linguistic adequacy.

This raises the question of the position that the assessor of a translation should adopt with regard to the ST. Should she at least initially place herself in the position of the translator? Should she place herself in the shoes of the end-user, which means for most translation assignments feigning ignorance of the ST as well as of the conditions of production of the translation? Or should she adopt the position of the expert judge whose job it is to protect the interests of the end-user and/or translation initiator? The first position, it seems to me, is one that can usefully be used for translation analysis and criticism — and hence as a preliminary step to evaluation, as advocated by Newmark (1988: 186–7), but it should not be the basis of evaluation itself; a translation must eventually be evaluated in its own right (cf. Chesterman 1997: 138), though the conditions of production (availability of time, sources, etc.) are obviously relevant.

The second position, that of the end-user, is one that has the advantage of corresponding with some kind of reality; after all, it is the end-user that the translation is produced for, and if he is satisfied with what he gets, why should anyone else cavil? One problem is that it is very difficult for the assessor to put herself in such a position. She may find it impossible to feign ignorance of the ST, as she has often chosen it herself, or at least has made herself familiar with it beforehand. Nor is it by any means always obvious just what kind of reader the typical end-user is, and even if we can estimate this with some degree of likelihood, his probable satisfaction is even more difficult to determine. He may be quite satisfied with a TT that misrepresents the ST because he is unaware of the fact, but would he be satisfied with it if knew of its shortcomings in this respect? And if he is, should the assessor be?

The third position seems to me to be the correct and, indeed, usually the only feasible one for the translation evaluator or critic (be she a university teacher, an examiner for an accreditation institution or for that matter a critic reviewing a translated work of literature) to adopt. This means that she will use a detailed comparison between the ST and the TT as one basis for her assessment. She will not, however, necessarily assume that the ST is the functional standard by which the TT must be measured. That said, even where a high degree of adaptation is involved in the translation, what Chesterman (1997) calls 'prospective assessment' is not enough; without a comparison between the ST and the TT, it is not possible to estimate the input of the translator in creating the TT. In her evaluation or criticism, the assessor will also take all the circumstances attending the production of the translation into account, including the strategy adopted by the translator, and ultimately she will have to estimate the suitability of the translation as a product for the end-user.

In view of the multiplicity of parameters that may be involved in evaluating a translation, it is hardly surprising that these have generally been reduced to the two broad categories mentioned above. However, I have argued that this artificially limits the range of translation texts that can be selected for evaluation purposes. This then may discriminate adversely against translators who have other (perhaps more original) talents than slavish reproduction. On the other hand, the lack of reliable, objective and practicable criteria for evaluating the communicative success of texts leaves the evaluator in a very difficult position. However, there are many areas of life where people are obliged to give a quantified evaluation of a product or performance. A typical example is the judge who awards points to competitors for their performances in sports like diving or figure skating, where the judge has fairly precise guidelines to use (for example so many triple jumps to be successfully completed). Nearer home, schemes are being evolved for criterion-referenced evaluation of levels of competence in foreign language learning, for example, in the Common Framework proposal of the Council of Cultural Cooperation of the Council of Europe. It should be possible to devise comparable guidelines for the evaluation of translations. Meanwhile, we really have little more to go on than Peter Newmark's statement which stands at the head of this contribution (Newmark, 1988: 192).

Notes

1. '[A] translation can only be analysed and evaluated by comparison with the original (editor's translation).
2. In the interest of equality, I use 'he' for the end-user and 'she' for the assessor.

References

Chesterman, A. (1997) *Memes of Translation*. Amsterdam: John Benjamins.
Common European Framework of Reference for Modern Languages: Learning, Teaching Assessment 1996. Draft 2 of a Framework Proposal. Strasbourg: Council of Europe, Council of Cultural Cooperation.
Gouadec, D. (1989) Comprendre, évaluer, prévenir. *TTR* 2 (2), 35–54.
Hatim, B. and Mason, I. (1997) *The Translator as Communicator*. London: Routledge.
Hewson, L. and Martin, J. (1991) *Redefining Translation. London: Routledge.*
House, J. (1981) *A Model for Translation Quality Assessment*. Tübingen: Gunter Narr Verlag.
House, J. (1997) *Translation Quality Assessment; A Model Revisited*. Tübingen: Gunter Narr Verlag.
Koller, W. (1979) *Einführung in die Übersetzungswissenschaft*. Heidelberg: Quelle & Meyer.
Kussmaul, P. (1995) *Training the Translator*. Amsterdam: John Benjamins.
Newmark, P.P. (1982) *Approaches to Translation*. Oxford: Pergamon Press.
Newmark, P.P. (1988) *A Textbook of Translation*. London: Prentice Hall.
Nord. C. (1991) *Text Analysis in Translation*. Amsterdam: Rodopi.
Reiss, K. (1971) *Möglichkeiten und Grenzen der Übersetzungskritik*. Munich: Hueber.
Sager, J. (1983) Quality and standards — the evaluation of translations. In C. Picken (ed.) *The Translator's Handbook* (pp.121–8). London: ASLIB.
Wilss, W. (1982) *The Science of Translation*. Tübingen: Gunter Narr Verlag.

Part 4 And Beyond

Chapter 17

Electronic Corpora as Tools for Translation[1]

Hans Lindquist

> *Collocations may override even meanings of powerful concepts*
> (Peter Newmark, 1993: 21)

Introduction

With the emergence of computer tools for translators, texts have become increasingly useful as a rich source of lexical data enabling translators not only to identify appropriate collocations but also to interpret lexical items in their pragmatic and linguistic contexts. Computer tools for translators have been around for quite some time. After all, machine translation research started in the late 1940s — so there has been fifty years of often intensive work — but it is only now, with today's computer memory sizes and processing capacity, that it really has become viable. Yet the uses of fully automatic machine translation are still very restricted (Sager, 1993; Arnold et al., 1994; O'Hagan, 1996).

For most purposes, interactive machine translation systems are more useful, especially the ones where users build up their own personal database of source texts (STs) and translations. With a new text to translate, the translator can access earlier work in the same area and check for recurring words, collocations and phrases. One could say that this is a matter of vastly improved bookkeeping and terminology administration. The document databases in the European Commission are used in this way by translators in Luxembourg, for example.

Term banks and electronic dictionaries are similarly becoming increasingly easy to access and use. There are term banks like *Termdok* from Tekniska Nomenklaturcentralen in Sweden, and in the European Union *Eurodicautom* (European Commission), which is constantly being enlarged (although it is still of limited use for translation into or out of the languages of the more recent member countries like Sweden and Finland, since it will take a while before the Swedish and Finnish terms have been entered). Electronic versions of general dictionaries are quickly becoming standard, although it has sometimes been claimed that printed dictionaries are at least as fast to access as electronic ones (and that they are more educational and fun). There is no doubt that paper dictionaries will continue to be used, but as electronic search programs continue to improve it is becoming quite clear that they are superior to the printed ones in several respects. It is possible, for instance, to:

179

- check several different sources at one go with some systems;
- search for a phrase or collocation and get to it directly without having to wade through several columns of sub-entries, perhaps not knowing under which main entry to look;
- make full text searches and look for any particular word used in any example sentence or even in the definitions in the dictionary;
- search on domain labels and be given all the words with, for example, the labels *forestry* or *philately*;
- subscribe to fairly frequent inexpensive updates.

For further ideas about possible future features of electronic dictionaries, cf. Svartvik (forthcoming), and for an interesting discussion and many useful references in relation to dictionaries and the lexicon, cf. Rogers (1996). The question whether the dictionary should be stored on a CD-ROM disc or be available on-line from the publisher's server is a matter of speed and reliability. CD-ROMs are fast and reliable; on-line access can be slow and erratic: sometimes the host server or the user's local network may be down. On the other hand, on-line dictionaries can be updated on a monthly, weekly or even daily or hourly basis. Also, it would be quite possible to devise a system whereby the user pays for each search, rather than having to invest initially in a number of expensive CD-ROM discs.

Corpus Linguistics

The use of electronic corpora for linguistic research started in the 1960s and has boomed in the 1980s and 1990s (cf. McEnery and Wilson, 1996 for the development of corpus linguistics and a survey of the field today). The early corpora, like the Brown corpus and the Lancaster–Oslo/Bergen Corpus (LOB), were relatively small (1 million words). This was sufficient for the study of common syntactic patterns, function words and many other frequently recurring phenomena in language, but not really for the study of the frequency of lexical words, collocations and the like. When corpora started reaching a size of tens or hundreds of millions of words, however, they became very useful for dictionary makers. It seems that British publishers were the quickest to latch on to this: the *Collins COBUILD English Dictionary* was the first and most typical example of a dictionary based on an electronic corpus (rather than excerpts on slips of paper), and Longman, Cambridge University Press and others have followed suit. Of course, electronic corpora are also becoming increasingly important for the production of grammars (examples are the *Collins COBUILD English Grammar* (1990) and the entirely corpus-based Mindt (1995).

A recent development in corpus linguistics which promises to be even more interesting for translators is the work on bi- or multilingual corpora. The idea here is to compile electronic corpora of texts in two or more languages, so that they consist either of STs and their translations, or STs belonging to the same genre and dealing with similar topics, but in different languages. Unfortunately there is some confusion about terminology. Since the term parallel text has long been used in translation studies to designate source language (SL) texts in different languages about similar topics (cf. for instance Neubert, 1986), the most convenient solution would be to call corpora of such texts *parallel corpora*, and corpora containing SL texts and their target language (TL) texts *translation corpora*. However, some of the research groups working on such translation corpora in fact call them *parallel corpora* (cf. Johansson and Ebeling, 1996). The neutral but rather infelicitous term *comparable corpora* has been proposed by Baker (1992).

Apart from supplying the texts with part-of-speech (word class) tagging, phrase tagging and, ideally, full syntactic tagging, the compilers of translation corpora have to devise a way to align them. Since bilingual corpora are intended to be sources for the comparison of expressions between languages, it is necessary to be able to go from one sentence (or word, or utterance) in one language to its translation (or source) in another language. This is not a trivial problem, as it is well known that sentence boundaries rarely occur in the same place throughout an SL text (ST) and a TL text (TT), and there rarely is a one-to-one relationship between items in the ST and the TT, but rather one-to-many or many-to-one. Advanced alignment programs have been developed, however, which will tag the texts in a way that makes them easy for a researcher or translator to use (cf. Johansson et al., 1996).

Some electronic corpora compiled for other purposes can be used by translators as well. Table 17.1 lists some of the best-known corpora of present-day English which have primarily been compiled to be used in linguistic research. It also includes newspaper CD-ROMs and the WorldWideWeb. These latter types of electronic information sources can also be highly useful for translators. For the calculations behind the astronomical figure for the English language part of the WorldWideWeb (as of summer 1996), cf. Bergh et al. (1998). For most lexical searches of the kind translators are likely to carry out, a corpus size of at least 20 million words is normally necessary.

Table 17.1 Selected electronic English language corpora

Name	Year of material	Kind of material	Size	Availability
Brown	1961	Written	1M	CD-ROM
LOB	1961	Written	1 M	CD-ROM
London-Lund	1960s–1980s	Spoken	0.5M	CD-ROM
CobuildDirect	1980s–1990s	Written & spoken	50M	On-line
British National Corpus	Mainly 1990s	Written & spoken	100M	CD-ROM. Requires 4 GB hard disk and preferably a workstation. Also becoming partially available on-line.
ICE corpora	1990s	Written & spoken	1 M each	Work in progress
Newspapers	Late 1980s and onwards	Written	15–40 M each year	CD-ROM
The World WideWeb	1990s	Written	8 billion	On-line

Using Newspaper Corpora for Translation Purposes

Newspaper CDs usually contain one complete year of the newspaper in question, often totalling as much 30 or 40 million words. One obvious drawback is that a search provides only the kind of language that is found in newspapers, which might differ from the kind of text on which a translator is working. On the other hand, newspapers, in their various sections, do in fact deal with almost all conceivable topics ranging in styles from the chatty on the family pages to the rather formal or technical in editorials and science columns. Bearing these limitations in mind, newspapers can be a rich source of data for translators. For many useful tips on how to use newspapers for teaching and research, cf. Minugh (1997, 1998).

The following example will show how a translator can benefit from searches on a newspaper CD-ROM when faced with the task of translating into English a Swedish information brochure for potential sufferers of osteoporosis. The Swedish term for the disease used in the brochure is *benskörhet*, literally 'bone-brittleness' (Swedish traditionally uses Germanic words for illnesses in general and saves the Latinate terms for professional use, although there are now some signs of change in this area). Looking up the word in the biggest Swedish-English dictionary, *Norstedts Comprehensive Swedish-English Dictionary* (1993), one finds the following gloss: *brittleness of the bones*. The smaller *Svensk-engelsk ordbok* (1992) gives *brittle-bone disease*, vet *osteoporosis* (the label 'vet' stands for *vetenskapligt språkbruk*, meaning 'scientific usage'). The question is, which term to use in a popular text in English?

A search for the two words *brittle* and *bone* in *The Times* CD-ROM for 1991 resulted in a fairly short list of articles, and after browsing through these for articles which seemed to be promising the following were selected:

(A) Anthea Gerrie, They're no longer women of a certain age. *Sunday Times* 7 July 1991; Menopause
(B) Liz Gill, The third age finds its second wind. *The Times* 18 July 1991; Health
(C) Victoria Glendinning, Change of life? Life of changes. *The Times* 12 October 1991; Books

It turns out that *brittle bone disease* is used in article (B) and *osteoporosis* in (B) and (C), while neither of the terms occurs in (A). Even if this does not provide a definitive answer, it does show that it is acceptable to use the Latinate term in non-technical contexts. It also shows that the more transparent term *brittle bone disease* can be used. But a number of other English terms needed for this particular translation also offer themselves in these three articles, without much research work from the translator, as indicated by Table 17.2.

Some of these can obviously be found in general bilingual dictionaries, and others may be found in monolingual medical dictionaries, but the great advantage of this use of parallel texts is that the translator can see the words and collocations in actual use in the appropriate type of text. In this way, the finished translation of the osteoporosis brochure is likely to sound more natural than it would have done otherwise. As Peter Newmark has noted, for the translator 'the collocation is the most important contextual factor'(1988: 212).

Table 17.2 Related words and phrases found in the *New York Times*

Swedish source text	Term(s) used in the articles
bruten underarm	wrist fracture (B)
lårbensfraktur	hip fracture (B)
bentäthet	bone density (A,B)
bentäthetsmätning	bone density screening (B)
benförluster	loss of bone density (A)
blodvallningar	hot flushes (B)
kalciumförluster	calcium loss (B)
övergångsålder	menopause (C), (female) climacteric(C)

Similarly, when translating a Swedish text dealing with pain, a quick trawl in *The Times* CD-ROM 1991 resulted in the following three useful articles:

(1) Jeremy Laurance, Migraine is a real pain, *The Times* 24 September 1991; Life and Times

(2) Victoria McKee, Whose time of the month?, *The Times* 7 June 1991; Psychosomatic illnesses; Life and Times

(3) Thomson Prentice, Pains in the neck can destroy a night of passion, *The Times* 26 July 1991

Among the terms and phrases in these three articles that might come in handy for the translator of an article on headache were the following:

> self-induced
> pulsating
> visual aura
> pain threshold
> migraine sufferer
> hormone replacement therapy (HRT)
> warning system, warning bells ring
> pain relief clinics
> mechanisms of pain
> total relief
> partial relief
> pain management
> palliative care
> non-prescription pain killers
> over-the-counter analgesics
> beta-blocker drug

Again, some of these look quite natural and unremarkable, but the point is that the translator in front of the word processor often hesitates, debating whether a seemingly natural and 'direct' translation is the one really used in the TL. The parallel text found in the newspaper corpus gives the answer, at the touch of a button (and a browse through a few interesting articles). In passing, the following interesting piece of sociological information was also found: 'every

Table 17.3 The 50-million-word CobuildDirect corpus

Subcorpus	Variety	Contents	Size
oznews	Australian	Newspapers	5M
ukephem	British	Ephemera (brochures, letters, etc.)	3M
ukmags	British	Popular magazines	5M
ukspok	British	Informal speech	10M
usephem	American	Ephemera	1M
bbc	British	BBC World Service radio	1M
npr	American	US National Public Radio	3M
ukbooks	British	Books (miscellaneous)	5M
usbooks	American	Books (miscellaneous)	5M
times	British	*The Times* newspaper	5M
today	British	*Today* newspaper	5M
Total size			50 M

headache in Hampstead is a migraine and every migraine in Lewisham is a headache'.

Using the CobuildDirect Corpus for Translation Purposes

The CobuildDirect corpus can be accessed direct on-line (for a fee) from any computer that is connected to the Internet and has a Telnet and an ftp program. It consists of a subset of the Bank of English (Birmingham) corpus, which at present consists of more than 300 million words, and is divided into subcorpora as shown in Table 17.3.

Returning to our example from the osteoporosis brochure, let us first search for the headword itself. The result is given in Table 17.4.

It turns out that *osteoporosis* occurs in all the subcorpora. The frequency varies somewhat, but since the figures are so low this could be due to chance — a single article or conversation or, indeed, brochure in one of the subcorpora could easily add another five or ten tokens and thus skew the results. For the translator, it is

Table 17.4 The frequency of *osteoporosis* in CobuildDirect

Subcorpus	f	Relative frequency
US ephemera	6	4.9/million
Australian newspapers	21	3.9/million
UK books	20	3.7/million
Today newspaper	19	3.6/million
BBC World Service radio	7	2.7/million
The Times newspaper	14	2.4/million
US National Public Radio	7	2.2/million
UK ephemera	6	1.9/million
US books	9	1.6/million
UK popular magazines	7	1.4/million
UK informal speech	5	0.5/million
Total (N)	121	2.4/million

be a protective factor against	osteoporosis,	as long as it is kept in
form, which may protect against	osteoporosis	and heart disease as well as
plump helps protect against	osteoporosis,	so it's quite important for
offer some protection against	osteoporosis,	or 'thinning of the bones',
of years ago to protect against	osteoporosis.	\<h> Peak of fitness at a
do sometimes develop	osteoporosis	in old age) and women should
they are more likely to develop	osteoporosis	# than those who are above
were just as likely to develop	osteoporosis.	\<p> Those who tended to
women who are developing	osteoporosis,	and they found that dairy
may be at risk of developing	osteoporosis	is that after the menopause,
in the risk of developing	osteoporosis	a weakening of the bones
at all against developing	osteoporosis.	These effects are not the
shown any signs of developing	osteoporosis,'	said Priscilla.
crumbling and she was developing	osteoporosis.	\<p> She is now about to

Figure 17.1 Collocations with *osteoporosis; protection* and *developing*

more interesting to peruse the actual examples. The program supplies the user with a concordance, which can be read on screen in one- or five-line contexts or saved to disk in the same formats. Even from the short one-line contexts, interesting information can be gathered. The following is a selection of some of the 121 concordance lines for *osteoporosis*, which give further information on its collocations and use in English.

First, it becomes clear that *protection* against *osteoporosis* is a must if you don't want to *develop* it. This is evidenced by Figure 17.1.

Sorting the concordance according to the word before the key word and looking for *and* in that position, we get the names of diseases which are mentioned in the same breath as *osteoporosis*: *heart disease* (f = 4), *arthritis* (f = 2), *stress fractures, cardiovascular disease, menopause, amenorrhoea, strokes* (see Figure 17.2).

women with heart # disease and	osteoporosis	# if cells in the artery of
of stress fractures and	osteoporosis	# eating disorders and
of cardiovascular disease and	osteoporosis.	\<p> Not all women require
In the risk of heart disease and	osteoporosis	is required. \<p> There are #
issues such as the menopause and	osteoporosis	— all in all — the wellbeing
protect against heart disease and	osteoporosis).	\< p \> High alcohol intake. \<
contribute. Amenorrhoea and	osteoporosis	Significant weight loss
became a prison as arthritis and	osteoporosis	further restricted her
spite of crippling arthritis and	osteoporosis	that slowly crushed her
of heart disease, strokes and #	osteoporosis	for post-menopausal women.

Figure 17.2 Collocations with *osteoporosis; and*

and excessive bone loss, known as	osteoporosis,	is particularly common in w
This condition, known as	osteoporosis,	is commonly associated with
the thinning out of bone called	osteoporosis	that occurs in many women
in treating bone loss disease,	osteoporosis.	In a carefully controlled
and the bone-thinning disease,	osteoporosis?	<p> WERTHEIMER: No, I
suffered from the bone disease,	osteoporosis,	and you have always # been
the # bone thinning disease	osteoporosis,	for example in some men
the bone-thinning # disease,	osteoporosis.	But fears that it could
the brittle bone disease #	osteoporosis;	keeps joints mobile and
for the # bone-thinning disease	osteoporosis,	which can be used on women
on the brittle bone disease	osteoporosis	when she discovered she was

Figure 17.3 Collocations with *osteoporosis; known as* etc.

In Figure 17.3 several examples seem to suggest that the Latinate term needs explaining.

Note also the alternative names here: *bone loss, bone loss disease, thinning out of bone, bone-thinning disease* (with or without hyphen) and *brittle bone disease*. To be certain, we can search for these terms as well. Their frequencies, together with that of *brittleness of the bones* (given by one of the dictionaries) are given in Table 17.5.

It seems that no term can compete with *osteoporosis*. Note that the translation suggested by one of the dictionaries, *brittleness of the bones*, scored zero. If we take a closer look at some of these terms, however, further useful collocations can be found.

In Figure 17.4, collocations like *brittle bone alert* and *brittle bone condition* might come in handy for the translator. Figure 17.5 gives the concordance for *bone density*, another important term in this field.

Useful phrases here might be *low bone density* (f = 2), *maintain(ing) bone density* (f = 2), *average bone density* (f = 1), *increased bone density* (f = 2), *loss of bone density, bone density test* (f = 2). Figure 17.6 then gives the concordance for *bone mass*, yet another term in this semantic field.

This gives phrases like *lay down new bone mass, increase in bone mass, deterioration of bone mass, lose bone mass*.

Table 17.5 The frequency of alternatives to osteoporosis in CobuildDirect

	f	Relative frequency
bone loss	6	0.12/million
bone loss disease	2	0.04/million
thinning out of bone	1	0.01/million
bone-thinning disease	4	0.04/million
brittle bone disease	3	0.06/million
brittleness of the bones	0	0

osteoporosis, the crippling	brittle-bone	disease that is prevalent
protects the elderly against the	brittle bone	disease #osteoporosis; keeps
and a poor disciplinary record. < h >	Brittle bone	alert #</h> <p> HUNDREDS of
women may be suffering from a	brittle bone	# condition which will leave
was making a programme on the	brittle bone	disease osteoporosis when
are now affected by blindness,	brittle bones,	nerve problems and
loss of bony tissue, resulting in	brittle bones	that are liable to fracture
Retarded bone growth in youth, or	brittle bones	in old age; over-excitable
Tories. She threw infected teeth,	brittle bones	and tragic victims being #
insomnia, osteoporosis	(brittle bones),	irregular heartbeat #

Figure 17.4 Collocations with *brittle bone*

It is clear from these examples that an electronic corpus and a concordance program can be helpful for the translator who is looking for natural TL expressions, phrases and collocations.

Using the WorldWideWeb for Translation

The corpora dealt with so far are not generally available without considerable cost. There is, however, one other source: the WorldWideWeb. Using one of the many available search engines, enormous amounts of information can be collected extremely fast. In the following examples, the browser Netscape and the search engine AltaVista were used. First, back to brittle bones. It is a common

that # they themselves have low	bone density.	<p> This is a perfectly
the difference in their	bone density	# <p> Osteoporosis is a major
have an effect on maintaining	bone density,	and osteoporosis is a loss of
those with below average	bone density	are # more anxious about it
K.F. 1989 # Determinants of	bone density	in normal women: risk factors
drinking include # increased	bone density	in the old and the inhibition
I lost 7 percent of my	bone density.	Now, that's scary.I mean,
researchers have measured the	bone density	of post-menopausal women who
seems to cause an increased	bone density,	perhaps helping to prevent
and osteoporosis is a loss of	bone density,	resulting in easily-fractured
whether this will result in	bone density	returning to normal, however,
exercises < f > helps maintain	bone density.	Since we may start to lose a
Many women will want to have a	bone density	test to assess their risk. <p>
I went to him, I had taken a	bone-density	test, which I think all
thought that to have low	bone # density	was especially serious and
accumulated # muscle mass and	bone density	which now stand them # in good

Figure 17.5 Collocations with *bone density*

Osteoporosis, a condition where	bone mass	is # greatly reduced, can
continue to lay down new	bone mass	throughout their 30s. <p>
Exercise <p> Learn how diet affects	bone mass	and how you can stay in
a small but significant increase in	bone mass.	Editronate has previously
well as preventing a deterioration of	bone mass	osteoporosis) which
the menopause that you lose most	bone mass.	<p> <h> I'll never be a

Figure 17.6 Collocations with *bone mass*

experience that the Web has given the phrase *embarras de richesses* a new meaning. A search for *osteoporosis* gave as many as 9,000 matches. A quick glance through the first hits, ten at a time, showed that there were many technical medical papers and reports, but also less specialised sites like *Women's Wisdom* and *Resources Catalogue for Secondary School Teachers* which offers 'Osteoporosis — Who Cares?' A beautifully produced video that talks to teenagers in their own language . . .'. In fact, quite a lot of information can be gleaned from the lists of hits, without going to the actual sites. For instance, from the list of the first ten (out of 10,000) matches for *brittle bone*, we learn that there is a site called *Osteoporosis* where the text begins: 'Osteoporosis. Known as the brittle bone disease, osteoporosis weakens bones in one out of four women over the age of 50. The loss of bone mass makes women more . . .' Here the two-line excerpt ends, but we have already learned a few things, for example that there is a term *loss of bone mass* which might be a closer translation of Swedish *benförlust* ('bone loss') than *loss of bone density* which we found in *The Times*. Finally, among the first ten out of 100,000 matches for *bone density* there is a site called *Bone Density Measurement*, a term which certainly seems to be another good candidate for the translation of the Swedish *bentäthetsmätning* ('bone-density-measuring'), together with *bone density screening* which was also found in *The Times*.

Conclusion

Although machine translation has caught the fancy of many people over the years, perhaps more outside the linguistic professions than inside, it may in the end be other electronic tools that turn out to be of the greatest practical use for translators. In addition to interactive translators' work stations, these include linguistic corpora, newspaper CD-ROMs and the WorldWideWeb.

Notes

1. I would like to thank Staffan Klintborg and Jan Svartvik for helpful comments on an earlier version of this chapter.

References

Anderman, G. and Rogers, M. (eds) (1996) *Words, Words, Words: The Translator and the Language Learner*. Clevedon: Multilingual Matters.

Arnold, D., Balkan, L., Humphreys, R.L., Meijer, S. and Sadler, L. (1994) *Machine Translation: An Introductory Guide*. Oxford: NCC Blackwell.

Baker, M. (1992) *In Other Words*. London: Rcutledge.

Bergh, G., Seppänen, A. and Trotta, J. (1998) Language corpora and the Internet: A joint linguistic resource. In A. Renouf (ed.) *Explorations in Corpus Linguistics*. Amsterdam: Rodopi.

Collins COBUILD English Dictionary (1995) London: Harper Collins. 2nd edition.

Collins COBUILD English Grammar (1990) London: Collins.

Johansson, S. and Ebeling, J. (1996) Exploring the English-Norwegian parallel corpus. In C.E. Percy, C.F. Meyer and I. Lancashire (eds) *Synchronic Corpus Linguistics*. Amsterdam & Atlanta: Rodopi.

Johansson, S., Ebeling, J. and Hofland, K. (1996) Coding and aligning the English-Norwegian parallel corpus. In K. Aijmer, B. Altenberg and M. Johansson (eds) *Languages in Contrast*. Lund: Lund University Press.

McEnery, T. and Wilson, A. (1996) *Corpus Linguistics*. Edinburgh: Edinburgh University Press.

Mindt, D. (1995) *An Empirical Grammar of the English Verb*. Berlin: Cornelsen.

Minugh, D. (1997) Using newspaper CDs in research and teaching. In G. Bjørhode and G. Rogne (eds) *Proceedings from the Sixth Nordic Conference for English Studies* (Tromsö, May 25–28, 1995), 2 vols.

Minugh, D. (1998) All the language that's fit to print: Using British and American newspaper CD-ROMs as corpora. In A. Wichman, S. Fligelstone, T. McEnery and J. Knowles (eds) *Corpora and Language Teaching* (Proceedings of the TALC94 Conference, Lancaster, April 1994). London: Longman.

Neubert, A. (1986) On the interface between translation theory and translation practice. In L. Wollin and H. Lindquist (eds) *Translation Studies in Scandinavia*. Lund: Lund University Press.

Newmark, P.P. (1988) *A Textbook of Translation*. New York: Prentice Hall.

Newmark, P.P. (1993) *Paragraphs on Translation*. Clevedon: Multilingual Matters.

Norstedts Comprehensive Swedish-English Dictionary (1993) Stockholm: Norstedts. 2nd edition.

O'Hagan, M. (1996) *The Coming Industry of Teletranslation*. Clevedon: Multilingual Matters.

Rogers, M. (1996) Beyond the dictionary: The translator, the L2 learner and the computer. In G. Anderman and M. Rogers (eds).

Sager, J. (1993) *Language Engineering and Translation*. Amsterdam: John Benjamins.

Svartvik, J. (forthcoming). Corpora and dictionaries. *Proceedings from a Symposium at Institut für Anglistik und Amerikanistik*. Universitet Erlangen Nürnberg. Lexicographica, Series maior. Tübingen: Max Niemeyer.

Svensk-engelsk ordbok (1992) Stockholm: Natur och Kultur.

Chapter 18

The Writing on the Screen. Subtitling: A Case Study from Norwegian Broadcasting (NRK), Oslo[1]

Sylfest Lomheim

> *There is no such thing as a law of translation, since laws admit of no exceptions. There can be and are various theories of translation, but these only apply to certain types of text, and all are at various points between the continuum of transmitter and receiver emphasis.*
>
> (Peter Newmark, 1981: 113)

Introduction

Subtitling is an essential part of everyday communication in Scandinavia. Since it is rare for non-Scandinavian programmes to be dubbed, watching a programme on television or at the cinema involves watching the subtitles as well. Given that most people watch programmes on television several times a week, clearly subtitles are some of the most widely read texts in the Scandinavian language community. Still, little analysis or research has been undertaken in this field. The lack of knowledge about the writing on the screen was my reason for carrying out the study presented here.

So what is subtitling? Most people would say it is a written translation of the foreign dialogue in a programme — which is true, but inaccurate. If we are to arrive at a more systematic definition, we must describe subtitling as a linguistic phenomenon encompassing three basic perspectives:

- the relationship between the spoken and the written language;
- the relationship between the foreign language and the target language (TL);
- the relationship between complete and partial translation.

The aim of this study is to chart the procedures involved in subtitling. How does the subtitler handle formulation and presentation? On the basis of this, I aim to arrive at both a terminology and a model that can be used in the analysis of subtitling.

My approach is limited inasmuch as I have looked at subtitling only from the point of view of the subtitler — the production aspect. Audience perception of the texts, how difficult or easy they are to read, how satisfactory they are for the viewer — in other words, the reception aspect — is a fundamental and wide-ranging subject for another study.

The material for the study was three programmes screened by Norwegian Broadcasting (NRK) in 1993: *Maigret chez les Flamands, Allo! Allo!* (one episode) and *Golden Years* (one episode) (henceforth, M, A and G respectively). I chose three very different programmes on the assumption that they might produce different approaches to subtitling. In the *Maigret* programme, despite its detective genre, the emphasis is on the depiction of milieu and characters. The tone is literary and contemplative. *Allo! Allo!* is set during the Second World War and is well known for its burlesque humour, poking fun at relations between the Germans, the French and the British. The humour is based largely on a constant stream of verbal jokes and situation comedy. *Golden Years* is an American series consisting of plenty of action, dramatic developments, and a science-fiction storyline about a caretaker who unwittingly consumes a top-secret substance that makes him grow younger — in short, sharp exchanges spoken out of the corners of a mouth full of chewing gum.

Reduction: Shrinkage between Original Dialogue and Subtitles

Given that reduction is such a characteristic feature of subtitling as a translation process, an objective way of measuring it is needed. A simple but not entirely satisfactory means of doing so is by counting the words in the dialogue and comparing this figure with the number of words in the subtitles. However, while the lexical structure of English, French and Norwegian differs — for instance, *the man* is two words, *l'homme* contains a contraction, and *mannen* is one word — the word-count approach has been used in this study because:

- There is no other straightforward means of comparison;
- The margin of inaccuracy due to different lexical structures seems to even itself out in longer texts.

It therefore seems reasonable to assume that such figures provide a useful and reliable indication of the overall extent of reduction. The figures are presented in Table 18.1.

According to these figures, the action-based programme (*Golden Years*) shows the greatest reduction. The two others, although completely different types of programme, display similar percentage reductions. However, it is true of all three programmes that the percentage reduction is clear enough to indicate that a significant reduction takes place during the transfer from dialogue to subtitles, and that the extent of this reduction varies between programmes.

Table 18.1 Comparison of original word counts and subtitle word counts

	Word count for original dialogue	Word count for subtitles	Subtitles as % of dialogue
Maigret	6,030	4,728	78%
Golden Years	3,716	2,235	60%
Allo! Allo!	2,675	2,059	77%

Table 18.2 Distribution of one- and two-line subtitles

	One-line subtitles	Two-line subtitles	One-line subtitles as % of total
Maigret	98	488	17% (98/586)
Golden Years	128	210	38% (128/338)
Allo! Allo!	101	185	35% (101/286)

Visual and Quantitative Aspects of Subtitling

As TV film viewers know, subtitles consist of one or two lines of text at the bottom of the screen. Each line accommodates 30–3 characters including spaces and punctuation. Part of the subtitler's job is to decide, where possible, whether to present the text in one or two lines, and where to divide the text in the case of two-liners.

One-liners and two-liners

Table 18.2 shows the distribution of one- and two-liners in the chosen programmes.

In general, one-line subtitles are easier for the viewer to follow than two-liners. However, we should be wary of concluding that one-liners are always easier to understand than two-liners. If one-liners contain greatly condensed information, coupled with a high degree of implied information, it is quite conceivable that they may be more difficult to interpret than two-liners. With this reservation in mind, we can say as a general rule that when there is a high percentage of two-liners, as in M, the viewer will have more to read.

This is a logical consequence of the fact that the subtitles in M are more crucial to conveying the content than those in G or A. Taken together with the fact that M also has the highest percentage reproduction of dialogue as subtitles (78%, see Table 18.1), this means that, at this stage of the analysis, we can describe M as the most 'literary' of the three programmes — literary in the sense that, in this programme, the subtitles demand more time and attention from the viewer than in the other two.

Subtitle layout

The distribution of the titles between the first and second lines has implications for the viewer's perception of the picture. In two-line subtitles, the shortest possible first line is the optimal solution from the visual perspective.

It is the received wisdom among NRK subtitlers that a short first line and full second line is a better arrangement than two lines of equal length. The worst arrangement is said to be a full first line and shorter second line. In Scandinavia this approach has been preferred by NRK and DR (Danish Broadcasting). Previously a full first line and shorter second line was considered entirely acceptable by SR (Swedish Broadcasting) subtitlers, but this approach now seems to have been reviewed.

Why do subtitlers hold this view? There are two main arguments. The first is purely visual — consideration of the information contained in the picture. In

Table 18.3 Distribution of two-line subtitles between first and second line

	Two-line subtitles	Two-liners with shorter first line	% two-liners with shorter first line
Maigret	488	181	37%
Golden Years	210	69	33%
Allo! Allo!	185	86	46%

most cases a short first line will obscure less of the action in the picture than a full first line. We can call this the cinematic argument. The second argument is that the viewer's eye takes less time to read subtitles with a short first line and full second line than those with a full first line and shorter second line. If the first line is short, the eye has a shorter distance to travel when it moves on to the second line. In addition, this arrangement makes it easier for the viewer, under time pressure, to understand longer sections of text at a glance. We can call this the readability argument.

Table 18.3 shows the distributions for the three programmes.

The remaining two-liners have either two lines of equal length or a shorter second line. Table 18.3 shows that, in all three programmes, most of the two-liners have either two lines of equal length or the first line longer than the second. There is nothing to suggest that the three subtitlers concerned were unacquainted with the above principle concerning the layout of two-liners, yet in practice their approach means that most two-liners do not conform to the received wisdom. Why? It is difficult to find an explanation other than that there were considerations weighing more heavily than those of visual aesthetics (cinematics) and readability.

In many cases the subtitler simply has no choice, for example when a two-liner comprises an exchange between two speakers, one on each line, as below (the Norwegian subtitle is shown on the left with an English gloss on the right; 'M3' refers to the third subtitle in *Maigret*):

M3
Er Joseph hjemme   [*Is Joseph at home?*
Nei.   *No*]

More interesting are cases where a two-liner contains the words of only one speaker and where the subtitler has space to spare. What then are the priorities? As an example we can look at subtitle M26, where the daughter of the house says to Maigret, 'Mor og jeg syns det er best at De bor på hotellet' [*Mother and I think it is best if you stay at the hotel*]. Including word spaces, this subtitle consists of 49 characters. The subtitler has space for about 65 characters, so there is plenty of excess capacity here. Three options are available — full first line, two lines of similar length, or full second line:

M26
Mor og jeg syns det er best at   [*Mother and I think it is best if*
De bor på hotellet.   *you stay at the hotel*]

Mor og jeg syns det er	[*Mother and I think it is*
best at De bor på hotellet.	*best if you stay at the hotel*]

Mor og jeg syns	[*Mother and I think*
det er best at De bor på hotellet.	*it is best if you stay at the hotel*]

M's subtitler chose the last option, in line with both cinematic and readability considerations. We can also see that, in purely linguistic terms, the break occurs at a structural division between a main clause and a subordinate clause.

However, the short first-line principle is not always followed. For example, subtitle M76, 'Be broren Deres komme bort på hotellet i kveld' [*Ask your brother to come over to the hotel this evening*], could have followed this principle:

M76

Be broren Deres	[*Ask your brother*
komme bort på hotellet i kveld.	*to come over to the hotel this evening*]

but the subtitler chose a different option:

Be broren Deres komme	[*Ask your brother to come*
bort på hotellet i kveld.	*over to the hotel this evening*]

We have to assume that the subtitler made his decision rapidly and spontaneously, but this is not to say that his choice was entirely arbitrary. In this case it is reasonable to suppose that coherence assumes a greater importance than a short first line in determining line divisions. The following example also demonstrates that sentence structure can be a more important factor than keeping a short first line (a division after 'God dag.' would lead to an overlong second line):

M44

God dag. Anna har fortalt	[*Good afternoon. Anna said*
at De vil hjelpe oss	*you would help us*]

Elsewhere, however, the subtitler retains a short first line by breaking the sentence in the middle of a phrase:

M97

Er De glad	[*Are you fond*
i kusinen Deres fortsatt?	*of your cousin still?*]

In fact, a short first line could be retained either by keeping the adjective and its extension together:

Er De	[*Are you*
glad i kusinen Deres fortsatt?	*fond of your cousin still?*]

or, by retaining the preposition 'i' [*of*] in the first line:

Er De glad i	[*Are you fond of*
kusinen Deres fortsatt?	*your cousin still?*]

The following example also illustrates a break in the middle of a phrase, since the noun phrase 'broren min' [*my brother*] has been split:

M59

Marguerite er forlovet med broren	*[Marguerite is engaged to my*
min. Det er mors store sorg.	*brother. Mother is very upset]*

However, in this case there was no alternative, since the text requires all the space available on both lines.

It seems therefore that subtitlers tend to choose a short first line only when this clearly does not conflict with other criteria, as the following examples confirm. In the subtitle 'Jeg kommer til Dem i ettermiddag som jeg sa i går' [*I'll come and see you this afternoon as I said yesterday*] a natural break can be made after either 'Dem' [*you*] or 'ettermiddag' [*afternoon*]. In this case the subtitler chose the option with the shorter first line:

M493

Jeg kommer til Dem	*[I'll come and see you*
i ettermiddag som jeg sa i går	*this afternoon as I said yesterday]*

G's subtitler, too, opts for a short first line when it is natural to do so:

G82

Tørk det	*[Don't wipe it*
i hvert fall ikke av på buksa	*on your trousers whatever you do]*

In the next example, there would have been room for both 'du' [*you*] and 'ikke' [*not*] on the second line, but the subtitler has chosen instead to follow the natural syntactic break between clauses:

G107

Enkelte menn presser du ikke	*[You don't threaten individual men*
hvis du har livet kjært.	*if you value your life]*

A's subtitler obviously adopted the same approach to two-liners. Syntactic coherence is a more important factor than the desire to keep the first line as short as possible, for example:

A64

Da står vi alle i det du veit	*[We're all standing in you-know-what*
opp til hit. Nei, hit.	*up to here. No, here]*

and:

A251

Eg trudde du hadde gifta deg	*[I thought you'd got married*
med madame Edith.	*to Madame Edith]*

A short first line is chosen only when it is also natural from a syntactic viewpoint, for example:

A256

Ein foreldrelaus	*[An orphan*
som vi fann utanfor døra	*we found outside the door]*

and:

A245
Eg høyrde   [*I heard*
at René snakka med han.   *that René had spoken to him*]

As a rule we find line breaks that defy syntax only where this is unavoidable —
in other words, in full two-liners:

A26
Dette er eit lite kart. Det tek   [*This is a small map. It'll take*
dagevis før dei kjem til Nouvion.   *days for them to reach Nouvion*]

Exposure time

The three programmes display clear differences as regards subtitle exposure
time. This is shown in Table 18.4.

The different distributions of subtitles across exposure times indicate that
reading times and rhythms differ greatly for each programme. Programme A
contains the fastest subtitles, with nearly one in ten on screen for less than two
seconds, and over 60 per cent (176/286) on screen for less than four seconds. The
subtitling of M shows an opposite trend. No subtitles are displayed for less than
two seconds, and only about one- quarter (153/586) for less than four seconds.
In fact, nearly three-quarters of M's subtitles are displayed for longer than four
seconds (433/586), and nearly 40 per cent for five seconds or more (224/586).
The corresponding figure for A for subtitles of over five seconds is only about
16 per cent (46/286). The subtitling of G falls into an intermediate category
between M and A, but on the whole the profile is closer to that of A. A little under
50 per cent of the subtitles (168/ 338) are displayed for less than four seconds,
and about 30 per cent (101/ 335) are on screen for five seconds or more.

A subtitle's exposure time is, of course, related to the number of words it
contains; long subtitles should be displayed for longer than short ones, and
two-liners for longer than one-liners. The rule of thumb for the relationship
between length and exposure is:

10 letters   2 seconds
30 letters   3 seconds
60 letters   6 seconds

However, if we look at the individual subtitled texts, we soon see that there is

Table 18.4 Number of subtitles shown according to exposure times and shown
as percentage of total number of subtitles (highest percentage for each
programme shaded)

	Total number of subtitles	<2 secs.	2–3 secs.	3–4 secs.	4–5 secs.	5–6 secs.	>6 secs.
Maigret	586	0 (0%)	27 (4.6%)	126 (21.5%)	209 (35.7%)	130 (22.2%)	94 (16.0%)
Golden Years	338	3 (0.9%)	66 (19.5%)	99 (29.3%)	69 (20.4%)	57 (16.9%)	44 (13.0%)
Allo! Allo!	286	25 (8.7%)	77 (26.9%)	74 (25.9%)	64 (22.4%)	34 (11.9%)	12 (4.2%)

another crucial factor: the pace of the dialogue. A subtitle must not overlap with the next line of dialogue; hence, a one-liner may be displayed for only two or three seconds if time is short (rapid dialogue), but for four or five seconds if there is plenty of time. For instance, at one point in M the mother of the family sighs, turns her gaze heavenwards and exclaims:

M15
Hvorfor, Herre?   [*Why God?*]

These two words are on screen for over four seconds. This length of exposure is good from the point of view of tone and theme, because the depiction of the characters and the Flemish small-town milieu is important. The slow pace is reinforced by an interval of three seconds before the next subtitle is displayed.

The following are examples of one-line subtitles in M that are displayed for less than three seconds:

M111
Hvor var De?   [*Where were you?*]

M106
Det er mulig.   [*It's possible*]

M130
Det er ungen til Germaine.   [*That's Germaine's boy*]

There are also instances of short two-liners displayed for under three seconds:

M149
Hvor gammel er De?   [*How old are you?*
30 år.   *Thirty*]

However, two-liners, short and long, may both be displayed for 3–4 seconds:

M564
Nei.   [*No.*
Hva?   *What?*]

M572
Sa De fra   [*Did you tell*
til søsteren Deres og Marguerite?   *your sister and Marguerite?*]

Once again, we see that it is impossible to lay down general guidelines for how long subtitles should be displayed. It appears, however, that exact exposure time (for example, whether a subtitle is displayed for 2.5 or 3.2 seconds) is determined more by the pace of the dialogue than by the information load of the actual subtitle, even though the subtitler constantly assesses the degree of linguistic difficulty and tries to reflect this when deciding exposure time.

The subtitler's opinion, of how difficult the words in the subtitle are, is probably responsible for the decision to display two simple words for only two seconds:

M262
En øl.   [*A beer*]

whereas a single word may be on screen for nearly four seconds, as in the
following example which presents the viewer with an unusual compound:

M263
Flamlenderpurken.   [*Flemish sow*]

On other occasions, however, it is evident that the action and the pace of the
dialogue, rather than the subtitler's view of what is necessary or ideal, ultimately
determine exposure times. The following two examples from G demonstrate
this:

G274
Vent litt!   [*Wait a second!*
Ikke rør deg!   *Don't move!*]

G277
Nei!   [*No!*]

These two subtitles — the first a short two-liner, the second a single word — are
both displayed for a similar length of time, 2–3 seconds. But G274 is tightly
squeezed between two other subtitles, which we must assume are essential (in
the subtitler's opinion). For G277 the subtitler has plenty of time before the next
subtitle, so he lets the single word remain on screen for a while.

We can summarise the findings concerning exposure times as follows: the
viewer of *Allo! Allo!* has to read quickly; the viewer of *Maigret* has to read a lot,
but does not need to read so quickly; and the viewer of *Golden Years* has to read
neither quickly nor a large amount. In this case, the viewer must have time to
follow a great deal of action — explosions, punch-ups, snarling investigators and
car chases.

Rhythm

In general, if a subtitler greatly condenses subtitles, longer pauses can be
achieved between them, and the rhythm is less frantic. However, the pace of the
dialogue varies from programme to programme and even within a single
programme, and it is this which largely determines the rhythm of the subtitles
(here meaning the length of the intervals between subtitles), together with the
subtitler's personal 'style'. At NRK, where the subtitlers have been working
together for many years and have similar views on condensing, it is reasonable
to assume that differences in subtitle rhythm between different programmes are
determined more by the genre and character of the programme than by the
subtitler's style and taste.

The subtitle intervals in all three programmes can be broken down as shown
in Table 18.5 (in television one second contains 25 frames).

The subtitling of A differs from that of the other two programmes through
the virtual absence of longer intervals. Only one interval is more than 30 seconds,
and only 11 are more than 10 seconds, indicating that there is a steady flow of
subtitles throughout the programme. This is not unexpected, since the dialogue

Table 18.5 Breakdown of subtitle intervals, showing number of intervals for time shown (highest percentage for each programme shaded)

	Maigret	Golden Years	Allo! Allo!
<2 frames	0	0	0
2 frames	324	0	0
3 frames	6	24	48
4–12 frames	33	88	96
13–24 frames	36	44	30
1–2 secs.	53	57	37
2–4 secs.	40	48	39
>4 secs.	93[a]	76[b]	35[c]

Notes:
[a] 15 of these 93 intervals are over 30 seconds, some over a minute.
[b] 7 of these 76 intervals are over 30 seconds.
[c] 1 of these 35 intervals is over 30 seconds

of this programme is characterised by humour and wordplay: the dialogue constitutes the action. At the very end the intervals are longer than at the start, the pace reducing somewhat. The episode under consideration is the last in the series, and the quieter pace of the dialogue in the last few minutes seems to help bring to a close the story of René, the café proprietor. In M the typical interval is clearly 2 frames. On the other hand, the viewer (reader) also finds the longest intervals in M, some of them lasting more than a minute.

Looking at the intervals in G, we might conclude that the programme was relatively slow in pace. There are no intervals under 2 frames, which was the typical interval in M, and the largest group is 4–12 frames. But when we see the programme, our impression of it is anything but slow; on the contrary, G is the typical action programme among the three. The fact that the subtitles in G change more slowly than in M should, I believe, be regarded as typical of this genre. The slightly longer intervals act as a counterbalance to the frantic pace of the action. However, the overall impression for the viewer is likely to be of a programme in which things happen quickly.

The opposite is the case in M. Here the subtitles change very quickly most of the time, but the action is slow and the cinematic depiction lingering. The pace of the subtitles can therefore be fast without creating the impression of a hectic programme.

My conclusion is that a rapid pace in the subtitles (short intervals) does not necessarily go hand in hand with a fast pace and dramatic action in the programme. On the contrary, the material in this study reveals that the programme with the slowest pace of action has the fastest pace of subtitling. The statistics for the three programmes show that pace of subtitling and pace of action follow each other only to a limited extent. In general the viewer does not regard reading the subtitles as a separate activity when watching a programme — everything appearing on screen is taken as a whole. It seems reasonable to assume that it is the speed of the spoken dialogue and the rest of the action which the viewer perceives as the 'pace'. However, this hypothesis can only be tested through viewer surveys, and reception analysis is beyond the scope of this study.

Subtitling as Translation?

To the viewing public, subtitling is primarily translation; they hear foreign dialogue and see a text in their own language on the screen, translated by a person called the subtitler, whose name they catch a glimpse of at the end of the programme. This is why, in the frequent correspondence in the press about subtitling, it is usually the translation that viewers complain about. We do not see them arguing about the rhythm of the subtitles or the visual positioning of the subtitles.

This concentration on the translation is by no means unreasonable; despite all the intensive discussions on exposure and line breaks that occur between subtitlers, the actual translation process, the transfer from foreign speech to, say, Norwegian text, is the main point of programme subtitling. Nevertheless, this type of translation is highly specialised, as indicated by its description as *subtitling* and not *translation*.

Main subtitling strategies

As a collective term for the process of converting speech to text during subtitling, I have chosen to use *transfer*. This allows me to use *translation* for that part of the transfer process which technically and professionally is covered by this term, meaning a linguistic transfer that meets the normal requirements for *equivalent translation* (cf., for example, Nida and Tabor's (1974: 12) definition: 'reproducing the closest natural equivalent of the source language message, first in terms of meaning and secondly in terms of style'). For instance, when programme G contains over 3,700 words of speech but only some 2,200 words (60 per cent) in the Norwegian subtitles (cf. Table 1), we can see that much of what takes place is not what is normally understood as equivalent translation.

As I understand the term *(equivalent) translation* the translator attempts to reproduce the sense in full. Thus translating '24 hours' or 'day and night' into idiomatic Norwegian as just one word, 'døgn', which lacks a one word equivalent in English, is an example not of Reduction but of Translation, because it reproduces the sense of the English accurately. In the same way, the translation of 'au Palais Bourbon on discute encore cette affaire' as 'i Palais Bourbon, den franske nasjonalforsamlinga, diskuterer dei framleis denne saka' [*in the Palais Bourbon, the French national assembly, they are still discussing this matter*] is not an example of Expansion, since it is essential for the Norwegian translation to be explicit in order to reproduce what is self-evident to a French reader (the fact that the Palais Bourbon is home to the national assembly). In both these cases, I believe, it is a question of obligatory transformations to achieve equivalence, so it is important to note that, in my model, Reduction, Expansion, Neutralisation, etc. represent alternative solutions to a possible, (more) equivalent translation. In Chomsky's syntactic terminology, they are optional transformations resulting in solutions that the subtitler would probably not have chosen if equivalence were the guiding principle.

The question is, what do we call this other process that is not equivalent translation? How far should we go in categorising the linguistic techniques that are applied with a communicative aim other than equivalent translation?

To date there has been only one major study of television subtitling in Scandinavia: Henrik Gottlieb's analysis of the subtitling by Danish Broadcasting of the programme *Frankenstein Junior*. Gottlieb arrived at a 'typology of subtitling strategies' (1994: 294), employing ten categories, expressed in English as follows:

Type of strategy	Character of translation
1. Expansion	Expanded expression, adequate rendering (culture-specific references)
2. Paraphrase	Altered expression, adequate content (non-visualised language-specific items)
3. Transfer	Full expression, adequate rendering (slow, unmarked speech)
4. Imitation	Identical expression, equivalent rendering (proper nouns; international greetings)
5. Transcription	Non-standard expression, adequate rendering (dialects; intended speech defects)
6. Dislocation	Differing expression, adjusted content (musical/visualised language-specific items)
7. Condensation	Condensed expression, concise rendering (mid-tempo speech with some redundancy)
8. Decimation	Abridged expression, reduced content (fast speech; low redundancy speech)
9. Deletion	Omitted expression, no verbal content (fast speech with high redundancy)
10. Resignation	Deviant expression, distorted content (incomprehensible or 'untranslatable' speech)

Gottlieb remarks that strategies 1–7 provide what he calls *correspondent translation*, but that Decimation and Deletion (8, 9) involve a reduction in the semantic and stylistic content which is of a qualitative nature. However, he claims that with both these strategies, the audio-visual feedback may complement the titles, often conveying the complete message. He further suggests that strategies 5–9 are 'all more common in subtitling than in printed translation', but that Resignation (10) is found in 'all types of verbal transmission' (1994: 295). Presumably, Expansion (1), Paraphrase (2), Transfer (3), and Imitation (4) are also strategies which are more commonly found in other types of translation.

The distinction which Gottlieb makes between strategies more prevalent in subtitling and those of translation in general are in my view crucial — so crucial that, after taking a few random samples from my material, I have considered it useful to adapt Gottlieb's detailed typology for those lines of dialogue that have been subject to what we are calling equivalent translation. As suggested earlier, I am calling this category (or strategy) 'Translation', referring to those cases where the strategy commonly occurs in other types of translation.

A quantitative analysis of the subtitles of our three programmes reveals large differences with respect to the number of titles which have been 'translated' and those in which other strategies have been used. *Maigret* contains the most Translation (about two thirds of titles) and *Golden Years* markedly the least (about one-third of titles) while *Allo! Allo!* falls exactly between the two (about half of titles). In this context it is understandable why some subtitlers do not like to describe themselves as 'translators'. They consider themselves media journalists who adapt texts; a more appropriate term, they say, is 'mediators'.

In attempting to classify the titles in my sample according to Gottlieb's typology, a number of difficulties arose, including the number of strategies falling outside what I have called here (equivalent) translation, and the somewhat fluid boundaries between them. Furthermore, not only does the difficulty of assigning subtitles to particular strategies increase with the number of available categories, underlying trends may also be harder to establish if the data are too fragmented. I am therefore proposing an alternative typology of strategies, based on a systematic evaluation of my data. The following six strategies, together with (equivalent) translation, are in my view essential to any attempt to analyse the subtitling process: Omission, Compression, Expansion, Generalisation, Specification and Neutralisation.

Subtitling Strategy Types

In this section I illustrate each of the strategies proposed on the basis of the three programmes analysed here. In the examples chosen to illustrate the various strategies, the original dialogue is shown above the Norwegian subtitles. An English gloss is provided in italics below the Norwegian subtitle and in some cases below the French dialogue.

1. Omission

M240–1
Elle s'est foulée la cheville dans la cour de son école. Je vous sers un genièvre?
Hun hap vrikket ankelen.   Vil De ha en sjenever?
[*She has twisted her ankle.   Would you like a genever?*]

The phrase 'dans la cour de son école' [*in the school playground*] disappears during the transfer from the French dialogue to Norwegian text.

2. Compression

G76–7
Until and unless we learn otherwise, the people in that car are asleep. No danger to us. But if they make a move against us, you do what you have to do.
Det ser ut til at de sover og ikke utgjør noen fare. Men finner de på noe, gjør dere det dere må.
[*It looks as if they're asleep and don't pose any danger. But if they think of anything, do what you have to*]

In this case it is not so easy to specify which phrases have disappeared during transfer. The simplest explanation is that the subtitler has condensed the whole expression, replacing for instance 'the people in that car' simply with the pronoun 'de' [*they*] in Norwegian.

3. Expansion

M199
Commissaire Maigret! Téléphone de Paris!
Fullmektig Maigret! Det er telefon fra Deres kone!
[*Maigret! It is telephone from your wife!*]

The subtitler has added in the Norwegian text the fact that the telephone call is from Maigret's wife, whereas in the programme Maigret is told only that it is from Paris. It is quite correct that it is Maigret's wife on the telephone, but no one actually says so; the subtitler adds this information, probably in an attempt to make it easier for the viewer.

4. Generalisation

M453
Je ne pense à rien du tout si non que ce Saint-Pourcain est très bon.
Jeg tenker ikke annet enn at denne vin er god.
[*I have no other thoughts other than that this wine is good*]

Although a wine connoisseur would know that Saint-Pourcain is a good burgundy, the subtitler has deemed the name unimportant or even confusing to Norwegian viewers, and has therefore replaced it with the general term 'vin' [*wine*]. In semantic terms we can call this Generalisation.

5. Specification

M182
C'est mon petit-fils.
Det er dattersønnen min.
[*It is my daughter's son*]

In this case the subtitler does the opposite of Generalisation and makes the text more specific. 'Petit-fils' [*grandson*] becomes 'dattersønn' [*daughter's son*] in Norwegian. If the subtitler had not known the specific family relationship, he could have simply chosen 'barnebarnet mitt' [*my grandchild*] in idiomatic Norwegian.

6. Neutralisation

G66
If that scumbucket wants anybody wasted, he can do it himself.
Vil han ha folk drept, får han gjøre det selv.
[*If he wants people killed, he can do it himself*]

The language of the English is colourful and rough, while the Norwegian is sober (in so far as describing killing can be sober). I have chosen to call this linguistic Neutralisation.

The opposite of Neutralisation is to retain the style, colour and spice, for example:

G71
You're a filthy son of a bitch!
Du er en råtten jævel!
[*You are a rotten devil*]

I do not claim that 'en råtten jævel' [*a rotten devil*] is exactly the same thing as 'a filthy son of a bitch', but it is not far off. Here the subtitler attempts to retain the tone and style, avoiding Neutralisation.

Summary
We can see from the above examples that it is difficult to maintain a clear distinction even between these relatively few categories. Thus the Neutralisation category contains elements of Generalisation. At the other extreme, doubts may arise over whether something should be classed as Expansion or Specification. In practice the strategies are closely interrelated.

It is also important to emphasise that a subtitler does not exclusively use one of the six strategies at a time when formulating the subtitles. The only fundamental choice to be made is whether to aim for complete or partial (or possibly no) translation. If the latter choice is made, there is nothing to prevent several strategies being used side by side. Neutralisation can therefore be combined with Omission, Expansion, Compression, Generalisation or Specification. The following example shows a subtitler using three strategies simultaneously — Compression, Neutralisation and Specification:

G48–50
Not at all, Captain Marsh. I want your men to open up on the tyres and the lower body of that car. Keep away from the gas tank. Flush them out. You copy?
Nei da. Be karene åpne ild mot dekkene og den nedre delen av bilen. Ikke bensintanken. Forstått?
[*No. Ask your men to open fire on the tyres and the lower part of the car. Not the fuel tank. Understood?*]

Not only is the Norwegian text much reduced in length (17 words in the subtitle against 33 in the original dialogue), but the American slang is rendered with more ordinary, neutral Norwegian words, for instance the implicit 'open up' is made explicit and specific in Norwegian: 'åpne ild' [*open fire*].

Dialogue: How Radical Are the Changes?
In addition to categorising the strategies for linguistic changes used by subtitlers, it is important to quantify the extent of the changes. As a starting point we need to use the dialogue in the script, or possibly on the soundtrack. Subtitlers often find that the details of the original script vary from the actual dialogue spoken. On the basis of a survey of every line, we can obtain statistics showing how often a subtitler uses the Translation strategy and how often other strategies are used.

Maigret contains 673 'units' or 'texts' (mainly dialogue, but also including notices, letters, etc.). In 139 of these units the subtitler uses Omission as the strategy, i.e. leaving out all or part of the dialogue. For example, names may be left out:

M7
Qu'est-ce qu'il y a, Germaine?
Hva er det?
[*What is it?*]

Or a whole line of dialogue may be ignored, for instance when we see (and hear) the daughter at the guest house showing Maigret to his room by saying 'Par ici, s'il vous plaît' [*This way please*], no subtitle is provided.

In 36 units the subtitler reduces the lines by summarising them, creating a synthesis to capture the sense without it being obvious which individual words have disappeared, for example:

M8
Je ne partirai pas sans avoir vu Joseph.
[*I won't leave without seeing Joseph*]
Jeg vil snakke med Joseph.
[*I want to speak to Joseph*]

M13
Allez, rentre chez toi . . .
[*Go on, go home . . .*]
Gå hjem.
[*Go home*]

Translations M8 and M13 do not render the spoken lines word for word, but the shorter solutions in Norwegian reproduce the sense well in the context.

Omission and Compression both result in shorter texts and can therefore be collectively labelled Reduction, even though in the first instance we have recorded them as two separate strategies. 175 units (139 omitted and 36 compressed) were reduced during transfer from speech to text; in other words, about 26 per cent of the units in M were subject to Reduction (Omission or Compression). If the subtitler neither reduces nor translates the units of content, but increases the volume by adding new units (present either implicitly or explicitly in the original), we can call this Expansion. In *Maigret* this applies to about 6 per cent of the translation units, for example:

M36
Mon père.
[*My father*]
Det er faren min.
[*This is my father*]

M37
Laissez-moi vous débarrasser.
[*Let me assist you*]
La meg ta sakene Deres.
[*Let me take your things*]

Table 18.6 Distribution (%) of subtitling strategies used in the three programmes

	Translation	Reduction	Expansion
Maigret	68%	26%	6%
Golden Years	50%	42%	8%
Allo! Allo!	33%	61%	6%

M13 and M36–7 both illustrate that discretion forms the basis of any classification of different strategies; a generous eye would view them as Translations, since they reproduce the sense. I have classified M37 as Expansion because a shorter translation, still fully equivalent in the context, would have been possible in Norwegian: 'La meg ta bagasjen.' [*Let me take the luggage*]

Reduction and Expansion

Using the above figures, the profile set out in Table 18.6 is obtained for the three programmes focusing on the three strategies Translation, Reduction and Expansion.

It is clear from these figures that the level of Expansion in all three programmes is similar, despite their different genres. The major differences are found in the relative levels of Reduction and Translation in each programme. These clear variations are probably due largely to the differences between the programmes — pace of dialogue, the role of the purely verbal in the programme, etc. — in other words, differences between programme genres. Admittedly there are differences in style and temperament, both between these three subtitlers and among subtitlers in general, but any such individual differences are largely expressed through particular characteristics of subtitle layout, timing and language usage, not through the strategy used.

Conclusion: A Model of Subtitling Strategies

Although there is no doubt that Reduction and Expansion are strategies frequently used by subtitlers, we have already examined the difficulties of quantifying the reduction and expansion of content. Such difficulties will always be present when the main categories are linked to judgements concerning content and message. This is the case even with the fundamental term in translation theory, equivalence, which also cannot be defined by means other than a subjective judgement of what the relevant message is, the message that the translator is seeking to reproduce. In any discussion of translation we therefore have to accept a degree of interpretation. One way of describing the subtitling process is to employ two planes or axes whose intersection represents equivalent translation, the focal point for any evaluation of sense transfer. The horizontal axis represents form, the vertical axis content. Generalisation and Specification are therefore the poles of the content axis, Reduction and Expansion those of the form axis. Since Neutralisation is so central to the subtitling process, in my view it should be treated as a separate strategy and placed centrally between the two axes, in the area between Reduction and Generalisation.

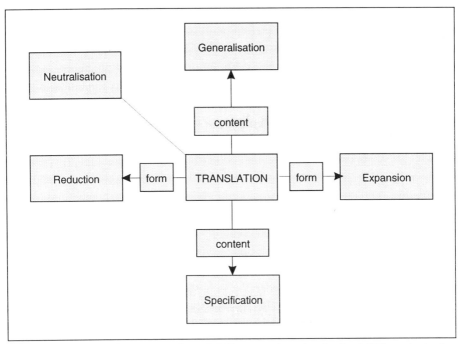

Figure 18.1 A two-dimensional model (form and content) of subtitling strategies

Translation, where the translator's aim is clearly to arrive at a formulation that is equivalent, lies at the centre, at the intersection of the two planes.

On the basis of the above, the model for analysing subtitling strategies can be presented diagrammatically as in Figure 18.1.

The aim of my model is to show how and to what extent a subtitler has departed from (equivalent) Translation, which is the central point of reference. The value of such a model is twofold: first, it is a (simplified) presentation of the characteristics of subtitling as a process; second, on the basis of detailed analysis and statistical calculations, it allows us to draw up a subtitle profile of an individual programme or subtitler. Hence we can reveal internal variations in subtitling practice, such as the extent to which subtitlers use Neutralisation, Reduction or Generalisation. In this way the model is able to deliver a schematic presentation of the subtitle profile of a programme or a subtitler.

Notes

1. A full report on this work is available as: S. Lomheim (1998) *Skrifta på skjermen*. Agder College, Kristiansand, Report No. 8.

References

Gottlieb, H. (1994) *Testning. Synkron billedmedieoverættelse*. Copenhagen: Center for Oversættelse, Københavns Universitet.

Newmark, P.P. (1981) *Approaches to Translation*. Oxford: Pergamon Press.

Nida, E. and Taber, C.R. (1974) *The Theory and Practice of Translation*. Leiden: Brill.

Chapter 19

Translating for Children

Eithne O'Connell

> *... the translation, like the original is written to delight as well as instruct*
> (Peter Newmark, 1991: 44)

Introduction

Children's literature has long been the site of tremendous translation activity and so it has come as something of a surprise to me to discover recently the extent to which this area remains largely ignored by theorists, publishers and academic institutions involved in translation research and training. I have also been struck by the fact that much of the recent material available in English on translating for children focuses on translations to and from lesser-used languages, in particular, Scandinavian languages or Hebrew.

It is now more than ten years since the Swedish educationalist, Göte Klingberg, listed in some detail five possible areas of research into the translation of children's books which he felt deserved urgent and detailed investigation. The potential areas for research activity he referred to were:

> statistical studies on which source languages yield translations in different target languages or countries;
> studies on economic and technical problems associated with the production of translations;
> studies on how books are selected for translation;
> studies of current translation practice and specific problems encountered by translations; and
> studies concerning the reception and influence of translations in the target language (TL) (Klingberg, 1986: 9).

Yet it is clear more than a decade later that many of these topics have still not been investigated thoroughly. This becomes easier to understand when one realises that the original subject matter, i.e. children's literature, is itself something of an undervalued or neglected area. According to Knowles and Malmkjaer (1996: ix) there is a 'curious discrepancy between the ubiquity and perceived importance of children's literature, and scholarly research in the field'. On the one hand, most parents and teachers must be aware of the importance of the genre and know that the development of good reading skills and a discerning attitude to one's reading materials are crucial for success in the education system and, indeed, in life in general. On the other hand, the public critical perception seems to be that works of children's literature, with a few notable and usually time-honoured exceptions, do not really deserve to be called 'literature' at all and are generally somehow second-rate and functional rather than of high quality, creative and deserving of critical attention in the way that serious adult literature clearly is. Consequently, a frank acknowledgement of the fact that children's literature has long suffered from relative neglect is a useful starting point for any discussion of the general topic of books for young readers and, more specifically, the challenges posed by their translation.

What Is Meant by 'Children's Literature'?

One of the primary difficulties in defining what is meant by 'children's literature' is the enormously inclusive scope and potentially vague nature of the semantic fields covered by the concepts referred to using the nouns 'children' and 'literature'. Some commentators such as Knowles and Malmkjaer (1996: 2) offer a very broad, pragmatic definition which seems to dodge the very difficult issues: 'For us children's literature is any narrative written or published for children and we include the "teen" novels aimed at the "young adult" or "late adolescent" reader.' The difficulty presented by the terms is addressed more frankly by Oittinen (1993a: 11):

> There is little consensus on the definition of child, childhood and children's literature. The definition . . . is always a question of point of view and situation: childhood can be considered a social or cultural issue; it can be seen from the child's or adult's angle . . . I see children's literature as literature read silently by children and aloud to children.

As a result of the fact that the term 'children's literature' lacks specificity, many of those writing critically about books for children feel obliged to restrict their terms of reference in some way as above. Klingberg, quoted in Reiß (1982: 7), opts for this working definition:

> . . . Literatur für Kinder und Jugendliche (von hier an einfach Kinderlitera-tur genannt) wird definiert nicht als diejenigen Bücher, die die Jugend gelesen hat (von Kindern und Jugendlichen wird und wurde eine umfan-greiche Literatur gelesen), sondern als diejenige Literatur, die für oder hauptsächlich für Kinder und Jugendliche veröffentlicht worden ist.

Adopting this as a functional definition, we can turn to address some of the most salient characteristics of children's literature as a genre. Firstly, books of this kind (while categorised by their primary target audience, i.e. young readers) in fact address two audiences: children, who want to be entertained and possibly informed, and adults, who have quite different tastes and literary expectations. The latter group, which comprises, in the first instance, editors and publishers, and, subsequently, parents, educators, academics and critics, is clearly much more influential than the former (Puurtinen, 1995: 19). It is adults, after all, who wield power and influence and it is they who decide what is written and, ultimately more importantly, what is published, praised and purchased.

Secondly, while it is true that some works of children's literature appeal essentially only to the primary audience, many are what Shavit (1986: 63–91) calls ambivalent texts such as *Alice in Wonderland*, which can be read by a child on a conventional, literal level or interpreted by an adult on a more sophisticated or satirical level as well.

Thirdly, children's literature is written by people who do not belong to the target group:

> Children's books are written for a special readership but not, normally, by members of that readership; both the writing and quite often the buying of them is carried out by adult non-members on behalf of child members. [Briggs, 1989: 4]

An unfortunate consequence can be that writers of children's literature may be out of touch or not convincing, guilty at times of a measure of condescension in their work. Some adult writers do not know their primary audience sufficiently well and write as much to please the secondary audience of critics, parents and teachers as they do to please their young readers.

Finally, as Puurtinen (1995: 17) has pointed out, the genre is unusual because of:

> the numerous functions it fulfils and the diverse cultural constraints under which it operates. Children's literature belongs simultaneously to the literary system and the social-educational system, i.e. it is not only read for entertainment, recreation and literary experience but also used as a tool for education and socialization. This dual character affects both the writing and the translation of children's literature, whose relationships with literary, social and educational norms make it a fascinating and fruitful field of research.

Children's Literature and Prestige

Despite this important dual function, there are understandable reasons for the tendency to regard children's literature as 'the cinderella of literary studies' (Shavit, 1992: 4) and these include the fact that children's literature has tended to remain uncanonical and culturally marginalised. This may be because books for young readers are written for a minority: the primary target audience is children and they and their literature, like women and women's literature, are treated in many cultural systems as, at worst, peripheral, and, at best, not really central to the concerns of 'high art' and culture.

According to Hunt (1992: 2):

> an instructive parallel can be drawn between the emergence of children's literature and other 'new literatures' (national, ethnic, feminist, post-colonial) that are becoming part of the institutional, cultural, critical map. Just as the literatures of colonial countries have had to fight against a dominant culture, so children's literature (as a concept) has had to fight against the academic hegemony of 'Eng. Lit.' to gain any recognition. Just as colonized countries have adopted a paternalistic stance towards the 'natives' and a patronizing stance to their writings, so, within what seems to be a single culture, the same attitude has been taken to children's literature books.

Hunt (1992: 2–3) maintains that the conventional literary system, reflecting the values implicit in the traditional hierarchical family system, tends to undervalue women's writing while children's literature fares even worse as it concerns children primarily and is seen very much as the domain of women — whether mothers or teachers.

> The conventional literary system is, after all, very like the traditional family: adult male literature predominates, women's literature is secondary (and grudgingly recognised), while children's literature is not only at the bottom of the heap, but (worse) it is very much the province of women. It was pointed out by the President of the Library and Information Science Education in the USA in 1987 that in the field of children's and young adult's literature, 92 per cent of the faculty were women, yet fewer than 10 per cent of those were full professors [Hearne, 1991: 111].

Other factors have also contributed to the evaluation of children's literature as inferior. In the first instance, books for children often deviate from conventional literary norms and pose problems as regards conventional evaluation and classification.

> Forced to describe themselves in terms of established norms, children's books do not shape up very well: their narratives are often novellas rather than novels; their verse is doggerel rather than poetry; their drama is improvisation rather than mediated text. As with other forms of literature, genre can degenerate rapidly into formula. [Hunt, 1992: 3]

As a consequence, critics often shun such writing because children's fiction 'thwarts would-be interpreters simply because so *few* children's novels move beyond the formulaic or stereotypical' (Nodelman, 1985: 5). In other words, the recurrent similarities in terms of structure, characters and language found in many works of children's literature are seen as contributing in a significant way to scholarly evaluation as 'inferior'.

But the fact that these works pose problems for those who would apply the tools of traditional literary criticism to them does not necessarily mean that it is the genre *per se* which is at fault. Perhaps, as Nodelman would have it, it is the means of interpretation which actually fail. 'Until we develop a new approach, we will not understand how a children's novel can in fact be unique even though its characters, its story, its "simple" language, and even its central core of patterns and ideas are not.' (1985: 20)

If the genre itself is not held in very high esteem by the world of scholarship, it is hardly surprising that the authors of books for children often suffer from problems of poor status and low pay. While in many countries there are awards for the writers of children's books, these same authors are not usually considered eligible for major literary awards under the general rubric of 'creative fiction'. Could someone like Astrid Lindgren, who was awarded the Hans Christian Andersen Award in 1958 and the International Book Award from UNESCO in 1993, ever be considered for the Nobel Prize for Literature? I think not, and yet Roald Dahl, who wrote for both adults and children, could at least in theory be a contender.

The Translation of Children's Literature

If children's literature has suffered from problems of low status, it is only to be expected that the translation of children's literature would have to endure a similar fate. For one thing, its very source material is considered of marginal interest and the professional activity, i.e. the translation carried out on this material, is, in itself, undervalued. This fact continues to find eloquent expression in the rates of pay and conditions offered to literary translators (Klingberg, 1978: 88) and the minimal formal acknowledgement of the translator's contribution on the cover or elsewhere in a translated work.

Poor status, pay and working conditions can perpetuate a vicious circle in which publishers are often presented with what they deserve, namely, translated work which could be a good deal better. One development which could have far-reaching implications in terms of breaking this cycle would be to improve the skills (and thus the professional confidence) of those who translate children's fiction. Academics are as guilty as anyone of contributing to this problem of poor public perception and low prestige. How many undergraduate or for that matter postgraduate programmes in Translation Studies offer students the chance to develop skills in this field in either core or optional courses? I must confess that my own institution, Dublin City University, has only recently developed an option in the very specific area of the translation of children's literature into Irish. If academic institutions involved in translator training were prepared to channel more resources in terms of research and teaching staff into investigations of the specific challenges of this field, it would surely make a difference, just as research into commercial and technical translation in the 1970s and 1980s enhanced the status and conditions of those engaged in that kind of work.

Of course, the full responsibility for the current state of children's literature translation cannot lie with the academic world alone. As already suggested, publishers are very active players in the field and, as a consequence, translators are not entirely free agents. Editors and publishers exert considerable influence over their output (Even-Zohar, 1992: 235), in a sense forcing an approach to the task of translation which has much more to do with conventions relating both to the TL, in general, and children's literature in the TL, in particular, as well as target culture stereotypes relating to the source culture:

> Policy-makers in the publishing and marketing world play an important role not only in forming images, but also in strengthening the received images of other nations through translation, particularly in the case of minority cultures in their relation to dominant cultures. These images are often the result of historical development and cultural interchange, and they are frequently images the source culture itself wishes to convey to the outside world for conscious marketing strategies, or simply because it regards them as an intrinsic part of its national identity. [Rudvin, 1994: 209]

Rudvin's conclusions are based on a study carried out in relation to the translation of Norwegian children's books into English. She points out that, apart from the works of writers such as Henrik Ibsen and Knut Hamsun, Norwegian literature is generally not well known in English-speaking countries. The genre of children's literature is an exception, according to Brudevoll, who is quoted by Rudvin (1994: 203) as claiming that while just a few hundred copies of any translation for adults from Norwegian are usually published in English, several thousand copies of translated children's books are published.

These books tend to be selected on the basis that their content corresponds to the prevailing positive British image of Norway as a natural, unspoilt country of mountains, lakes and forests. Such a policy in relation to the selection of texts for translation leaves 'the classical canon unchallenged, boundaries unstretched, perpetuating stereotypes rather than giving room for innovative thinking and thereby introducing new literatures and authors' (Rudvin, 1994: 203).

Future Research Directions in Translating for Children

We now need more studies, like Rudvin's, of the translation of children's literature which address the topics suggested back in 1986 by Klingberg for research purposes. Furthermore, we need appropriate research tools and methodology. To this end, we must look beyond Klingberg who has been described as 'dogmatic and inflexible' in his approach to the translation of children's literature (Puurtinen, 1993: 59). His analyses of Swedish-English and English-Swedish translations of books for children were very much source language orientated in marked contrast to the polysystems TL approach developed by Israeli academics such as Even-Zohar and Toury and so successfully applied to investigations of the Scandinavian translation trends in the 1990s referred to in this chapter. Klingberg was highly critical of translators taking what he saw as unnecessary liberties with the text. This does not mean that he totally opposed any form of adaptation, for he conceded that this may be necessary, for example in the case of certain foreign, historical, geographical or cultural references. But his prescriptive approach advocated 'faithfulness' to the source text where at all possible.

A more descriptive approach to the translation of a particular literature, in this case children's literature, can, as Shavit (1986: 171) and Even-Zohar (1992: 231) illustrate, shed light on the norms which operate within a particular target system since 'none of the choices made by the translator or, for that matter, the author, are manifestations of individual whims or inspiration, but are made within the (poly-)system in which they operate' (Even-Zohar, 1992: 231). Thus, contemporary target-orientated writers on these matters tend to shy away from Klingberg's tendency to apply some 'preconceived, fixed idea of the permissible extent of manipulation of the Source Text' (Puurtinen, 1995: 60). For the adherents of the polysystems approach, the focus is the TL and target culture and, as a result, 'the translator's decisions are likely to be based on prevalent norms and expectations, and the purpose of the translation' (Puurtinen, 1995: 60), rather than on some general code of good translator practice that could apply more or less equally to the translation of children's literature in different countries and eras.

Screen translation for children

In recent years minority language cultures, in particular, have started to show more interest in the important area of the translation of children's literature. However, it must be remembered that the major technological advances in the field of audio-visual communications over the last twenty years have had an important impact on the role of the printed word in the education and development of young people. Even highly literate children with extensive access to books, comics and magazines rely much more on oral/aural communication than the previous generation. The Swedish author of children's books, Lennart Hellsing, sees children's literature as a very broad field which encompasses everything that a child reads or hears (Oittinen, 1993b: 37). Viewed from this perspective, plays, puppet shows, computer and video games, radio and TV programmes, films, videos, etc. are just as important as books in terms of the education and entertainment of young people. Since, in the case of such texts, it is more accurate to speak of 'listeners' or 'viewers' rather than 'readers', Oittinen (1993b: 10) suggests the general term of 'receptor' is now more appropriate. In view of the long hours spent by most children in front of television screens, in particular, studies of translations produced for children must broaden their scope to include the analysis of screen translation for children as it is currently practised.

The two most prominent forms of screen translation are subtitling and dubbing. Although cost is usually an important factor in the production of children's programmes, and subtitling can prove up to ten times cheaper than dubbing, subtitling is rarely used because of anticipated problems relating to the variable reading abilities and speeds of young viewers. As a consequence, foreign language TV programmes, films and videos aimed at children and/or adolescents are invariably dubbed. When a film or video is to be dubbed, a script translator usually provides a complete draft translation which serves as a basis for the final, usually somewhat adapted, version that emerges when dubbing actors, producers and directors get together in the dubbing studio. The dubbing script translator usually faces many of the same linguistic challenges as those associated with the drafting of foreign language versions of other oral/aural material, for example radio and theatre plays. But the task is typically complicated by the constraints imposed by, for example, the need to achieve good quality lip synchrony whenever a close-up shot appears on screen and match, as closely as possible, syllable count and sentence length in the source and target versions. The problems and challenges associated with the translation of children's texts in general, and such scripts in particular, constitute an area well worth investigating and would include consideration of the particular difficulties associated with endeavouring to achieve satisfactory lip-synchrony while using the kind of constrained language and limited vocabulary which would be appropriate in view of the low mean age of the primary audience.

Major to lesser-used language translation

As we have seen, translation, like all other cultural activity, is conducted according to certain norms. In the case of translation for children, these may be didactic, ideological, ethical, religious, etc. They determine what is translated when and where and they change continually. Furthermore, the norms may vary from language to language, culture to culture and generation to generation. Thus, while specific norms exist in all cultures for the writing and translation of children's literature, it does not follow that the same approach is adopted in the case of any two languages. As Even-Zohar (1992) and Toury (1995) have pointed out, translations for children produced early in the century from German to Hebrew (a case of translation from a major to lesser-used language) were highly literary and intended to enrich the young readership's vocabulary. Now that the Hebrew language has established itself as a more stable, multifaceted contemporary language with distinct registers and oral and written styles, translated children's books are starting to reflect more colloquial varieties of the language tending more towards entertainment and less towards education.

My own particular research in this field has investigated the particular dynamic of the dubbing translation of animation programmes from a major language, German, into a lesser-used language, Irish. Children's stories by the German author, Janosch, were adapted in the 1990s for use as scripts for an animated children's TV series in Germany. The animation series was subsequently dubbed into Irish. Although the German scripts used a variety of registers and extensive vocabulary, the Irish versions tended to adopt a more colloquial style throughout and avoided the specialised terminology of the fairly sophisticated German scripts. One possible reason for the preferred use of a lower register in the Irish version relates to the norms of the TL, Irish, as it exists today. Although the classical scholarly tradition of the language continues at academic institutions and new poetry, prose, criticism, journalism, etc. is written and published every year, Irish is, at least for most native speakers, primarily a language for oral rather than written communication. This is fairly typical of the plight of lesser-used languages in decline or *extremis* and is in stark contrast to the case of German which has many millions of native speakers, a large number of dialects, an extensive range of special languages and a highly developed range of registers to suit every oral and written situation.

Conclusion

Hebrew and Irish translations of German storybooks and TV animation aimed at children during different periods in this century are mentioned here only as illustrations of the wide range of factors (language pairs, text type, historical period, status, i.e. major/lesser-used language, primary target audience, literary, educational, translation, broadcasting and/or other norms, etc.) which all may play a part in determining the final shape of a particular translated text, whether written or aural. There is clearly wide scope for further detailed investigations of a descriptive kind which may add to the insights gained in recent years from preliminary research based on Scandinavian and German literature translated for children.

Notes

1. Reiß does not give a precise source for Klingberg's definition. The translation given here is the editors': *Literature for children and young people (referred to simply as children's literature from now on) is defined not as those books which they read (children and young people read and always have read a wide range of literature), but as literature which has been published for — or mainly for — children and young people.*

References

Bamberger, R. (1978) The influence of translation on children's literature. In G. Klingberg, M. Ørvig and S. Amor (eds) *Children's Books in Translation: The Situation and the Problems* (pp. 19–27). Stockholm: Almqvist & Wiksell.

Briggs, J. (1989) Reading children's books. *Essays in Criticism* XXXVIX 1,1–17.

Chambers, N. (ed.) (1980) *The Signal Approach to Children's Books*. Middlesex: Kestrel Books.

Even-Zohar, B. (1992) Translation policy in Hebrew children's literature: The case of Astrid Lindgren. *Poetics Today* 13:1 Spring, 231–45.

Even-Zohar, I. (1979) Polysystems theory. *Poetics Today*, Autumn 1, 237–310.

Hunt, P. (ed.) (1992) *Literature for Children: Contemporary Criticism*. London: Routledge.

Klingberg, G. (1986) *Children's Fiction in the Hands of the Translators*. Malmö: CWK Gleerup.

Klingberg, G., Ørvig, M., Amor, S. (eds) (1978) *Children's Books in Translation: The Situation and the Problems*. Stockholm: Almqvist & Wiksell International.

Knowles, M. and Malmkjaer, K. (1996) *Language and Control in Children's Literature*. London: Routledge.

Newmark, P.P. (1991) *About Translation*. Clevedon: Multilingual Matters.

Nodelman, P. (1985) Interpretation and the apparent sameness of children's novels. *Studies in the Literary Imagination* 18:2, Fall, 5–20.

Oittinen, R. (1989) On translating for children: A Finnish point of view. *Early Child Development and Care* 48, 29–37.

Oittinen, R. (1993a) On the dialogics of translating for children. In C. Picken (ed.) *Translation: The Vital Link. XIII FIT World Congress* (pp.10–16). London: Institute of Linguists.

Oittinen, R. (1993b) *I am Me — I am Other*. Tampere: University of Tampere.

Puurtinen, T. (1995) *Linguistic Acceptability in Translated Children's Literature*. Joensuu: University of Joensuu.

Reiß, K. (1982) Zur Übersetzung von Kinder- und Jugendbüchern. *Lebende Sprachen* 1 Feb., 7–13.

Rudvin, M. (1994) Translation and 'myth': Norwegian children's literature in English. *Studies in Translatology* 2:2, 199–211.

Shavit, Z. (1986) *Poetics of Children's Literature*. Athens, Georgia: University of Georgia Press.

Shavit, Z. (1992) The study of children's literature: The poor state of the art. Why do we need a theory and why semiotics of culture? *Barnboken* 1, 2–9.

Toury, G. (1980) *In Search of a Theory of Translation*. Tel Aviv: The Porter Institute for Poetics and Semiotics, Tel Aviv University.

Toury, G. (1995) *Descriptive Translation Studies and Beyond*. Amsterdam: John Benjamins.

Chapter 20

Translation and Language Games in the Balkans

Piotr Kuhiwczak

> *Translation is concerned with moral and factual truths.*
> (Peter Newmark, 1991: 1)

Introduction

In his well-known book *Sociolinguistics*, published for the first time in 1974, Peter Trudgill (1974: 61) writes the following about Yugoslavia:

> ... different ethnic groups speak the same language, and here language may act as an *identifying* characteristic (although not, today, a particularly important one). This is true of Sarajevo, the capital of Bosnia, where the three main ethnic groups in the city, Serbs, Croats, and Moslems, all speak Serbo-Croat, the most widely used Yugoslavian language. Historically speaking this ethnic-group differentiation in Sarajevo has to do with religion (Serbs are or were Orthodox, Croats Catholic) and partly to do with geographical origin (Serbia is to the East of Bosnia, Croatia to the west). Today [i.e. in 1974] these factors are of no very great importance, but individuals are still aware of their ethnic group membership.

In 1987 a specialist in Slavonic languages, Greville Corbett, could still say with full confidence that:

> Serbo-Croat is the major language of Yugoslavia; it is spoken in the Yugoslav republics of Bosnia and Hercegovina, Croatia, Montenegro and Serbia, by a total of over 17 million according to the 1981 census. Slovenia and Macedonia have their own languages but many Slovenes and Macedonians know Serbo-Croat (as do large numbers of the sizable populations of Albanians and Hungarians living in Yugoslavia and of the smaller groups of Bulgarians and Rumanians). Many hundreds of thousands of Serbo-Croat speakers now live abroad, notably in the United States and Australasia, and in West Germany and Sweden. [Corbett, 1987: 128]

What sounded so authoritative only a decade ago reads now like a report from another epoch. The country called Yugoslavia still exists, but in a truncated form, and the factors which Trudgill once dismissed as of no great importance — religion and ethnicity — are more important in the Balkans than anything else.

217

Macedonia and the Macedonian language are questioned by both the Greeks and Bulgarians, and the Serbo-Croatian language, for which both Serbs and Croats made sacrifices and fought the Austrians, Germans, Italians, Turks, Hungarians and who knows who else, has been removed from the register of known languages. It is not surprising that many Yugoslavs see the war as a breakdown in communication — a language war in which translation has been used as an effective and dangerous weapon.

This is neither the place nor time to discuss the political implications of the collapse of Yugoslavia. But after the 1992–4 war, negotiations, and the fragile peace settlement, it is time to ask what we have learned from the Yugoslav crisis, and whether anything can be done to prevent the spread of what is euphemistically called 'the Balkan problem'. In the limited space available I want to look only at the consequences of the Yugoslav war which might alter our thinking about the nature of language and the role of translation.

Language and Nationhood

There is no doubt that the common attitude to language is full of paradoxes. Sometimes, looking at languages, we behave like dispassionate archivists and arrange them into neat groups according to a variety of often arbitrary typological or historical criteria. But as soon as languages are linked to social and political realities, emotions begin to run high, and abstract linguistics and philology give way to a passionate quarrel about language rights and policies. We are equally confused in our attitudes towards diversity. On the one hand, we would like get back to the time before Babel and construct one universal language for everyone (like Dr Zamenhof's Esperanto); on the other hand, we deeply believe that even the smallest language is sacred, and should be preserved, perhaps not at all costs, but certainly at the cost of reducing the importance of Esperanto or the current lingua franca.

What has happened with the languages of Yugoslavia exemplifies very well our conflicting attitudes to language. But the Yugoslav disaster has brought home yet another truth, namely that many of the late eighteenth- and early nineteenth-century ideas about the relation between language, nation, and state are not buried corpses, but living ideas capable of further development. Herder's hypothesis that the spirit of nations is expressed in their language, presented in *Ideas Toward a Philosophy of the History of Mankind (1784–91)*, has recently enjoyed a revival on both sides of the Atlantic. It is not Herder's fault that his hypothesis has stirred minds in countries as different as Canada and Yugoslavia, to name just two conspicuous examples. His primary concern was with the state of German identity. Since the Germans had no political unity, the poet cum philosopher claimed, the essence of what it meant to be German must be located in the German language and culture. We know how seriously the Germans took Herder's idea, and where that translation of philosophy into life took not only Germany, but the whole of Europe earlier this century. But it was not only the Germans who believed Herder's theory. Many Central European nations dominated by oppressive powers also liked his ideas. Being under foreign occupation, Czechs, Poles, Serbs, Croats, Hungarians and many other smaller nations were not able to express their civic identity by establishing political institutions. Instead, they tried to derive their sense of national unity from a link between their 'sacred' languages and 'essential' national characteristics.

In a very interesting essay on the Czech national revival, J.P. Stern (1992: 29–43) asks a very uncomfortable question: 'But what happens to Herder's theory of language in a country in which two languages are used?'(1992: 30). Anyone who knows the story of the Czech national revival will certainly recognise this question, since, at the time of the revival, Bohemia was inhabited not only by Czech speakers but also by Bohemian Germans and Jews. The answer was predictable: the Czech-speaking revivalists had little patience with their German-speaking compatriots, as did the German speakers with the Czechs, and the consequences of this unwillingness to compromise have troubled the Czech lands until very recently.

Yugoslavia Revisited: The Concept of a 'Language'

The origins and evolution of both the Serbo-Croatian language, and the concept of Yugoslavia, are too complex to explain in this short chapter. But there is no doubt that at the time of their conception both phenomena were impressive and very innovative. Unlike anybody else in this part of Europe, the South Slavs decided that their future did not lie with the Herderian principle of one nation — one language, but in a much more civilised construct: the union of South Slav peoples with a common language. If the political unification caused problems, the linguistic reform carried out by Vuk Karadzić (1787–1864) had only minor hitches. The outcome was workable and impressive. Serbo-Croatian became a real language, and what's more, could be written in two alphabets: Latin and Cyrillic. There is no doubt that under Communist rule the Yugoslav idea, like any other sensible idea for that matter, was effectively perverted, but the basic principles of the union, including the common language, managed to survive. In an article with the ominous title 'Language War — War Language', Jasna Levinger (1994: 229–36) describes the situation in Yugoslavia when political demagogy began to filter down to everyday language. When the conflict in Bosnia erupted, Croats, Serbs and Slav Muslims began rapidly to undermine the common Yugoslav heritage and to emphasise their distinct national identities. Levinger identifies four ways of manifesting distinct identities by means of language: newly-coined words, euphemisms, loan words of Turkish origin, and late nineteenth-century Croatian words brought into use during the Second World War. It was the media that initially championed the language change, but eventually the language of the street also became infected. At the end of her analysis Levinger (1994: 235) writes:

> Finally, there is not only the official, but an individual language war, within a building, among neighbours, in a store or anywhere where more than three people meet. It starts with greetings: will one be recognized as a member of a particular ethnic group, will one accordingly be rejected or accepted? How to decide which form of a greeting to use — the one one usually uses, or the one the other party uses; will he interpret this as provocation, offence or courtesy? But the same question arises if the selected form is the other one, not the one he uses. The problem is also practical — will one get a piece of bread if he calls it *hljeb* (Serbian) instead of *kruh* (Croatian)?

That was the first stage of language separation. With the recognition of Croatia and Bosnia by the European Union, further changes took place. Soon, it was generally accepted that Serbo-Croatian was 'out', and two politically distinct languages emerged: Serbian, spoken in Serbia, and Croatian spoken in Croatia. At more or less the same time, the Croats began to behave as if they had never seen the Cyrillic script. The Serbs could not do the same to Latin, but the number of printed texts in Cyrillic and the number of public signs in this script has grown considerably. In both countries, but in Croatia in particular, the respective Academies of Science began to churn out new histories of the language, and dig up nineteenth-century phrases and invent 'indigenous' words. The media and some politicians began to use the new language, although President Tudjman has been heard to forget his new language and slip back into his old Communist idiolect. But if Serbia and Croatia could fall back on the antique, the newly created would-be multicultural Bosnia and Hercegovina had little ancient identity to turn to. From time immemorial Bosnia has been a multicultural area, often described as a European fault line and the meeting point of three religions — Western Christianity, Orthodox Eastern Christianity, and Islam.

In language terms, Bosnia has also been the place where the Eastern and Western varieties of Serbo-Croatian merged. Under Yugoslavia, Bosnia had the status of a republic, but neither Croats, nor Serbs, nor Slav Muslims, nor Jews were obliged to prove their distinct Bosnian identity. But once the new Bosnian establishment decided to set up Bosnia as an independent country, the whole arsenal of nineteenth-century tricks was deployed. It is not surprising that the language issue came to the fore, and after some preparatory work the Bosnian language was revealed to the outside world in 1995, when the government-sponsored Language Commission published the *Pravopis Bosanskoga Jezika*.

It is difficult to find an adequate English equivalent of the word *pravopis* (it literally means 'correct writing' rather than 'dictionary'), but on the Continent the legal codification of what is correct in a language, and what is not, is not uncommon. Similar works exist in German and in Polish, and any linguistic change to be recognised as real must find its way into these compendia of correct spelling. What interests us here, however, is what kind of language Bosnian is. The *Pravopis* does not supply readers with a lot of information. The author (Halilović, 1995: 6–7) states that from time immemorial Bosnian has been related to Slavonic languages, but he does not say which Slavonic languages these might be. Only once is it hinted that since 1960 Bosnians have been using the *pravopis* based on the Novi Sad convention, but the words Croat, Serb or Yugoslav are not mentioned. The mystery is dispelled when one begins to analyse the new language, and quickly finds out that what is called a 'new language' reads exactly the same as the old one, i.e. Serbo-Croatian. It is at this point that translation becomes important.

The Political Role of Translation

One of the first books presented as a translation into Bosnian was one of the major founding texts — *The Q'ran*. Then came the time for bilingual dictionaries. Not surprisingly, it was the *Englesko-Bosanski i Bosansko-Engleski Rječnik* ('English-Bosnian and Bosnian-English Dictionary') which appeared first, in 1996.

Normally, dictionaries are not the most exciting kind of reading, Dr Johnson's English Dictionary being the only exception. But the Bosnian-English Dictionary is exciting for different reasons. The author's name, printed on the title page, is Dr Branko Ostojić who died some time ago. Ostojić was well known in the old Yugoslavia as the author of the Serbo-Croatian- English Dictionary published in pre-war Sarajevo. It does not take a moment to realise that the 'new' Bosnian-English Dictionary is simply Ostojić's old Serbo-Croatian-English Dictionary, with new covers and a new title page. There are plans to publish Ostojić's dictionary in Serbia early next year, and the Serbian editors are putting a lot of effort into making it clear that the new dictionary has a distinctly Serbian flavour. It is most likely then that Ostojić's dictionary will acquire yet another title — Serbian-English Dictionary.

An uninformed visitor from the outside might simply say that the whole affair with the new post-Yugoslav languages is either a publisher's con-trick to multiply profits, or a mad politicians' dream. But neither linguists nor historians should be surprised that, although the Serbs, Croats and Bosnians do share the same language, they have decided to not to recognise this obvious fact any more. Perhaps, if we compare them with the famous nationalist literary forgeries of the previous century in Scotland and the Czech lands,[1] for instance, these post-Yugoslav tricks do not seem so spectacular or even particularly well disguised, but the impulse behind the old and the new cases is not dissimilar. What the Yugoslav crisis should help us to realise is that, contrary to our everyday experience in peaceful times, translation in times of international conflict may be used for other purposes than to bridge the linguistic and cultural gap. To dedicated nationalists, translation in its conventional sense poses a major danger — because it serves as a channel of communication between parties who would not otherwise be able to communicate. To subvert this positive role of translation, they turn it into a tool which helps not to link but to separate, and to prove that communities which once happily used a common language are now so deeply divided and distinct that they need to be interpreted to each other and the outside world.

When the international agreements on Bosnia were being negotiated in Switzerland and the United States, all the post-Yugoslav delegations used interpreters to communicate, not only with the EU and US delegates, but among themselves. In this way they emphasised the fact that they represented distinct nations with distinct languages. It remains to be seen whether the successor states will manage to complete their project. At the moment all the available energy is concentrated on widening the gaps. The Croats have stopped teaching Cyrillic in schools, which means that the next generation of Croatian readers will not have direct access to many Serbian texts. The majority of the population either supports the changes, or is not interested in the issue at all, but many intellectuals are playing an active role in speeding up the change.

If the first stage of the cultural and linguistic separation of the former Yugoslavia has been engineered and implemented by the governments and central administration, the more recent developments have had a much more decentralised and less official character. It is also clear that the post-Yugoslav states are now concerned that the outside world should accept their point of view and collaborate in constructing the new linguistic and cultural realities. The

Croatia's new self-image

range of methods and strategies each successor country employs is very wide. Croatia, for instance, has put considerable emphasis on constructing a new image. There is no doubt that the propaganda campaign is driven as much by nationalist ideology as by the need to attract tourists to the Adriatic coast. What the Croatian tourist organisations stress is the country's distinctly Mediterranean flavour, and its proximity to the Latin heritage of neighbouring Italy. Maps reproduced in publications sponsored by Croatian tourist agencies and their foreign associates manipulate geography in such a way as to change our habitual association of Croatia with the Balkan Peninsula.[2]

At the textual level, the main strategy is to dissociate the name of the country from the recent war, and establish a link with a set of positive associations, such as proximity to Western Europe, old traditions, and cultural heritage. One typical attempt to change our perceptions, taken from an advertisement distributed by the Croatian National Tourism Office in London, reads like this:

> We are currently sitting outside a little cafe in *ancient* Dubrovnik which is an architectural jewel: endless renaissance towers, statues, and stepped side streets. *Hard to believe it only took two and a half hours to fly here.* We've been exploring and have never seen so much history, *completely undisturbed*. Many of the towns are *medieval*, each with their own fascination: local churches, chapels and art treasures. [Emphasis added]

Since image is always associated with linguistic expression, Croatia and Serbia manipulate commercial texts to enhance linguistic, political and cultural difference. This happens even at the most trivial level of information on ordinary packaging. The Balkan states have succeeded in involving even multinational companies in producing labels which reflect their constructed reality. Common products such as washing powders, sweets, toys, and other consumer goods, which normally carried information in Serbo-Croatian as well as many other languages, now provide separate Serbian and Croatian entries. In all these cases the manufacturers need to be very ingenious to write the two texts in such a way that they pass for texts written in two distinct languages. The big chocolate manufacturer Ferrero, for instance, has gone for a simple strategy: texts marked YU (Yugoslavia) are printed in Cyrillic, while those marked HR (Croatia) are in Latin script. McDonald's preference, on the other hand, is for use of style as a differentiating factor. Their texts marked 'Srpski' (Serbian) and 'Hrvatski' (Croatian) are written in the same script, but the message is phrased differently:

SRPSKI — Igračka je testirana za uzrast *dece* od 3 god i više. Pažnja: može sadrzati sitnije delove pa se ne preporučuje za decu ispod 3 godine.

(This toy has been safety tested for children aged 3 and over. Caution: it may contain small parts and is not intended for children under 3.)

HRVATSKI— Ova igračka je namijena za djecu od 3 i više godina. Upozorenje: Može sadržavati manje dijelove i nije namijenjena za djecu mladu od 3 godine. Molimo sačuvajte ovu obavijest.

(This toy is intended for children aged 3 and over. Caution: it may contain small parts and is not intended for children under 3. Please retain information for reference.)

The one conspicuous difference in spelling and pronunciation (*dece — djecu —* Eng. child) has traditionally distinguished the Western from the Eastern variety of Serbo-Croatian, and only recently has begun to be used by Serbs and Croats as a linguistic difference. Other differences result simply from the different choice of approximately equivalent lexical items and syntactic structures. Thus *testirana* ('tested') in Serbian, is *namijenjena* ('intended for') in Croatian. So the difference, as represented in English, would look as follows:

Serbian: The toy has been *tested* for children over the age of 3.
Croatian: This toy is *intended* for children aged 3 and over.

The last sentence in the Croatian text (*Please retain this information*) has been dropped from the Serbian entry altogether, since the Serbs do not share a Croatian habit of overusing polite phrases inherited from the Austro–Hungarian empire.

   The fact that the strategies are not consistent, and that many obvious changes like the removal of plaques with both Latin and Cyrillic street names have not been made, does not mean that there is no will to implement the changes more vigorously. Simply, the countries involved are too impoverished by the war to launch a major purifying *Kulturkampf*. In some cases, the lack of consistency produces surrealistic effects. For instance, throughout the whole period of the Yugoslav conflict, the major motorway junctions west of Belgrade were still signposted 'Zagreb', although travel to Zagreb was out of the question. Today when it is theoretically possible to drive to Zagreb along the motorway of 'brotherhood and unity', the sign has regained only a fraction of its pragmatic significance, because Croatia consistently refuses to grant entry visas to Yugoslav nationals.

Conclusion

Those who oppose the process of pushing Yugoslavs into tribalism by trying to prevent these surrealistic language wars are few and far between. One of the most conspicuous of 'cosmopolitan' Sarajevans carries out his anti-nationalist project on the waves of a private Sarajevo broadcasting station, *Radio Zid*. His strategy depends on the patient repetition of the fact that every sentence he says is valid and well understood in all possible combinations of the Serbo-Croatian language, and that the former Yugoslavs do not need interpreters to communicate. What they badly need is a minimum of common sense and a great deal of good will.

Just before the conflict in Yugoslavia erupted, Peter Newmark (1991: 42) wrote:

> Translation is linked with an awareness of democratic potential; it is a weapon against obscurantism, the realisation that the material, social and cultural inequalities often associated with ethnic and linguistic groups as well as with gender, race or class, are not God-given or natural, that they have to be at least drastically reduced. And so you have Canada, Spain, Belgium, Yugoslavia — all countries where social equilibrium is related to free interlinguistic communication, and the publication of their statutes in all their national languages.

But a few pages later in the same book (1991: 161), he also warns us that translation 'can be a weapon, a cutting tool, a hatchet'. One hopes that one day the Yugoslavs will bury the hatchet and rediscover translation's democratic potential. For us outside the Balkan tragedy, the Yugoslav case should be a reminder that what matters most is not what language one speaks, but whether what is spoken makes sense and does not get wilfully lost in translation.

Notes

1. In 1817 and in 1818 two manuscripts of supposedly medieval Czech poetry were discovered in Kraluv Dvur and in Zelena Hora. The discovery gave rise to an unprecedented series of investigations, and literary quarrels which continued until the end of the 19th century. The Czech case strongly resembled James Macpherson's (1736–96) forgeries of old Scottish poetry.
2. Maps similar to the one reproduced are frequently published in tourist brochures and other promotional materials, including advertisements in the national press in many countries.

References

Corbett,G. (1987) Serbo-Croat. In B. Comrie (ed.) *The Major Languages of Eastern Europe* (pp. 125–44) London: Routledge.

Halilović, S. (1995) *Pravopis Bosanskoga Jezika*. Sarajevo: Preporod.

Levinger, J. (1994) Language war — war language. *Language Sciences* 16(2), 229–36.

Newmark, P.P. (1991) *About Translation*. Clevedon: Multilingual Matters.

Ostojić, B. (1996) *Englesko-Bosanski i Bosansko-Engleski Rjecnik*. Sarajevo: IP Svjetlost.

Stern, J.P. (1992) *The Heart of Europe*. Oxford: Blackwell.

Trudgill, P.(1974) *Sociolinguistics*. Harmondsworth: Penguin Books.

Chapter 21

ADNOM — A Project that Faded Away

Patrick Chaffey

> *. . . it is desirable that translating teams employed by national governments*
> *should make official translations of their principal institutional terms so*
> *that foreign translators should at least be able to use the correct versions, if*
> *they wish to respect the (source language) SL country's interests.*
>
> (Peter Newmark, 1981: 81)

Introduction

In 1984 and 1988, ADNOM, the Norwegian Project for Multilingual Administrative Nomenclature, produced two dictionaries, *ADNOM* (1984) and *Norsk-engelsk administrativ ordbok* (1988). An important contribution to both projects was made by the Centre for Translation Studies at the University of Surrey, in particular by Professor Nigel Reeves, at the time head of the Department of Linguistic and International Studies, who collaborated as a member of the editorial board.

The Original Need

ADNOM was first started in January 1982, when the late Odd Sandal, then Head of the Translation Division of the Ministry of Foreign Affairs in Oslo, and I decided to attempt to standardise in English and perhaps also in other languages the names of Norwegian institutions as well as the terms used for various Norwegian occupational designations, especially throughout the Norwegian Civil Service. This collaboration was timely. As a civil servant and academic, teaching the Theory and Practice of Translation at the University of Oslo, it was clear to me that in the teaching of translation in Norway the type of problem in question was normally avoided. Literary passages were naturally preferred, for example at Oslo University, for translation at all levels, usually a culturally neutral kind. Texts that contained the names of any Norwegian institutions that were not readily translatable into English were avoided because their names did not 'shine through', to use Newmark's term. Texts containing specifically Norwegian occupational designations were also rejected on the grounds that students and teachers had no means of knowing what would be the preferred or indeed official translation.

Newmark (1981: 81), discussing the translation of proper names and institutional and cultural terms, makes the point that '. . . it is desirable that translating teams employed by national governments should make official translations of their principal institutional terms so that foreign translators should at least be able to use the correct versions if they wish to respect the (source language) SL country's interests'. This is exactly what Odd Sandal and I wanted to do, and it was precisely this aim that led us to establish ADNOM. Our intention was to produce in the first instance a glossary listing the names of a large number of Norwegian state institutions in both Norwegian and English, but we did not exclude the possibility of including organisations such as trade unions, firms and associations falling outside the public sector. We also wished to include the main occupational designations used throughout the Norwegian Civil Service, but again we did not reject the idea of including certain occupational designations occurring in the private sector. Furthermore, we hoped to include cultural terms, such as legal terminology, but soon realised that such a task would probably be insurmountable. Legal terminology should really be a matter for a bilingual law dictionary, rather than for a dictionary of administrative nomenclature.

My personal view was that the project would be fairly straightforward and that we ought to be able to compile such a glossary in a relatively short space of time. Odd Sandal, a law graduate from the University of Oslo who was bilingual in English and Norwegian, warned me that such a project would be sure to meet with a certain amount of resistance. He feared that there would be objections to such a project in principle: firstly, because the need for it would not be immediately obvious, on the assumption that all Norwegians speak English and automatically translate the name of any Norwegian institution into English in the same way; and secondly, because there would be serious objections to any attempt to standardise the translation of such names, on the grounds that this would seem high-handed and undemocratic. One must bear in mind that although English is a compulsory subject in Norwegian schools, English is not an official language in Norway. Strictly speaking any translator is free to translate the name of any Norwegian state institution into English or any other language in whatever way he or she chooses. In other words, there was in fact a great need in Norway for official lists of the names of Norwegian institutions in English, and a similar need for such lists of occupational designations and so forth, but the way towards solving these problems was not going to be easy.

Administrative Nomenclature and Terminology

From the start we adopted the terms 'administrative nomenclature' and 'administrative terminology' to cover the two aspects of our work. The first term was used to cover the names of Norwegian institutions, including the names of any departments, divisions or offices into which they might be divided. The second term was used to cover terminology that was culture-bound, such as the terminology that arises through the passing of national legislation or through the process of collective bargaining and other forms of negotiation.

Catford (1965: 93–103) had drawn attention to the phenomena of linguistic and cultural untranslatability, but we felt that there was no term used by translation theorists to cover precisely the area of terminology we had in mind. For example, we are faced with an instance of cultural untranslatability if we have to find an English equivalent for a Norwegian word like *vardøger*. This is a common word in Norwegian which is used in the following situation: if you hear or see for a brief moment a person who is not actually physically there and if the person in fact appears about twenty minutes later, then you have heard or seen that person's *vardøger*. The majority of Norwegians have had experiences of this kind, usually in sound, and indeed I have myself had many such experiences in Norway, although I always see the person in advance; I never hear the *vardøger*. The closest cultural equivalent in the English-speaking world would be the *fetch*, since it refers to the spirit of a living person, but the phenomenon is only generally known in Ireland, and it may not have the pleasant associations of the Norwegian term. Haugen (1965: 473) uses the English translation 'premonitory sound (or sight) of person shortly before he arrives'.

Clearly terms of this kind, which would come under the general category of 'cultural terms', were of no interest to us in our context. We needed to narrow down and restrict the range of terminology for our glossaries, and we chose to adopt the term 'administrative terminology' for elements of standardised language used in processes and procedures resulting from the way in which different societies decide to administer their affairs. We all know that different societies have different legal systems, different educational systems, different forms of government and so forth, and that such differences do not arise as easily when different societies speak the same or almost the same language. This is why the same monolingual law dictionaries are often used throughout the English-speaking world; even if the terms may differ slightly, the basic concepts are usually the same. The same would be true of Norway, Sweden and Denmark, where the similarity of language leads to a fundamental similarity of concepts if not of actual terms.

A good example of an administrative term would be the Norwegian word *storfag*, which belongs to the set of terms relating to university degrees in Norway. Clearly one cannot translate *storfag* into English or into any other language unless the degree system of that culture is identical to the system we have in Norway. A student who takes the *storfag* examination in a subject will have studied that subject for four semesters. After two semesters of study the student must have passed the *grunnfag* examination in that subject, and after a third semester of study s/he must have passed the *mellomfag* examination. In other words, a person who has achieved *storfag* level has taken that subject for two years in modules of one year, one semester and one semester, not necessarily without interruption. The student may have studied other subjects between some of the modules. Even the term *study* may itself be tricky. In the English-speaking world it may imply an attendance or residence requirement imposed by the university concerned, while in Norway there are not normally any such requirements except in subjects like Medicine and Dentistry.

As the Norwegian educational system needs to be described in English, a term equivalent to *storfag* must be found in English, cultural differences notwithstanding. The term cannot easily be borrowed into English. It is composed of two Norwegian words, *stor* ('big') and *fag* ('subject'), and will immediately be recognisable as an educational term to anybody who knows Norwegian, but the word does not fit into English either phonologically or morphologically, something which would make the word difficult for English speakers to pronounce or remember.

For translation purposes, consistency is of the essence. At the University of Oslo we decided to use the term *'major subject'*, and this is used consistently in all our documents relating to degree structure. Obviously we could have chosen other terms, and indeed some people object to the term we have chosen, but the point here is that we needed a label for a particular element in our degree system. On many occasions I have pointed out in lectures and in print that a less than perfect term that is used consistently in this kind of situation is ten times better than a number of good terms that are used inconsistently, although it is not always easy to define a good term or a bad term. In this area there are not really any rights and wrongs in an absolute sense; there are simply felicitous and less felicitous choices with consistency of use being the prime concern, because we are dealing with items of standardised language in the SL culture.

It is clear that there are no obvious problems describing our own society in our own language. Most monoglots are blissfully unaware of the problems that arise for the translator of texts containing administrative nomenclature and terminology, since they tend to assume that all words must have some equivalent in any language. Many also assume considerable cultural similarity between societies speaking different languages and fail to see the kinds of problem the translator has to face. One has only to think of the English notions of 'joint' and 'common' property to illustrate the point. Walker (1980: 667) draws a clear distinction between the two concepts, but the English notion of joint property applies in Norway only between marriage partners who have not expressly contracted otherwise. The Norwegian term for this is *felleseie*, composed of two Norwegian words, *felles* ('joint' or 'common') and *eie* ('property' or 'ownership'). Chaffey and Walford (1997: 38) chose to call the concepts 'co-ownership of marital property' and 'community property' respectively, precisely to avoid the confusion and misunderstanding that would arise if terms were simply adopted from Anglo-American law.

The difficulties posed by such cultural terms for transfer into another language and culture are illustrated by the behaviour of bilingual speakers who make use of what Catford (1965: 21) calls 'partial translation', as in the following example:

Marit lives in a small *borettslag* where the *innskudds* were not very high.

What is interesting about this sentence is the fact that the terms *borettslag* and *innskudd* are examples of standardised language, that is to say administrative terms, that are difficult to translate into English for cultural reasons. These terms are to be found in the legislation relating to housing co-operative associations, which have always been more popular in Norway than in the English-speaking world, probably because of both the political climate and the different traditions concerning the provision of housing. By the same token it is difficult to translate the term *building society* into Norwegian, since there is no cultural equivalent in Norway.

The occurrence of 'partial translation' among bilingual speakers is always of interest to the translation theorist and terminologist, since it reveals elements of one of the two languages that they find difficult or impossible to translate. Part of the problem is that since there is no readily available translation equivalent, they are afraid of inventing one because it may not be understood. When we are dealing with standardised language, we must have standardised translation equivalents. It is also essential to have standardised translation equivalents if people who are not bilingual are to be able to understand the administrative realities of a country whose language they do not know. This problem becomes particularly acute in the case of institutional names, which often consist of administrative terms, and it is to this question I should now like to turn.

The Problem of Name versus Description

Firstly, names serve to identify, and if we did not need to identify or label persons, places and institutions, we should have no need for names. Identification is the essence of names: if institutional names, for example, are not translated consistently, then there will be confusion as to which institution is intended and there may even be total loss of identity. We probably do not immediately think of proper names as being translatable, since personal names are not normally translated except in the case of some kings and queens, for example. The reason that institutional names are translatable is that they are normally composed of ordinary words in the language concerned.

Secondly, names may contain a descriptive element. This is not essential but it is usually the case with institutional names since they tend to be composed of ordinary words in the language. If we take the English *Ministry of Agriculture*, for instance, people readily appreciate that it belongs to the category of institutions known as ministries and they would be astonished if they were then told that it was responsible for education. It is basically irrelevant whether my name is Patrick, Peter or Paul, provided the name is used consistently for purposes of identification, but in the case of the name of a ministry, there will normally be a descriptive element that is meaning-bearing, and if a ministry deals with education, it must be called the *Ministry of Education* and not the *Ministry of Agriculture*. It is this descriptive element of institutional names that is problematic for the translator, because very often the words constituting the descriptive element will be administrative terms. In a sense, names are not strictly translatable, but descriptions always are. This sometimes leads to a desire for a translated name that has a far longer descriptive element than is the case in Norwegian, sometimes so long that the translation could no longer be considered a name. There is clearly a restriction on how long a name can be, but there is no such constraint in the case of a description. It is nevertheless true that descriptions are sometimes used for the purpose of identification when no name is available.

Thirdly, names carry associations. However dispassionate we try to be as linguists, we cannot deny the fact that names arouse emotions, and it may be the case that they do so to a greater or lesser degree in different cultures. Norway has a high level of what I call name-consciousness, and the changing of any name can easily lead to controversy. In Britain the ministry of finance is called the *Treasury* and the minister is called the *Chancellor of the Exchequer*. In Norway the ministry of finance is called *Finansdepartementet* and the minister is called *finansministeren*, yet it would seem culturally inappropriate to call the Norwegian minister the *Chancellor* or to speak of the Norwegian ministry as the

Treasury. On the other hand there would no doubt be controversy in Britain if anybody proposed changing the name of the Treasury to the *Ministry of Finance* or calling the Chancellor the *Minister of Finance.* We have only to think of a ministry like the Home Office to make the point. Even though the Home Office deals with such areas as immigration control, prisons and police, the name does not sound unpleasant. However, if, as in Anthony Burgess's novel *A Clockwork Orange,* the name is changed to the *Ministry of the Interior,* this is no longer the cosy Britain we know. It is a frightening Britain in which the Minister of the Interior is a man to be feared. In Norway the corresponding ministry is called *Justisdepartementet;* it could never be called *Innenriksdepartementet,* because that name was used for a ministry that existed during the period of Vidkun Quisling's National Socialist government which assumed power as a result of the German occupation. Yet in Norwegian, the British Home Office is always referred to as *Det britiske innenriksdepartement.*

In Norway a very good example of how high feelings can run with respect to the translation of names was provided by a letter written to the national daily newspaper *Aftenposten* in January 1985. It was a letter of protest caused by the ADNOM proposal that all institutions in Norway having the word *høgskole* in their names should have the word *college* in their English names. The writer argued that in the case of a particular institution this pattern could not be followed and that *school* should be used in place of *college,* largely because it was felt that the term *school* indicated a higher status. No objection was raised to the use of the word *college* as such for institutions of higher education, only to the case of a particular institution. Interestingly enough, before ADNOM was ever started, Kirkeby (1979: 460) had used the word *college* for this particular institution and ADNOM was not aware that there had been any objections when Kirkeby included it under his entry for the Norwegian term *handelshøyskole.* It seems that criticism of the project stemmed largely from an objection to standardisation, an idea that was fundamental to the project.

The Problem of Standardisation

From the very outset ADNOM adopted four basic principles for its work. These were soon formulated as four maxims by Nigel Reeves, who was involved in ADNOM from the establishment of the project until the completion of the manuscript for *Norsk-engelsk administrativ ordbok.* The maxims ran as follows:

(1) The English name must not arouse British (or American etc.) cultural connotations alien to the Norwegian context.
(2) The English name must not misinform the reader about the nature or status of an institution.
(3) The English name must be grammatically acceptable and it must not sound absurd.
(4) The English name must reflect the underlying Norwegian nomenclature in a consistent and systematic way.

These principles are quoted in both English and Norwegian in the Preface to *Norsk-engelsk administrativ ordbok,* the resulting publication on Norwegian-English administrative terminology (Chaffey: 1988).

It was the standardising aspect of ADNOM's work that was to prove the greatest challenge and present the greatest difficulty. In accordance with Principle 4, for instance, we argued that all institutions with *høgskole* in their Norwegian name should have *college* in their English name, all those with *departement* in their Norwegian name should have *ministry* in their English name, and so forth. Since nomenclature is relatively systematic in Norwegian when it comes to state institutions, we felt this should be reflected in the English translations. The fact that a ministry in the United Kingdom might be called *ministry, office, department, agency* and so on, and might not have any of these terms in its name, as is the case with the Treasury, makes the system opaque. Those studying British Constitution often find it very confusing that there are, for instance, three Cabinet ministers with the title of *Chancellor*, while others have the title of *Secretary of State* or *Minister*. Non-standardised terms may lead to communication problems in so far as the same term may refer to two different entities (polysemy) or two different terms may refer to the same entity (synonymy). Any subject is easier to understand if the terminology is systematic and above all consistent but, surprisingly, many people in Norway objected to the form of standardisation proposed, often because they wanted their institution to have a name modelled on the name of what they believed to be an equivalent institution in the United Kingdom or the United States. This meant that a standardised term in Norwegian, such as *høgskole*, would be translated by a variety of terms in English, such as *college, school, institute, academy, university* or *polytechnic*, leaving the English reader unsure whether the same or different types of institution are meant. Not infrequently there would be disagreement between members of the same institution about the appropriate English translation of its name.

The Power of Decision

It was probably the thorny problem of the power of decision in matters of standardisation that brought about the demise of the project. Norway is a social democratic state with a high degree of management by committee, meaning that collective responsibility rather than any notion of personal responsibility prevails in matters of this kind. In other words one goes for consensus. In accordance with this principle, no entry was included in *Norsk-engelsk administrativ ordbok* for an institution on which no consensus had been reached, even though it is difficult to achieve a balance between linguistically well-motivated proposals from academic linguists on the one hand and the need for consensus on the other, particularly in a situation where the proposals emanate from those academics as civil servants who have no legal right to prescribe usage. Judgements of linguists, including both translation theorists and applied linguists, are also more vulnerable to criticism than those of many other professional groups such as doctors or lawyers. In matters of language, everyone claims to know best. Basically this was not satisfactory but we saw no alternative. English is not an official language in Norway and nobody has the power to decide what any institution is to be called in any language except Norwegian, and even that can be very controversial.

In 1988 the Ministry of Foreign Affairs assumed full responsibility for the

ADNOM project but little or nothing was heard of any work being done on a new edition of Norsk-engelsk administrativ ordbok. In 1992 the Ministry wanted to blow new life into ADNOM and invited a team of linguists at the University of Oslo including myself to participate on a purely voluntary basis, but this time there was a difference. The Ministry hoped to lay down translations of names in English and other languages with or without consensus, but this was, in our view, not the role of a university, which is to conduct research. In our case we could carry out research that would lead to a basis on which various possibilities could be evaluated, but we could not ourselves be party to a prescription of terms. If the Ministry of Foreign Affairs wished to prescribe translations, then it must do so without us. In reality the Ministry has no such power in law, but it could argue that for the sake of practical common sense its Translation Division simply had to operate with standardised translations on the lines of Newmark's suggestion (cf. above). The Ministry appreciated our point of view and it was agreed that it would contact us again if it felt the need to use us in a purely advisory capacity.

Since March 1992 I had heard absolutely nothing of ADNOM until the end of November 1997, when I was contacted by one of our former students who is now working in the Translation Division of the Ministry of Foreign Affairs. He is hoping to revive the project and make the nomenclature available to the public, possibly via the Internet. I am not in any way involved myself, but it will be very interesting to see whether this new attempt meets with greater success. If it does, then we may see the appearance of such lists as Newmark has in mind during the course of 1999.

In conclusion I think it is only true and fair to say that in a social democratic state with a monocultural national language as its only official language, it is extremely difficult to solve the problems that ADNOM faced. The problems were acute in the case of English, because most people have some familiarity with English; they were less acute in the case of French or German; they were non-existent in the case of Finnish.

References

Adnom (1984) *ADNOM*. Oslo: Universitetsforlaget.
Catford, J.C. (1965) *A Linguistic Theory of Translation*. London: Oxford University Press.
Chaffey, P. (1988) *Norsk-engelsk administrativ ordbok*. Oslo: Universitetsforlaget.
Chaffey, P. and Walford, R. (1997) *Norsk-engelsk juridisk ordbok*. Oslo: Universitetsforlaget. 2nd edition.
Haugen, E. (1965) *Norsk-engelsk ordbok*. Oslo: Universitetsforlaget.
Kirkeby, W. (1979) *Norsk-engelsk ordbok*. Oslo: Kunnskapsforlaget.
Newmark, P. (1981) *Approaches to Translation*. Oxford: Pergamon Press.
Walker, D. (1980) *The Oxford Companion to Law*. Oxford: Clarendon Press.

Chapter 22

From Anonymous Parasites to Transformation Agents — A 'Third World' Vision of Translation for the New Millennium

Simon S.C. Chau

> *[Translators] must be seen as key figures in promoting better*
> *understanding among peoples and nations. They must not be regarded as*
> *anonymous. They are responsible for all definitive, therefore written,*
> *bilingual and interlingual communications.*

(Peter Newmark, 1991: 41)

How should one translate? If there is one question that forms the backbone of translatology, translation criticism and translation education, this must be it. Clearly, the answer to this question depends on WHO is doing the job for WHOM, working on WHAT texts under what circumstances, and WHY. I would like to discuss this familiar question in the context of developments outside the Western world, where the work of the translator can be seen as a catalyst to action which is of benefit to society as a whole. I would like to argue that in this context, notions of equivalence become less important than social effectiveness.

As the twentieth century draws to a close, the world of translating is undergoing a sea change — particularly in the misnamed 'developing' or 'Third World'. Based on my experience of working in this environment, this is my vision of the translation profession in the new era.

Past and Present

> *A hundred years ago, English translators were considered as leisured and*
> *literary figures: often a professor of classics or a diplomat who translated in*
> *their spare time.*

(Peter Newmark, 1991: 40)

We are all familiar with these pre-professional age practitioners, with their amateurish vigour and dedication, turning out translations of their favourite classics with various degrees of success. They did play an important role in bridging cultures, when the Western civilisation 'spread' to all corners of the earth. After all, it was the European missionaries who first introduced a full canon of classical Chinese thinking and literature to the Western reader, again translating in their spare time between sermons and baptisms. Translating quality was left to chance and to the individual translator's ingenuity. The contrast with current practice is clear:

> Now they are seen in various main roles: in UNO, UNESCO, EC, OCED, Council of Europe and other international organisations, translating working papers, reports, journals, pamphlets, brochures, publicity to facilitate communication between representatives of member countries . . .; as freelancers, they may be translating original papers for academic journals to help researchers to keep up with what their foreign colleagues are doing . . . [Newmark, 1991: 40–1]

The age of professional translating has come to some Western countries (notably in North America and Western Europe) thanks to the needs of the market and the admirable efforts of some practitioners who fought for the right and integrity of the profession. Today, translators in those countries are often specifically trained. They may be bound by a common code of professional ethics, and enjoy a level of remuneration in line with their training and experience, although their contribution is not always recognised by the community. We have a generation of reliable wordsmith mercenaries, working for a decent living, and usually getting it. While being far more indispensable than their pre-professional predecessors, they prefer to function like well-oiled machines — efficient but characterless. As we shall see, this is less applicable to the role of the translator outside the West.

The Future

Looking to the future role of translators, Newmark sees this to be a socially active one:

> [Translators] must be seen as key figures in promoting better understanding among peoples and nations. They must not be regarded as anonymous. They are responsible for all definitive, therefore written, bilingual and interlingual communications. [Newmark, 1991: 41]

Looking out of his metaphorical window, Newmark is viewing the world from an Anglocentric position. All very well. However, while the sentiment of his prediction is impressive, other things are happening in different ways in the 'remaining' parts of the world, where 'development' often follows in the footsteps of the West. Functioning at the receiving end of the information tidal flow, translators sometimes find other modes of operation in order to be effective in countries such as Brazil, China, Iraq, Nigeria, Thailand and the like.

If we look back over the history of many positive developments in human civilisation in the West, such as human rights, environmental protection, healthy eating, animal rights, consumer rights, breast versus bottle feeding, the fight against tobacco, women's rights, chemical versus organic farming, vegetarianism, the credit for starting such campaigns is shared among a number of people. First there were the thinkers who dared to dream and innovate, as well as the researchers who gathered the necessary information, followed by the activists who, inspired by the thinkers and researchers, and empowered by the facts they provided, launched the battle.

In other parts of the world, where over three quarters of humanity live, it is a different story. The battle, and with it social transformation, begins with the transfer of information.

It is unlikely that people just wake up one fine morning and feel the agony of political prisoners on another continent, understand the implications of the ozone hole, realise how unwise chemical farming and animal testing are, or attain enlightenment concerning the threats of tobacco fumes and formula milk. It is here that the translator plays an essential role. Typically, it is a translator who has waded through the flood of information and passed on the message, *with his/her heart and in an effective way*, that eventually persuaded local activists, scholars, and finally politicians in the corridor of power to change things. In those parts of the world, translators serve as windows on the world for their communities. The people hear about the 'reality out there' only through the filter of translation. Thus, what gets translated, and how, charts the future of such societies.

Conclusion

There will still be amateur translators turning out translations of literary and philosophical classics into and out of English. There will be the majority in the translation profession who feed their families by serving as multilingual mercenaries in the government and the private sector, ensuring that diplomatic literature, business contracts as well as the Bible are rendered in the time-honoured ways. Yet, it is the increasing number of those that we might call conscientious 'Information Transfer Activists' who play the most influential role in the shaping of history. Well versed in translatology or otherwise, these subversive cultural transformers translate in ways they consider most effective, with the ultimate goal of 'A.I.D.A.' (attracting Attention, passing on Information, triggering Decision leading to Action).

Until there is a critical mass of literature on organic farming, breastfeeding, feminism, and vegetarianism in the local language and delivered in appropriate forms, there is little activists on the ground can do. The success of such campaigns, to some extent, depends on the dedication and art of the translators behind the scenes. In this sense, translating becomes a matter of life and death — babies survive on their mother's milk (one million of them are dying each year as an indirect result of formula milk, according to WHO), and cattle and pigs escape the knife.

Understandably, this new breed of translators in an 'exotic' setting adapts a kind of ethos different from those traditionally held. Their primary allegiance is to the cause, the desired outcome, and society at large, rather than to the author, the original text, the original message, or the client. The success of their toil is often measured not by any kind of equivalence to the original text, but by the quality of the 'A.I.D.A.' impact described above. The progress of a large part of human civilisation is at their fingertips.

References
Newmark, P.P. (1991) *About Translation*. Clevedon: Multilingual Matters.

Index